CUET

(UG) & Integrated PG

2022

Biology

DU | BHU | JNU | JMI | TISS & etc.

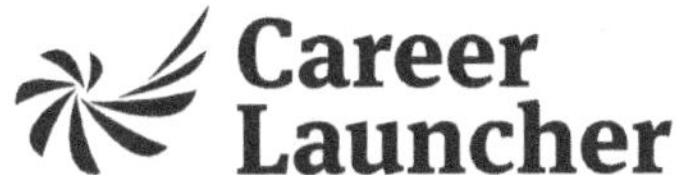

Career
Launcher

Title   : CUET 2022 : Biology

Language   : English

Editor's Name   : Sneha Gurkha

Copyright ©   : 2022 CLIP

No part of this book may be reproduced in a retrieval system or transmitted, in any form or by any means, electronics, mechanical, photocopying, recording, scanning and or without the written permission of the Author/Publisher.

Typeset & Published by :

Career Launcher Infrastructure (P) Ltd.

A-45, Mohan Cooperative Industrial Area, Near Mohan Estate Metro Station, New Delhi - 110044

Marketed by :

G.K. Publications (P) Ltd.

Plot No. 9A, Sector-27A, Mathura Road, Faridabad, Haryana-121003

ISBN   : **978-93-95101-28-8**

For product information :

Visit *www.gkpublications.com* or email to *gkp@gkpublications.com*

CONTENTS

About CUET

A year ago, it would have been unimaginable that cut-offs in Delhi University would skyrocket to 100% for some of the undergraduate courses! While DU has always been known for its high cut-offs, there are several other universities where the story is no different.

However, the National Education Policy 2020 (NEP) aims to do away with the tyranny of the ever-rising cut-offs by introducing a Common Entrance Test for all the Central Universities in the country. NEP not only proposes a holistic approach in evaluating the students by giving them the option to select subjects based on their interest, but it also aims to simplify the process of admission to higher-education institutes.

To start with, there would be a Common Entrance Test for all the Central Universities, which would be conducted twice a year from 2022. While this might sound like a new concept to many, the fact is, there is already a CUET, which is conducted for the Central Universities established in or after 2009. As many as 14 of them already admit students based on their performance in the entrance test. The CUET scores are also accepted by four state universities of the country.

The proposed CUET aims to assess conceptual understanding and application of knowledge; and also, to lessen the burden of appearing in multiple tests.

CUET Eligibility

Getting into a premier University is every student's dream. The brand value of the University not only facilitates securing a seat in a master's program in a national/international institute, but also helps in getting job offers through campus placements.

Entry to a Central University, in most cases earlier, was based on merit, i.e., marks secured in Class XII Board exams. However, from the academic year 2021, all Central Universities will also consider the CUET score for admissions into their Undergraduate programs.

CUET 2022: Eligibility Criteria

While the official criteria will be learnt once the CUET 2021 notification is released, the stipulations are not expected to change much from those of previous years.

- A candidate must have passed Class XII (10+2) or equivalent from a recognized education Board.
- If the respective Board awards grades (or CGPA), the conversion factor given by the Board must be used to compute the percentage of marks.
- Candidates, who have completed their Class XII in 2021, and have passed the Board exams, will also be eligible to apply for CUET 2022.

Eligibility: Class XII Students

While CUET is for students who have passed the Class XII (or equivalent) Board exams, any student who is appearing for the Class XII Board exam in 2022 is also eligible to apply for CUET 2021. The candidate would be required to produce the marksheets and relevant certificates as mandated by the participating Central University, and follow the timelines provided for admissions.

Key Points

- Each participating Central University is free to decide its own eligibility criteria for admissions.

- The weightages for CUET and Class XII Board exam results(if, applicable) will be at the sole discretion of the Central University, to which admission is being sought.

- As of date, CUET does not have an age limit. However, Central Universities can fix minimum & maximum age limit for admissions to all (or any) of the programs on offer.

Reservation of Seats

As CUET is an entrance exam for admissions to Undergraduate courses at the Central Universities, which have been established under an Act of the Parliament, each Central University must follow the norms set by the Government of India, with respect to intake and reservation of seats.

Generally, the following break-up is followed:

Category	Reservation
Scheduled Castes	15%
Scheduled Tribes	7.5%
Other Backward Classes (Non-Creamy)	27%
Persons with Disability	5%

Some institutions might even have provisions for the Economically Weaker Sections, which can account for 10% of the total seats. These EWS seats are carved out from the Open Category.

To avail of the reservation benefit based on caste (or any other category as specified), a candidate must be able to produce valid documents/certificates to support such claims.

Conclusion

It is essential for every candidate to check the validity of their candidature for CUET, as well as the Central University he/she is applying to. The candidate should be aware of the documents that might be required while applying for the exam, or during the admissions.

CUET 2022 notification is expected in March 2022, and registration is also going to start then.

CUET: Exam Pattern

Examination Structure for CUET (UG) -2022:

CUET (UG) –2022 will consist of the following 4 Sections:

    Section IA –13 Languages

    Section IB –19 Languages

    Section II –27 Domain specific Subjects

    Section III –General Test

Choosing options from each Section is not mandatory. Choices should match the requirements of the desired University.

Broad features of CUET (UG) -2022 are as follows:

Section	Subjects/ Tests	Questions to be Attempted	Question Type	Duration
Section IA – Languages	There are 13* different languages. Any of these languages may be chosen.	40 questions to be attempted out of 50 in each language	Language to be tested through Reading Comprehension (based on different types of passages–Factual, Literary and Narrative, [Literary Aptitude and Vocabulary]	45 Minutes for each language
Section IB – Languages	There are 19** Languages. Any other language apart from those offered in Section I A may be chosen.			
Section II - Domain	There are 27*** Domains specific subjects being offered under this Section. A candidate may choose a maximum of Six (06) Domains as desired by the applicable University/Universities.	40 Questions to be attempted out of 50	• Input text can be used for MCQ Based Questions • MCQs based on NCERT Class XII syllabus only	
Section III- General Test	For any such undergraduate programme/ programmes being offered by Universities where a General Test is being used for admission.	60 Questions to be attempted out of 75	• Input text can be used for MCQ Based Questions • General Knowledge, Current Affairs, General Mental Ability, Numerical Ability, Quantitative Reasoning (Simple application of basic mathematical concepts arithmetic/algebra geometry/mensuration/s tat taught till Grade 8), Logical and Analytical Reasoning	

*** Languages (13):** Tamil, Telugu, Kannada, Malayalam, Marathi, Gujarati, Odiya, Bengali, Assamese, Punjabi, English, Hindi and Urdu

**** Languages (19):** *French, Spanish, German, Nepali, Persian, Italian, Arabic, Sindhi, Kashmiri, Konkani, Bodo, Dogri, Maithili, Manipuri, Santhali, Tibetan, Japanese, Russian, Chinese.*

***** Domain Specific Subjects (27):** 1. Accountancy/ Book Keeping 2. Biology/ Biological Studies/ Biotechnology/Biochemistry 3. Business Studies 4. Chemistry 5. Computer Science/ Informatics Practices 6. Economics/ Business Economics 7. Engineering Graphics 8.Entrepreneurship 9. Geography/Geology 10. History 11. Home Science 12.Knowledge Tradition and Practices of India 13. Legal Studies 14. Environmental Science 15. Mathematics 16. Physical Education/ NCC /Yoga 17.Physics 18.Political Science 19. Psychology 20. Sociology 21. Teaching Aptitude 22. Agriculture 23. Mass Media/ Mass Communication 24. Anthropology 25. Fine Arts/Visual Arts (Sculpture/ Painting)/Commercial Arts, 26. Performing Arts – (i) Dance (Kathak/ Bharatnatyam/Oddisi/ Kathakali/Kuchipudi/ Manipuri (ii) Drama- Theatre (iii) Music General (Hindustani/ Carnatic/ RabindraSangeet/ Percussion/ Non-Percussion), 27. Sanskrit *[For all Shastri (Shastri 3 years/ 4 years Honours) Equivalent to B.A./B.A. Honours courses i.e. Shastri in Veda, Paurohitya (Karmakand), Dharamshastra, Prachin Vyakarana, Navya Vyakarana, Phalit Jyotish, Siddhant Jyotish, Vastushastra, Sahitya,Puranetihas, Prakrit Bhasha,Prachin Nyaya Vaisheshik, Sankhya Yoga, Jain Darshan, Mimansa, AdvaitaVedanta, Vishihstadvaita Vedanta, Sarva Darshan, a candidate may choose Sanskrit as the Domain].*

- A Candidate can choose a maximum of **any 3 languages** from Section IA and Section IB taken together. (One of the languages chosen needs to be in lieu of Domain specific subjects)
- Section II offers 27 Subjects, out of which a candidate may choose a **maximum of 6 Subjects.**
- Section III comprises **General Test.**
- For choosing Languages (upto 3) from Section IA and IB and a maximum of 6 Subjects from Section II and General Test under Section III, the Candidate must refer to the requirements of his/her intended University.

Mode of the Test	Computer Based Test-CBT
Test Pattern	Objective type with Multiple Choice Questions
Medium	13 languages (*Tamil, Telugu, Kannada, Malayalam, Marathi, Gujarati, Odiya, Bengali, Assamese, Punjabi, English, Hindi and Urdu)*
Syllabus	**Section IA & IB:** Language to be tested through Reading Comprehension (based on different types of passages–Factual, Literary and Narrative [Literary Aptitude & Vocabulary]
	Section II : As per NCERT model syllabus as applicable to Class XII only
	Section III : General Knowledge, Current Affairs, General Mental Ability, Numerical Ability, Quantitative Reasoning (Simple application of basic mathematical concepts arithmetic/algebra geometry/mensuration/stat taught till Grade 8), Logical and Analytical Reasoning

Level of questions for CUET (UG) -2022:

All questions in various testing areas will be benchmarked at the level of Class XII only. Students having studied Class XII Board syllabus would be able to do well in CUET (UG) – 2022.

Number of attempts:

If any University permits students of previous years of class XII to take admission in the current year also, such students would also be eligible to appear in CUET (UG) – 2022.

Choice of Languages and Subjects:

Generally the languages/subjects chosen should be the ones that a student has opted in his latest Class XII Board examination. However, if any University permits any flexibility in this regards, the same can be exercised under CUET (UG) -2022 also. Candidates must carefully refer to the eligibility requirements of various Central Universities in this regard. Moreover, if the subject to be studied in the Undergraduate course is not available in the list of **27 Domain Specific Subject** being offered, the Candidate may choose the Subject closest to his choice for e.g. For Biochemistry the candidate may choose Biology.

Candidates are advised to visit the NTA CUET (UG)-2022 official website **https://cuet.samarth.ac.in/** for latest updates regarding the Examination.

CUET Syllabus

Before you start your preparation for any entrance exam, it is important to understand the syllabus. Otherwise, your prep will be directionless, and you might be left wondering where things might have gone wrong!

With more than 1.68 lakh seats on offer for the undergraduate courses at the 54 Central Universities, CUET is one the most competitive examinations. For this very reason, while preparing for the exam, you will need to adopt a structured approach. And in doing that, understanding the syllabus is a critical step.

CUET 2022 Overview

CUET 2022 will be a Computer-Based Test (CBT), commonly referred to as an online exam. However, there is a difference between the two terms: CBT and online. In CBT, the questions are kept constant and simply presented in an online format; whereas in an Online Test, questions are stored as a bank, and the system decides which questions are to be presented to the candidate, based on a pre-defined logic.

CUET 2022 is likely to be a General Ability Test, with focus on English Language, Numerical Ability, Logical & Analytical Reasoning, along with General Awareness and Current Affairs.

CUET 2022 Syllabus

The CUET 2022 exam pattern gives a good idea about what is in store for the candidate and how one needs to prepare for the exam.

- **English Language:** The questions in this section will test one's proficiency in the language, based on comprehension passages, fundamentals of grammar, and vocabulary. In the Comprehension section, candidates will be evaluated on their understanding of a passage and its central theme, meanings of words used therein, etc. The Grammar section entails correcting grammatically incorrect sentences, filling of blanks in sentences with appropriate words, etc. Questions on synonyms & antonyms will check one's command over English vocabulary.
- **Numerical Ability:** Questions on Numerical Ability will test the candidate's knowledge of elementary mathematics. Areas like arithmetic, number system, basics of algebra, and modern maths will be central to these types of questions.
- **Logical & Analytical Reasoning:** This section tests the candidate's ability to identify patterns & logical links, and rectify illogical arguments. It can include a variety of Logical Reasoning questions, such as those on syllogisms, logical sequences, analogies, etc., along with Analytical Reasoning questions on series, directions, clocks & calendars, arrangements, and puzzles to name a few.
- **General Awareness and Current Affairs:** The General Awareness section includes static general knowledge, while questions on Current Affairs will gauge a candidate's knowledge of national & international current affairs.

CUET 2022 may or may not have a section on subject knowledge. Once the exam notification is out in March, there will be more clarity on this matter.

While there is no syllabus explicitly mentioned by CUET, the broad idea is always presented. One must look at the previous years' papers and solve the sample papers available to form a basic understanding.

About University of Delhi

University of Delhi (commonly known as DU) was established in 1922 and is one of the largest Universities in the country. With 16 faculties, 86 academic departments, 90 colleges and 540 programs on offer, Delhi University is no doubt one of the sought-after University in the country.

With 1, 96,000 students enrolled in UG programs, Delhi University is a valued university and constantly ranked among the top in the country. DU bagged 11th Rank in NIRF 2020 and ranked 6th in QS India Rankings 2020. The University has two Campuses: North and South.

DU UG Programs

Delhi University offers several programs at the undergraduate level. With more than 60 constituent colleges, the Delhi University offers many undergraduate courses.

Please refer to the table below for the important undergraduate courses offered by the DU and the intake across each program.

Program	Intake
B. A (Pass)	11249
B. A (Hons) Geography	788
B. A (Hons) Economics	2754
B. A (Hons) History	2791
B. A (Hons) Political Science	3657
B. A (Hons) Sociology	596
B. A (Hons) Psychology	670
B. A (Hons) Applied Psychology	252
B. A (Hons) Social Work	133
B. A (Hons) Philosophy	783
B. A (Hons) English	2886
B. A (Hons) Hindi	2829
B. A (Hons) Sanskrit	1407
B. A (Hons) Punjabi	214
B. A (Hons) Urdu	207
BA(Hons) French	49

Program	Intake
BA(Hons) German	49
BA(Hons) Spanish	49
BA(Hons) Italian	49
B. Com (Hons)	7953
B.Com (Pass)	7854
Program	Intake
B.Sc. (H) Biomedical Science	162
B.Sc. (H) Botany	937
B.Sc. (H) Chemistry	1487
B.Sc. (H) Computer Science	1265
B.Sc. (H) Electronics	624
B.Sc. (H) Mathematics	2428
B.Sc. (H) Physics	1659
B.Sc. (H) Zoology	944
B.Sc. Life Sciences	1515
B.Sc. Physical Science with Chemistry	703
B.Sc. Physical Science with Computer Science	553
B.Sc. Physical Science with Electronics	247
B. Sc (Hons.) Statistics	476
B. Sc. (Prog.) Applied Physical Science Industrial Chemistry	96
B.Sc. (Hons.) Home Science	900
B. Sc. (Hons.) Psychology	57
B.Sc. (H) Food Technology	179
B.Sc. (H)Instrumentation	99
B.Sc. (H) Microbiology	238
B.Sc. (H) Polymer Science	59
B.SC. Mathematical Science	224
B.SC. (Hons.) Biochemistry	146
B.SC. Industrial Chemistry	78
B.Sc. (Prog.) Physical Science	940
B.SC. (Hons.) Geology	98

DU UG Programs Eligibility:

As the University offers multiple programs and separate intake for male and female candidates, it is important to check the university official website regularly to keep oneself updated about the eligibility for each program, which can change.

DU UG Admissions:

Until 2021, Delhi University admitted students on the basis of class XII marks. From the academic year 2022, admissions to UG programs offered Delhi University will be based on CUET. CUET will be a common entrance for admissions to UG programs offered by all the Central Universities in the country.

Delhi University UG Programs Reservation:

DU being a Central University offers reservations in admissions according to central government rules.

Schedule Caste (SC): 15% of the total seats are reserved for students who belong to SC category.

Schedule Tribe (ST): 7.5% of the total seats are reserved for students belonging to ST Category.

Other Backward Classes (OBC): 27% of the total intake is reserved for students from Other Backward Classes (OBC), excluding those from creamy layer.

Economically Weaker Section (EWS): The University has reserved 10% seats for EWS category, in accordance with the directive of Ministry of Education.

Persons with Disability (PWD): 5% of the seats are reserved on horizontal basis for students from PWD category.

About BHU

Banaras Hindu University (BHU), situated in the holy city of Varanasi, was founded by Pandit Madan Mohan Malviya in cooperation with Dr. Annie Besant, in 1916 under the act of Parliament-B.H.U Act, 1915. BHU, which is a Central University, comprises of 6 Institutes, 14 Faculties, 144 academic departments, and 4 Inter-disciplinary centers, spread over 1300 acres. The University consists of 15,000 students, 1700 teachers and 8000 non-teaching staff.

BHU was ranked 3rd among the Universities in India in 2020. According to university submissions for NIRF 2021, BHU has 10, 585 students pursuing UG programs, of which 236 students are foreign nationals.

BHU UG Programs

BHU offers a host of undergraduate programs including medical and engineering. Through its various faculties, BHU offers a range of programs which caters to students learning abilities. The University along with its main campus, also offers the undergraduate courses from the following colleges: Mahila Mahavidyalaya (MMV); Arya Mahila Post Graduate College (AMPGC), Vasant Kanya Mahavidyalaya (VKM); Vasanta College for Women (VCW); DAV Post Graduate College (DAVPGC) and Rajiv Gandhi South Campus (RGSC).

Please refer to the table below for the important undergraduate courses offered by BHU and the intake across each program/campuses.

Faculty of Arts				
Course	Campus	Intake	Status	Duration
B.A (Hons) Arts	Faculty of Arts	765	Co-Ed	3 Years
	Mahila Mahavidyalaya	286	Women	3 Years
	Arya Mahila Post Graduate College	383	Women	3 Years
	Vasant Kanya Mahavidyalaya	286	Women	3 Years
	Vasanta College for Women	412	Women	3 Years
	DAV Post Graduate College	309	Co-Ed	3 Years
Faculty of Social Sciences				
Course	Campus	Intake	Status	Duration
B.A (Hons) Social Sciences [incl. B. A (Hons) Economics]	Faculty of Social Sciences	573	Co-Ed	3 Years
	Mahila Mahavidyalaya	193	Women	3 Years
	Arya Mahila Post Graduate College	383	Women	3 Years
	Vasant Kanya Mahavidyalaya	249	Women	3 Years
	Vasanta College for Women	210	Women	3 Years
	DAV Post Graduate College	326	Co-Ed	3 Years

Faculty of Commerce				
Course	Campus	Intake	Status	Duration
B. Com (Hons)	Faculty of Commerce	286	Co-Ed	3 Years
	Vasant Kanya Mahavidyalaya	96	Women	3 Years
	Arya Mahila Post Graduate College	96	Women	3 Years
	DAV Post Graduate College	227	Co-Ed	3 Years
	Rajiv Gandhi South Campus, Mirzapur	114	Co-Ed	3 Years
B. Com (Hons) Financial Markets Management	Faculty of Commerce	62	Co-Ed	3 Years
	Rajiv Gandhi South Campus, Mirzapur	62	Co-Ed	3 Years
Institute of Science				
Course	Campus	Intake	Status	Duration
B.Sc (Hons) Maths Group	Faculty of Science	573	Co-Ed	3 Years
	Mahila Mahavidyalaya	96	Women	3 Years
B.Sc (Hons) Bio Group	Faculty of Science	383	Co-Ed	3 Years
	Mahila Mahavidyalaya	193	Women	3 Years

Faculty of Visual Arts				
Course	Campus	Intake	Status	Duration
B.F.A (Bachelor of Fine Arts)	Faculty of Visual Arts	96	Co-Ed	4 Years
Faculty of Arts				
Bachelor of Vocation (Retail and Logistics Management)	Rajiv Gandhi South Campus	62	Co-Ed	3 Years
Bachelor of Vocation (Hospitality & Tourism Management)	Rajiv Gandhi South Campus	62	Co-Ed	3 Years
Bachelor of Vocation (Fashion Designing and Event Management)	Rajiv Gandhi South Campus	62	Co-Ed	3 Years
Bachelor of Vocation (Modern Office Management)	Rajiv Gandhi South Campus	62	Co-Ed	3 Years
Bachelor of Vocation (Food Processing & Management)	Rajiv Gandhi South Campus	62	Co-Ed	3 Years
Bachelor of Vocation (Medical Lab. & Technology)	Rajiv Gandhi South Campus	62	Co-Ed	3 Years

BHU UG Programs Eligibility:

Each of the courses have different eligibility for admissions. To be eligible for admissions, one must fulfil all the criteria as laid down by the respective faculties of the University.

B.A (Hons) Arts/ B.A (Hons) Social Sciences: Candidate must not be more than 22 years of age and must have passed class XII or equivalent with minimum 50% marks in aggregate.

B.A (Hons) Economics: Candidate must not be more than 22 years of age and must have passed class XII or equivalent with minimum 50% marks in aggregate along with mathematics as one of the papers.

B. Com (Hons)/B. Com (Hons) Financial Markets Management: Candidate must not be more than 22 years of age and must have passed class XII or equivalent with minimum 50% marks in aggregate with Commerce/Economics/Maths/Computer Science/Finance/Financial Markets Management as one of the subjects.

B. Sc (Hons) Maths Group: Candidate must not be more than 22 years of age and must have passed class XII or equivalent with minimum 50% marks in aggregate in the subjects Physics, Maths plus any one of the following: Chemistry, Statistics, Geology, Computer Science, Information Technology and Geography and must have passed in each of the concerned three subjects.

B. Sc (Hons) Bio Group: Candidate must not be more than 22 years of age and must have passed class XII or equivalent with minimum 50% marks in aggregate in the subjects Physics, Chemistry plus any one of the following: Biology, Geology and Geography and must have passed in each of the concerned three subjects.

B. F. A (Bachelor of Fine Arts): Candidate must not be more than 22 years of age and must have passed class XII or equivalent with minimum 50% marks in aggregate.

Bachelor of Vocation: Candidate must have passed class XII or equivalent in any stream (Science for Food Processing and Medical Lab Technology) or level 4 NSQF certificate.

BHU UG Admissions:

Until 2021, admissions to BHU UG courses were based on Undergraduate Entrance Test (UET) conducted by the University. From the academic year 2022, admissions to UG programs offered by BHU will be based on CUET, which will replace the UET. CUET will be a common entrance for admissions to UG programs offered by all the Central Universities in the country.

BHU UG Programs Reservation:

BHU being a Central University offers reservations in admissions according to central government rules.

Schedule Caste (SC): 15% of the total seats are reserved for students who belong to SC category.

Schedule Tribe (ST): 7.5% of the total seats are reserved for students belonging to ST Category.

Other Backward Classes (OBC): 27% of the total intake is reserved for students from Other Backward Classes (OBC), excluding those from creamy layer.

Economically Weaker Section (EWS): The University has reserved 10% seats for EWS category, in accordance with the directive of Ministry of Education.

Persons with Disability (PWD): 5% of the seats are reserved on horizontal basis for students from PWD category.

About JNU

Ever wondered which University, the cadets from National Defence Academy (NDA) graduate from? Yes. It is Jawaharlal Nehru University (JNU). JNU started in the year 1969, three years after the act of Parliament in 1966. With several academic centres of JNU declared "Centres of Excellence" by the University Grants Commission, JNU has been ranked No. 1 by National Assessment and Accreditation Council (NAAC). JNU has been ranked No. 2 by National Institutional Ranking Framework (NIRF) 2020 and has been awarded the Best University Award by the President of India in 2017. The European Commission has awarded the Jean Monnet Centre of Excellence for European Union Studies in India (CEEUSI) to Jawaharlal Nehru University in 2018. This is one of the highest international recognition for any European Studies programme.

JNU was the first University to start integrated five-year Master of Arts in Language Courses. JNU actively collaborates with National and International Universities for student and faculty exchange programs.

According to university submissions for NIRF 2020, JNU has 1,048 students pursuing UG programs, of which 46 are foreign nationals.

JNU UG Programs

JNU offers a limited program at the undergraduate level, unlike other universities. The focus at undergraduate has been largely on language courses. In 2018, JNU started two programs in engineering and plans to add a few more specializations in future.

Please refer to the table below for the important undergraduate courses offered by JNU and the intake across each program.

School	Program	Intake	Duration
School of Language, Literature and Cultural Studies	B. A (Hons) Pashto	19	3 Years
	B. A (Hons) Persian	39	3 Years
	B. A (Hons) Arabic	39	3 Years
	B. A (Hons) Japanese	48	3 Years
	B. A (Hons) Korean	39	3 Years
	B. A (Hons) Chinese	44	3 Years
	B. A (Hons) French	48	3 Years
	B. A (Hons) German	48	3 Years
	B. A (Hons) Russian	68	3 Years
	B. A (Hons) Spanish	39	3 Years

School of Sanskrit and Indic Studies	B. Sc - M. Sc Integrated Program in Ayurveda Biology	20	5 Years
School of Engineering	B. Tech in Computer Science and Engineering & MS/M. Tech in Social Sciences/Humanities/Science/Technology	25	5 Years
	B. Tech in Electronics and Communication Engineering & MS/M. Tech in Social Sciences/Humanities/Science/Technology	25	5 Years

JNU UG Programs Eligibility:

Each of the courses have different eligibility for admissions. To be eligible for admissions, one must fulfil all the criteria as laid down by the respective faculties of the University.

B.A (Hons) Language Courses: Candidate must not be less than 17 years of age and must have passed Senior School Certificate (10+2) or equivalent examination with minimum of 45% marks.

B. Sc - M. Sc Integrated Program in Ayurveda Biology: Candidate must not be less than 17 years of age and must have passed Senior School Certificate (10+2) or equivalent examination with minimum of 45% marks.

B. Tech-M. Tech: Based on JEE Mains

JNU UG Admissions:

Until 2021, admissions to JNU UG courses were based on JNU Entrance Examination (JNUEE) conducted by the National Testing Agency (NTA). From the academic year 2022, admissions to UG programs offered by JNU will be based on CUET, which will replace the JNUEE. CUET will be a common entrance for admissions to UG programs offered by all the Central Universities in the country.

JNU UG Programs Reservation:

JNU being a Central University offers reservations in admissions according to central government rules.

Schedule Caste (SC): 15% of the total seats are reserved for students who belong to SC category.

Schedule Tribe (ST): 7.5% of the total seats are reserved for students belonging to ST Category.

Other Backward Classes (OBC): 27% of the total intake is reserved for students from Other Backward Classes (OBC), excluding those from creamy layer. Also, Central List of Caste to be followed.

Economically Weaker Section (EWS): The University has reserved 10% seats for EWS category, in accordance with the directive of Ministry of Education.

Persons with Disability (PWD): 5% of the seats are reserved on horizontal basis for students from PWD category.

About Jamia Milia Islamia

Jamia Milia Islamia (JMI) was founded in 1920 in Aligarh and became a Central University in 1988 by the act of Parliament. Jamia in Urdu stands for University and Milia means National, making Jamia Milia Islamia a National University. Jamia Milia Islamia moved to Delhi in 1925 and shifted to its present campus in Okhla in 1935.

Jamia Milia Islamia is a NAAC accredited University with grade "A" and was placed 10th in NIRF Rankings 2020. According to submissions made by University for NIRF 2021, Jamia Milia Islamia has a total of 5,911 students pursuing undergraduate courses at the University, of which 105 are foreign nationals. The University also manage to place a total of 681 UG students with an average salary ranging 4.2 Lacs-6.0 Lacs.

JMI UG Programs

Jamia Milia Islamia (JMI) offers a host of undergraduate programs for students. Through its various faculties, JMI offers a range of programs which caters to students learning abilities.

Please refer to the table below for the important undergraduate courses offered by Jamia Milia Islamia and the intake across each program.

Faculty	Course	Intake	Duration
Faculty of Humanities and Language	B. A (Hons) English	60	3 Years
	B. A (Hons) Hindi	40	3 Years
	B. A (Hons) Mass Media-Hindi	40	3 Years
	B. A (Hons) History	60	3 Years
	Bachelor of Hotel Management (BHM)	40	3 Years
	Bachelor of Tourism and Travel Management	40	3 Years
	B. Voc (Food Production)	40	3 Years
Faculty of Social Sciences	Bachelor of Arts (B. A)	68	3 Years
	B. Com (Hons)	55	3 Years
	BBA (Bachelor of Business Administration)	44	3 Years
	B. A (Hons) Economics	53	3 Years
	B. A (Hons) Sociology	42	3 Years
	B. A (Hons) Political Science	42	3 Years
	B. A (Hons) Psychology	42	3 Years
Faculty of Natural Sciences	B. Sc (Bachelor of Science)	50	3 Years
	B. Sc Biosciences	40	3 Years
	B. Sc Biotechnology	35	3 Years
	B. Sc (Hons) Chemistry	40	3 Years
	B. A/B. Sc (Hons) Geography	60	3 Years
	B. Sc (Hons) Mathematics	45	3 Years
	B. Sc (Hons) Applied Mathematics	45	3 Years
	B. Sc (Hons) Physics	45	3 Years
Faculty of Fine Arts	Bachelor of Fine Arts (Applied Art)	30	4 Years
	Bachelor of Fine Arts (Art Education)	20	4 Years
	Bachelor of Fine Arts (Painting)	20	4 Years
	Bachelor of Fine Arts (Sculpture)	10	4 Years

JMI UG Programs Eligibility:

Each of the courses have different eligibility for admissions. To be eligible for admissions, one must fulfil all the criteria as laid down by the respective faculties of the University.

B. Com (Hons) /BBA /B. A (Hons) Economics: Candidate must have passed class XII or equivalent with a minimum of 50% marks in five subjects.

BHM/BTTM/B. Voc (Food Production): Candidate must have passed class XII or equivalent with a minimum of 45% marks in five subjects.

B. A (Hons) Mass Media/B. A (Hons) Hindi: Candidate must have passed class XII or equivalent with a minimum of 45% marks in five subjects.

B. Sc/B. Sc (Hons): Candidate must have passed class XII or equivalent with minimum 50% marks in each of the science subjects i.e. Physics, Chemistry and Mathematics and 50% marks in aggregate of best 5-subjects.

JMI UG Admissions:

Until 2021, admissions to JMI UG courses were based on Entrance Test (JMI-ET) conducted by the University. From the academic year 2022, admissions to UG programs offered by JMI will be based on CUET, which will replace the JMI-ET. CUET will be a common entrance for admissions to UG programs offered by all the Central Universities in the country.

JMI UG Programs Reservation:

JMI is a minority reservation-based University and accordingly, seats are reserved for candidates as per the norms laid down by the University.

Muslim Minority: 30% of the total seats are reserved for Muslim applicants; 10% of the total seats are reserved for women applicants who are Muslim; 10% of the total intake is for OBC-NC candidates who are Muslims.

Persons with Disability (PWD): 5% of the seats are reserved for students from PWD category.

Jamia Students: 5% seats in all Undergraduate Programs shall be filled by internal students of Jamia who have passed their qualifying examination of the concerned programme (X or XII) from Jamia Schools as regular students.

In addition, Jamia Milia Islamia has supernumerary seats for Kashmiri Migrants and students from Jammu and Kashmir.

About Aligarh Muslim University

Aligarh Muslim University also referred as AMU was established by Sir Syed Ahmad Khan in 1875. The University started as Muhammadan Anglo-Oriental College and became a University (AMU) in 1920. The university has been ranked 801–1000 in the QS World University Rankings of 2021 and 17 in India by the National Institutional Ranking Framework in 2020.

Aligarh Muslim University is institution of national importance, under the seventh schedule of the Constitution of India.

AMU UG Programs

Aligarh Muslim University offers several programs at the undergraduate level. With 7 constituent colleges, the Aligarh Muslim University offers many undergraduate courses.

Please refer to the table below for the important undergraduate courses offered by the AMU and the intake across each program.

Course	Intake	Duration
B. Sc (Hons) Home Science	30*	3 Years
B.Sc (Hons) Agriculture	40	4 Years
B. A (Hons) Arabic	20+10*	3 Years
B. A (Hons) Communicative English	15+20*	3 Years
B. A (Hons) English	40+35*	3 Years
B. A (Hons) Hindi	40+25*	3 Years
B. A (Hons) Geography	50+20*	3 Years
B. A (Hons) Linguistics	20+25*	3 Years
B. A (Hons) Persian	15+25*	3 Years
B. A (Hons) Philosophy	20+10*	3 Years
B. A (Hons) Quaranic Studies	10+10*	3 Years
B. A (Hons) Sanskrit	15+10*	3 Years
B. A (Hons) Urdu	40+50*	3 Years
Bachelor of Fine Arts	15+15*	3 Years
B. Com (Hons)	180+100*	3 Years
B. Voc Production Technology	50	3 Years
B Voc Polymer and Coating Technology	50	3 Years
B. Voc Fashion Design and Garment Technology	50	3 Years
B. A (Hons) Chinese	20	3 Years
B. A (Hons) French	20	3 Years
B. A (Hons) German	20	3 Years

B. A (Hons) Russian	20	3 Years
B. A (Hons) Spanish	20	3 Years
B. Sc (Hons) Biochemistry	30+30*	3 Years
B. Sc (Hons) Botany	60+40*	3 Years
B. Sc (Hons) Zoology	60+45*	3 Years
B. Sc (Hons) Physics	120+35*	3 Years
B. Sc (Hons) Chemistry	120+65*	3 Years
B. Sc (Hons) Mathematics	120+40*	3 Years
B. Sc (Hons) Geography	45+30*	3 Years
B. Sc (Hons) Geology	100+30*	3 Years
B. Sc (Hons) Statistics	60+30*	3 Years
B. Sc (Hons) Industrial Chemistry	20+10*	3 Years
B. Sc (Hons) Computer Applications	40+20*	3 Years

AMU UG Programs Eligibility:

As the University offers multiple programs and separate intake for male and female candidates, it is important to check the university official website regularly to keep oneself updated about the eligibility for each program, which can change.

AMU UG Admissions:

Until 2021, AMU conducted its own entrance test to admit students for the UG programs. From the academic year 2022, admissions to UG programs offered by Aligarh Muslim University will be based on CUET. CUET will be a common entrance for admissions to UG programs offered by all the Central Universities in the country.

University of Allahabad UG Programs Reservation:

Allahabad University being a Central University offers reservations in admissions according to central government rules. Kindly check the university website for further details.

BIOLOGY

CHAPTER 1

Reproduction in Organisms

Asexual Reproduction

Reproduction and its basic features

Reproduction can be defined as the production of offspring by a sexual or asexual process. Formation of reproductive bodies or units can be done by,

- Replication of DNA
- Development of reproductive bodies into offsprings
- Cell division

Types of Reproduction

Production of offsprings by a single parent is known as asexual reproduction. The offsprings produced are identical to one another and also to their parent. This type of reproduction is usually found in unicellular organisms and also in simple plants and animals.

Methods of Asexual reproduction

- **Fission-** In this type of asexual reproduction, the cell divides into two or more individuals. For example - Monerans and Protists.

Fission can be divided into two types:

- Binary fission: It is a division of parent cell into two individuals. For example: Amoeba.
- Multiple fission: It is a division of parent cell into multiple individuals. For example: Plasmodium.
- **Budding-** In this type of asexual reproduction, a daughter individual is formed from a small projection (bud) arising on the parent body. It can be found in Yeasts, Hydra and Sponges.

Other reproductive structures

- Zoospores (motile spores): Found in some algae, fungi and protists.
- Conidia (non-motile spores): Penicillium
- Gemmules (internal buds of sponges): sponges

Vegetative propagation

In certain plants, vegetative propagules arise from the nodes of modified stems. When the nodes come in contact with damp soil or water, they produce roots and new plants. For example: Eyes in potato, Rhizomes of banana and ginger, Bulbil.

Sexual reproduction

In sexual reproduction, formation of male and female gametes is achieved, either by the same individual or by different individuals of the opposite sex. It results in offsprings that are not exactly identical to their parents or amongst themselves.

Juvenile phase: The period of rapid growth to attain maturity for sexual reproduction. In plants, it is known as the vegetative phase.

Reproductive phase: It is the phase of life cycle wherein the growth of the individuals is slowed down but it attains the maturity to reproduce. Annual and biennial plants show visible vegetative, reproductive and senescent phases but it is quite difficult to identify these phases in perennial plants.

Oestrus cycle: The females of placental mammals exhibit cyclic changes in the activities of ovaries and hormones, during reproductive phase. These cyclic changes are known as Oestrus cycle.

Senescence: Also known as 'Old age' in plants. It is the last phase of their life span and end of reproductive phase. In this phase, metabolism slows down, finally leading to death.

Events in Sexual reproduction

- **Pre-fertilization Events-** The events prior to the fusion of gametes.

Gametogenesis- Process of gamete formation for both male and female

- **Homogametes/Isogametes:** Gametes cannot be classified into male or female. Fusion of such gametes is known as Isogamy.

- **Heterogametes:** Male and female gametes can be easily differentiated. Female gamete is known as ovum or egg and the male gamete is known as antherozoid or sperm.

Sexuality in organism

- Heterothallic/dioecious: Plants that have only one sex organ.

- Homothallic/monoecious: Plants that have both male and female sex organs.

- Unisexual: Animals that have only one type of reproductive system. For example: cockroach.

- Bisexual: Animals that have both male and female reproductive system. Example: earthworms or leech. Fungi maybe bisexual (homothallic) or unisexual (heterothallic).

Cell division

Diploid parental body produces haploid gametes by the process of meiosis. It can be observed in angiosperms, gymnosperms and animals.

Haploid parental body produces haploid gametes by mitosis. It can be observed in Algae, Fungi, Monera.

Gamete transfer: For fertilization, male gametes need a medium to transport towards female. A large number of male gametes are produced to compensate the loss of male gametes during their movement toward the female gametes.

In plants like bryophytes and algae, the medium for the transfer of gametes is water.

- **Fertilization Events-** Fusion of gametes to form a diploid zygote.

The female gamete develops into a new organism without fertilization in honeybees, turkey, some lizards. This is called parthenogenesis.

There are two types of Fertilization (Syngamy):

- **External fertilization-** In this, the fertilization occurs outside the body of the organism. For example- Aquatic organisms like amphibians, algae. The offsprings produced from this type of fertilization are extremely vulnerable to predators threatening their survival.

- **Internal fertilization-** In this the fertilization occurs inside the body of the organism. For example- angiosperms, gymnosperms and bryophytes. The number of eggs is very low while the sperms are produced in large quantity.

- **Post-fertilization Events-** The events that take place after the formation of zygote.

- **Zygote:** Every sexually reproducing organism begins its life as a zygote. Zygote is formed after fertilization. The development of zygote depends on the life cycle off the organism and nature of environment. Organisms having diplontic life cycle, zygote divides by the process of mitosis whereas organisms having haplontic life cycle, zygote divides by the process of meiosis to produce haploid spores.

- **Embryogenesis-** The process of development of zygote into an embryo.

Cell division increases the number of cells in the embryo. Cell division (mitosis) and cell differentiation occurs in zygote.

Animals that lay eggs and the zygote development takes place inside the egg are known as Oviparous. For example- Reptiles and birds

Animals that give birth to the young ones are known as Viviparous. The zygote is developed inside the body of the female.

EXERCISE

1. Which animal have developed capacity of regeneration?
   - (*a*) Hydra, Starfish
   - (*b*) Plasmodium
   - (*c*) Earthworm
   - (*d*) Spongilla

2. Sporulation occurs in ______.
   - (*a*) Rhizobium
   - (*b*) Hydra
   - (*c*) Starfish
   - (*d*) Spongilla

3. Which plant reproduce vegetatively by roots?
   - (*a*) Oxalis
   - (*b*) Bryophyllum
   - (*c*) Onion
   - (*d*) Dahlia

4. How does Amoeba reproduce?
   - (*a*) Binary fission
   - (*b*) Budding
   - (*c*) Division
   - (*d*) Both a and c.

5. In which method of asexual reproduction the division of cytoplasm is not possible?
   - (*a*) Amitotic division
   - (*b*) Binary fission
   - (*c*) Division
   - (*d*) Budding

6. In which method of asexual reproduction the off spring's are genetically identical, to the parents?
   - (*a*) Amitotic division
   - (*d*) Multiple fission
   - (*c*) Division
   - (*d*) Binary fission

7. In which type of reproduction single parent is essential for reproduction.
   - (*a*) Asexual
   - (*b*) Sexual
   - (*c*) Vegetative
   - (*d*) Fragmentation

8. In which type of organism asexual reproduction is seen?
   - (*a*) Unicellular
   - (*b*) Bicellular
   - (*c*) Multicellular
   - (*d*) Both a and c.

9. Having two copies of each chromosome
   - (*a*) diploid
   - (*b*) biploid
   - (*c*) haploid
   - (*d*) triploid

10. This is the method by which bacteria reproduce.
    - (*a*) Fusion
    - (*b*) Binary fusion
    - (*c*) Budding
    - (*d*) Gametogenesis.

11. Each and every organism can live only for a certain period of time. The period from birth to the natural death of an organism represents its
    - (*a*) Asexual reproduction
    - (*b*) Sexual reproduction
    - (*c*) Development
    - (*d*) Life span

12. Whatever be the life span, death of every individual organism is a certainty, i.e., no individual is immortal, except
    - (*a*) Human beings
    - (*b*) *Amoeba* and *Paramoecium*
    - (*c*) Single-celled organisms
    - (*d*) Both (*b*) and (*c*)

13. Select correct statement with respect to life span
    - (*a*) It is related to the size of organisms
    - (*b*) It is correlated with complexity of organisms
    - (*c*) Peepal tree has much shorter life span as compared to a mango tree
    - (*d*) It is a specific trait of each organism

14. Which of the following statements is correct ?
    - (*a*) All the individuals of a species have exactly the same life span
    - (*b*) Smaller organisms always have shorter life span and *vice versa*
    - (*c*) Life span of an organism is the time period from its birth to its natural death
    - (*d*) No organism may have a life span of several hundred years

15. A biological process in which an organism gives rise to young ones (offspring) similar to itself is called
    - (*a*) Reproduction
    - (*b*) Fertilisation
    - (*c*) Parthenogenesis
    - (*d*) Gametogenesis

16. As compared to the asexual reproduction, the sexual reproduction is
    - (*a*) Elaborate, complex and slow process
    - (*b*) Elaborate, simple and fast process
    - (*c*) Diffused, complex and slow process
    - (*d*) Elaborate, simple and fast process

17. The growth phase of an organism before attaining sexual maturity is referred to as
    - (*a*) juvenile phase
    - (*b*) vegetative phase
    - (*c*) both (*a*) and (*b*)
    - (*d*) none of these

18. The end of juvenile/vegetative phase marks the beginning of the
    - (*a*) Reproductive phase
    - (*b*) Senescent phase
    - (*c*) Flowering period
    - (*d*) Maturation phase

19. Mark the incorrect statement.

(*a*) Perennial species shows clear cut vegetative, reproductive and senescent phases

(*b*) End of vegetative phase marks the beginning of reproductive phase

(*c*) Bamboo species flower only once in their lifetime

(*d*) The reproductive phase is of variable duration in different organisms

20. Which of the following plant shows unusual flowering phenomenon ?

(*a*) Bamboo and banana

(*b*) Banana and Neelakurinji

(*c*) Bamboo and *Strobilanthes kunthiana*

(*d*) All of the above

21. The most vital and critical event of the sexual reproduction is

(*a*) Gamete formation   (*b*) Gamete transport

(*c*) Gametic fusion   (*d*) Embryogenesis

22. In fungi, bryophytes and pteridophytes, the fertilization is

(*a*) External   (*b*) Internal

(*c*) Both (*a*) and (*b*)   (*d*) Can't say

23. Match the following columns.

Column-I	Column-II
a. External fertilisation	1. Human beings
b. Internal fertilisation	2. Algae and fishes
c. Ovipary	3. Bryophytes, pteridophytes and birds
d. Vivipary	4. Reptiles and birds

	a	b	c	d
(*a*)	4	1	2	3
(*b*)	3	1	4	2
(*c*)	2	3	4	1
(*d*)	4	2	1	3

24. Which is the vital link that ensures continuity of species between organisms of one generation and the next ?

(*a*) Sexual reproduction   (*b*) Embryo

(*c*) Zygote   (*d*) Fertilisation

25. Every sexually reproducing organism, including human beings, begins life as a single cell called

(*a*) Gamete   (*b*) Spore

(*c*) Embryo   (*d*) Zygote

Answer Keys

1. (*a*)	2. (*a*)	3. (*d*)	4. (*a*)	5. (*a*)	6. (*d*)	7. (*a*)	8. (*d*)	9. (*a*)	10. (*c*)
11. (*d*)	12. (*d*)	13. (*d*)	14. (*c*)	15. (*a*)	16. (*a*)	17. (*c*)	18. (*a*)	19. (*a*)	20. (*c*)
21. (*c*)	22. (*a*)	23. (*c*)	24. (*c*)	25. (*d*)					

Solutions

1. Hydras reproduce asexually by producing buds in the body wall which grow to be miniature adults and simply break away when they are mature. By this method new hydra is formed.

2. Sporulation refers to the formation of spores from Vegetative cells during unfavourable environmental conditions. Sporulation occurs in Plasmodium.

3. Plants like Dahlia can reproduce asexually without the fertilization of gametes, by either vegetative reproduction or apomixis.

4. Amoeba reproduces by the common asexual reproduction method called binary fission. After replicating its genetic material through mitotic division, the cells divides into two equal sized daughter cells.

5. Amitotic is also called Direct cell division. In amitotic division there is no chromosome formation and spindle formation occuring and hence the two daughter cells are approximately two equal halves of the parental cells.

6. Binary fission occurs when a parent cell splits into two identical daughter cells of the same size which allows the offsprings to be genetically identical to the parents.

7. Asexual reproduction occurs when an organism makes more of itself without exchanging genetic information with another organism through sex.

8. Both unicellular and multicellular organism can reproduce asexually. Many multicellular organism give birth to their young one's by asexual method.

9. An organism in which the two copies of the gene are identical that is, have the same allele is called diploid organism.

10. Bacteria reproduce by Budding method. In this a new organism develops from an outgrowth or bud due to cell division at one particular site.

11. Each and every organism can live only for a certain period of time. The period from birth to the natural death of an organism represents its **life span.**

12. Whatever be the life span, death of every individiual organism is a certainty, i.e. no individual is immortal, except **single-celled organisms.** Actually single celled organisms are considered to be **biologically immortal.** This is because they do not die as the grow old. This technically means that the same organisms keep getting split into new young ones (daughter cells) by binary fission.

13. Life spans of organisms are not necessarily correlated with their size or complexity. A mango tree has a much shorter life span (200 years) as compared to a peepal tree (2,500 years).

14. Each and every organism can live only for a certain period of time. Life span of an organism may be few minutes to several thousand years. Smaller organisms not necessarily have shorter life span. Life-span may be as short as a few days or as long as a few thousand years. A mango tree has 200 years life span while that of peepal tree has 2,500 years. Banyan tree has 200-300 years life span while that of *Sequoia* has 3000-4000 years.

15. Reproduction is defined as a biological process in which an organism gives rise to young ones (offspring) similar to itself.

16. As compared to the asexual reproduction, the sexual reproduction is **elaborate, complex** and **slow process.**

17. The period of growth is called the **juvenile phase.** It is known as **vegetative phase** in plants. This phase is of variable durations in different organisms.

18. The end of juvenile/vegetative phase marks the beginning of the reproductive phase in higher plants when they come to flower.

19. Plants, which are of annual and biennial types, show clear cut vegetative, reproductive and senescent phases, but in the perennial species it is very difficult to clearly define these phases.

20. **Bamboo** and *Strobilanthus kunthiana* show unusual flowering phenomenon. Bamboo species flower only once in their life time, generally after 50-100 years, produce larger number of fruits and die. Another plant, *Strobilanthus kunthiana* (neelakuranji) flowers once in 12 years. The last time this plant flowered during July-August, 2018.

21. The most vital and critical event of the sexual reproduction is **gametic fusion.** In many terrestrial organisms, belonging to fungi, higher animals such as reptiles, birds, mammals and in a majority of plants (bryophytes, pteridophytes, gymnosperms and angiosperms), syngamy occurs inside the body of the organism hence the process is called **internal fertilization.**

22. In most aquatic organisms, such as a majority of algae and fishes as well as amphibians, syngamy occurs in the external medium (water), i.e., outside the body of organism. This type of gametic fusion is called **external fertilization.**

23. (c)

24. **Zygote** is the vital link that ensures continuity of species between organisms of one generation and the next.

25. Every sexually reproducing organism, including human beings begins life as a single cell called **zygote.**

CHAPTER 2

Sexual Reproduction in Flowering Plants

Flowers and its parts

Structure of Flower

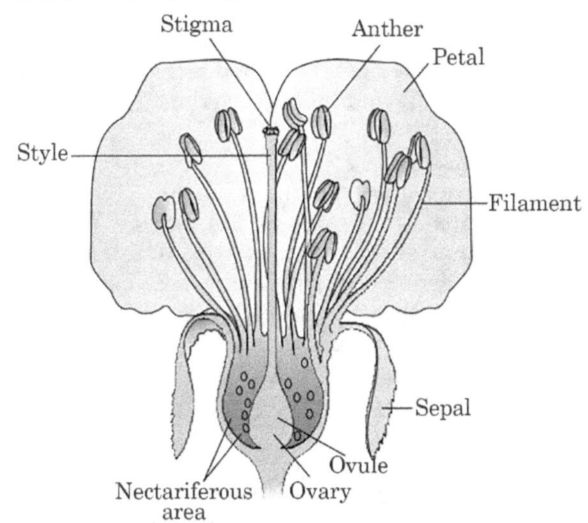

Fig.: Structure of Flower

Flower is the reproductive structure in plants. This is where male and female gametes fuse.

Structures and Events of pre-fertilization

The male reproductive system in a flower is called androecium that contains whorl of stamens and a female reproductive part known as gynoecium consisting pistil.

- Stamen: It is the organ of the flower that produces pollen.

It consists of three main parts namely: filament which is a lean and long stalk and has a bilobed extension known as an anther.

There are four microsprorangia located at the four sided structure of anther, two in each lobe. The further development of microsprorangia takes place and converts into pollen sacs. Microsporogenesis can be defined as the process in which microspores are formed from the pollen/microspore mother cell. They are divided by the process of meiosis.

Pollen grain: The pollen grains represent the male gametophytes.

The presence of sporopollenin ensures the pollen grains are well preserved as fossils. Generative cell and the vegetative cell are the two cells present in a matured pollen grain.

- Pistil: The gynoecium represents the female reproductive part of the flower. Gynoecium consisting of single pistil is known as monocarpellary and of multiple pistils is known as multicarpellary.

Gynoecium consists of pistils and each pistil has three part, the stigma, style and the ovary. From the placenta, megasporangia arises which are also called as ovules. An ovary may have one ovule such as in paddy or mango or it may have several ovules such as in water melons.

The pollen grains lands on stigma. Beneath the stigma is a lean part known as style. The bottom bulged part is ovary.

Megasporangium (Ovule)

The megaspore is responsible for formation of a single egg cell. The process in which megaspores are formed from the mother cell is coined as megasporogenesis.

Female gametophyte

Monosporic development is the method of embryo sac formation from a single megaspore. In general an angiosperm embryo sac at maturity, is 8 nucleate, 7 celled structure.

Pollination

- Pollination is the transfer of pollen grains from anther to stigma of a pistil.
- Pollination can be conducted through abiotic agents like wind and water and biotic agent like animals.
- We can prevent self- pollination by various practices like, In some species pollen release and stigma receptivity cannot take place simultaneously. In some species anther and stigma are at different positions, Another way to prevent self pollination and encourage cross pollination is production of unisexual flowers.

There are three types of pollination, on the basis of source of pollen:

- Autogamy: When the pollination is attained within the same flower and pollen grains transfer from the anther to the stigma of the same flower.
- Geitonogamy: When pollen grains transfer from the anther to the stigma of a different flower of same plant.
- Xenogamy: When the pollen grains transfer from anther to the stigma of another plant.

Pistel- Pollen Interaction

- Emasculation is the process carried out in bisexual flowers by removing their anthers using a pair of forceps before the anther bursts open.
- A bag of convenient size, usually made up of butter paper is used to cover the flowers that are emasculated to prevent contamination of that flowers's stigma with unwanted pollen is called bagging.

Double-Fertilisation

- When two types of fusions happen inside the embryo sac the first being triple fusion and the other syngamy this event is called double fertilization. After triple fusion, the central cell becomes the primary endosperm cell and is developed into endosperm. The zygote is developed into an embryo.

Post-fertilisation: Structure and Events

Post-fertilisation events is a collective term given to transformation of ovary into fruits, ovules into seeds and the development of embryo and endosperm that starts after the double fertilisation process.

Endosperm

Before the development of the embryo, endosperms develop. The cells of the endosperm tissue contain banked food materials and are also used to provide nutrition to the developing embryo. It is either to be entirely eaten up by the developing embryo (e.g., pea, groundnut, beans) before the seed matures or it may exist in the mature seed. For example- coconut.

The Embryo

- At the micropylar end of embryo sac the embryo development begins, this is where zygote is situated. Embryogeny refers to the early stage of embryo development which is common in both dicotyledonous and monocotyledonous embryo.

Seed

- The mature may be of two types either non-albuminous or ex- albuminous. The non albuminous seeds have no residual endosperm as it is consumed during embryonic development where as in albuminous seeds a part of endosperm is retained as it is not completely used up during embryonic development.

Apomixis and Polyembryony

- Some species of Asteraceae and grasses and few other flowering plants have evolved a special mechanism to produce seeds without fertilization and this is called 'Apomixis'.
- The event of presence of more than one embryo in a seed is referred to as polyembryony.

EXERCISE

1. Water is absorbed by
   - (a) Root hairs
   - (b) Root caps
   - (c) Root
   - (d) Root apex

2. Pneumatophores occur in plants of
   - (a) Sandy soil
   - (b) Saline marshy soil
   - (c) Marshy soil
   - (d) Water

3. Roots developing from plant parts other than radicle are
   - (a) Epiphyllous
   - (b) Epicaulous
   - (c) Adventitious
   - (d) Fibrous

4. Roots are feebly developed in
   - (a) Hydrophytes
   - (b) Mesophytes
   - (c) Xerophytes
   - (d) Halophytes

5. Nodulated roots occurs in
   - (a) Pea
   - (b) Wheat
   - (c) Mustard
   - (d) Rice

6. Root cap takes part in
   - (a) Formation of new cells
   - (b) Absorption of Water and Minerals
   - (c) Protection of root meristem
   - (d) Storage of food.

7. Conical fleshy roots occur in
   - (a) Sweet Potato
   - (b) Dahlia
   - (c) Asparagus
   - (d) Carrot

8. Napiform roots are recorded from
   - (a) Radish
   - (b) Carrot
   - (c) Beet
   - (d) Sweet Potato

9. Fusiform roots are found in
   - (a) Solanum tuberosum
   - (b) Calocasia
   - (c) Daucus carota
   - (d) Raphanus Sativus

10. Plants which flower only once in their life is
    - (a) Polycarpic
    - (b) monocarpic
    - (c) Cleistocarpic
    - (d) Pesicarpic

11. Third whorl in flower is of
    - (a) Petal
    - (b) Sepal
    - (c) Stamen
    - (d) Pistil

12. Flower is modified shoot because
    - (a) in some flowers thalamus become elongated and shows distinct nodes and internodes
    - (b) flowers aggregate to form inflorescence
    - (c) epicalyx is present in some flowers
    - (d) essential organs are present in some flowers.

13. In monoecious plants
    - (a) male and female parts are borne by the same plant but not by the same flower
    - (b) male and female parts are borne by the same flower
    - (c) male and female parts are borne by the different plant
    - (d) none of the above.

14. A flower is said to be complete when it has
    - (a) Corolla
    - (b) androecium and gynoecium
    - (c) Calyx and corolla only
    - (d) all the four whorls

15. Protandry is the situation when
    - (a) anthers and stigma mature at the same time
    - (b) anthers mature later than the stigma of the flower
    - (c) anthers mature earlier than the stigma of the same flowers.
    - (d) anthers of the flower pollinate the stigma of the same flower.

16. In a bisexual flowers when the gynoecium matures earlier than the androecium it is called
    - (a) Protogyny
    - (b) Protandry
    - (c) Autogamy
    - (d) Heterogamy

17. In which of the following plants do the male and female flowers occur in the same individual.
    - (a) pumpkin
    - (b) rose
    - (c) hibiscus
    - (d) both (b) and (c)

18. In a flower, when the ovary is situated on the torus above all other floral whorls, the flower is said to be.
    - (a) Perigynous
    - (b) epigynous
    - (c) inferior
    - (d) hypogynous

19. A flowers is brightly colored, scented and secrete nectar. It is most probably.
    - (a) pollinated by insects
    - (b) sterile
    - (c) pollinated by wind
    - (d) an insectivorous plant

20. A bisexual flower which never open in its life span is called.

(*a*) homogamous   (*b*) heterogamous

(*c*) polygamous   (*d*) cleistogamous.

21. Which one of the following in an example of cleistogamy.

(*a*) Sunflower   (*b*) Vallisneria

(*c*) Commelina   (*d*) Calotropis

22. When pollen grains of a flower pollinate the stigma of another flower of the same plant, it is called

(*a*) Dichogamy   (*b*) Herkogamy

(*c*) Geitonogamy   (*d*) Autogamy

23. Which prevents self pollination

(*a*) Self sterility

(*b*) Herkogamy

(*c*) Dichogamy

(*d*) All of the above.

24. Dichogamy which helps in cross pollination is a floral mechanism in which

(*a*) Pollen sac and stigma are at different heights

(*b*) Anther and stigma mature at different times

(*c*) Structure of pollen sac and stigma functions as hurdles

(*d*) Pollen grain is unable to germinate on the stigma of the same flower.

25. Pollination by slug and snails in called

(*a*) Ornithophilous

(*b*) Malacophilous

(*c*) Anemophilous

(*d*) Chiropterophilous

26. Pollination by water is seen in

(*a*) Nelumbium   (*b*) Vallisneria

(*c*) Eichornia   (*d*) Nymphaea

27. A close relation between flower and pollinating agent is best exhibited by

(*a*) Cocos   (*b*) Salvia

(*c*) Yucca   (*d*) Avena

28. Wind pollination is common in

(*a*) orchids   (*b*) legumes

(*c*) lilies   (*d*) grasses

29. The pollination which occurs in one plant is

(*a*) Herkogamy   (*b*) Cleistogamy

(*c*) Dichogamy   (*d*) Dicliny

30. In which of the following pollination takes place by lever mechanism.

(*a*) Salvia   (*b*) Ficus

(*c*) Antirhinum   (*d*) Ocimum.

31. Feathery stigma is present in

(*a*) Wheat   (*b*) Pea

(*c*) Caesalpinia   (*d*) Datura

32. In sausage tree (Kigelia africana) the pollination takes place by

(*a*) Birds   (*b*) Bats

(*c*) Winds   (*d*) Insects.

33. Anemophilous pollination is mainly observed in

(*a*) Gramineae   (*b*) Annonaceae

(*c*) Papilionaceae   (*d*) Euphorbiaceae

34. Flowers preventing self-pollination is called

(*a*) Dichogamy   (*b*) Protandry

(*c*) Herkogamy   (*d*) Protogyny

35. Both, autogamy and geitonogamy are prevented in

(*a*) Papaya   (*b*) Cucumber

(*c*) Castor   (*d*) Maize.

36. In which one of the following pollination is autogamous

(*a*) cleistogamy   (*b*) Geitonogamy

(*c*) Xenogamy   (*d*) Cosmogony

37. The pollination of two flowers on different plants is known as.

(*a*) Xenogamy   (*b*) Geitonogamy

(*c*) Cleistogamy   (*d*) Dichogamy

38. Syngamy means

(*a*) fusion of similar spores

(*b*) fusion of dissimilar spores

(*c*) fusion of cytoplasm

(*d*) fusion of gametes

39. When the pollen tube enters through the micropyle it is termed as.

(*a*) Chalazogamy   (*b*) Mesogamy

(*c*) Porogamy   (*d*) Name of the above

40. Female gametophyte of a typical dicot at the time of fertilization is

(*a*) 8 celled   (*b*) 7 celled

(*c*) 6 celled   (*d*) 4 celled

41. Double fertilization was discovered by

(*a*) Karl Scharf   (*b*) P. Maheshwari

(*c*) S.G. Nawaschin   (*d*) B.G.L. Swamy

42. Fertilization of egg takes place inside
   (a) Anther   (b) Stigma
   (c) Pollen tube   (d) Embryo sac
43. Which pollen tube enters by integuments, then the process is called.
   (a) Mesogamy   (b) Porogamy
   (c) Chalozogamy   (d) Pseudogamy
44. Double fertilization is a characteristic of
   (a) Gymnosperms
   (b) Bryophytes
   (c) Angiosperms
   (d) Pteridophytes
45. A pollen tube groups down the style because
   (a) It helps in fertilization
   (b) It takes nutrients from the style
   (c) Filiform apparatus of synergids attracts the pollen tube
   (d) of chemical attraction.
46. Germination of pollen grain on the stigma is
   (a) Autogamy
   (b) In vivo germination
   (c) In vitro germination
   (d) None of there
47. Number of nuclei taking part in double fertilization is.
   (a) 2   (b) 3
   (c) 4   (d) 5
48. The phenomenon of syngamy (fertilization) in angiosperms was discovered by
   (a) Svedberg
   (b) Strasburger
   (c) Nawaschin
   (d) Coulter and chamberlin.
49. The cells that divides to form two male nuclei in angiosperms is.
   (a) Vegetative cell
   (b) Generative cell
   (c) Tube cell
   (d) Antheridial cell

50. Growth of pollen tube towards embryo sac is
   (a) Geotropism   (b) Thigmotaxis
   (c) Chemotaxis   (d) Phototaxis
51. In an angiospermic plant, endosperm is formed due to fertilization of secondary nucleus but it is absent in same of the seeds Viz. Pea, bean, Phaseolus (moong) etc.; It is due to lack of
   (a) Certain enzymes
   (b) Dicotyledonous hormone
   (c) Growth hormone
   (d) None of the above.
52. Through which route the pollen tube enters the ovule
   (a) Chalaza   (b) Micropyle
   (c) Funiculus   (d) All of these
53. Which of the following is without exception in angiosperms
   (a) Secondary growth
   (b) Presence of vessels
   (c) Double fertilization
   (d) Autotropic nutrition
54. The formation of embryo without fusion of gametes is termed as
   (a) Apospory   (b) Isogamy
   (c) Apogamy   (d) Syngamy
55. Which of the following is not true for double fertilization
   (a) Discovered by Nawaschin
   (b) Male gamete and secondary nucleus fused to form endosperm nucleus
   (c) Endosperm nucleus is diploid
   (d) Endosperm provide nutrition to embryo.
56. Through which cell of the embryo sac, does the pollen tube enter the embryo sac.
   (a) Egg cell
   (b) Central cell
   (c) Persistent synergid
   (d) Degenerated synergid
57. After fertilization the outer integument forms.
   (a) Testa   (b) Tegmen
   (c) Perisperm   (d) Pericarp

Answer Keys

1. (a)	2. (c)	3. (c)	4. (a)	5. (a)	6. (c)	7. (d)	8. (c)	9. (d)	10. (b)
11. (c)	12. (a)	13. (a)	14. (d)	15. (c)	16. (a)	17. (a)	18. (d)	19. (a)	20. (d)
21. (c)	22. (c)	23. (d)	24. (b)	25. (b)	26. (b)	27. (b)	28. (d)	29. (b)	30. (a)
31. (a)	32. (b)	33. (a)	34. (c)	35. (a)	36. (a)	37. (a)	38. (d)	39. (c)	40. (b)
41. (c)	42. (d)	43. (a)	44. (c)	45. (c)	46. (b)	47. (d)	48. (b)	49. (b)	50. (c)
51. (d)	52. (d)	53. (c)	54. (c)	55. (c)	56. (d)	57. (a)			

Solutions

1. The root hairs enhance the exposed surface area of the root, for the absorption of water from the soil.

2. Some plants growing in salty marshes some branches of top root grow vertically upwards in to the air from horizontally secondary roots. There roots are called pneumatophores.

3. In monocotyledonous plants the radicle dies immediately after germination of seeds and later these roots arise from any portion (stem, leaves etc.) of the plant

4. Root system is very much reduced in some floating plants and in submerged plants the roots are absent.

5. The primary top root and its branches of leguminous plants, i.e, plants belonging to sub family papilionatal of family leguminosae (e.g. pea, gram, and groundnut etc) bear nodule like swellings, called root nodules.

6. It is a cap like parenchymatous multicellular structure which protects the root-apex. As the root is continuously growing downwards into the soil, friction with soil particles wears out the root-cap while its outer cells are being constantly replaced by new growth from its base.

7. The swollen root is broad at the base and tapers gradually towards the apex.

8. The root is nearly globular or spherical in shape. The basal portion of root is much swollen which suddenly tapers towards the apex giving a top shaped appearance, e.g., Turnip and Beet.

9. The storage root is like a spindle, narrow towards both base and apex. It occurs in Raphanus sativus. The basal part of it is made of tap root.

10. Monocarpic plants are those that flower, set seeds and then die. The term was first used by Alphonse de candolle.

11. The stamen is the third whorl of a flower, the male reproductive part. The stamen is made of a thin vertical thread-live structure called a filament topped with a circular or a oblong structure called an anther. The anther produces pollen, which is the male contribution to be reproduction process in plants.

12. The thalamus is the short abbreviated axis bearing the four sets of floral leaves. It is the swollen end of the peduncle or pedicle with four nodes and very much compressed internodes. The floral leaves remain inserted on the nodes in whorls or spirally. The axis nature of the thalamus becomes quite evident in some flower in which thalamus is considerably long and the internodes are distinct.

13. Monecious plants have both male and female flowers rather than perfect flowers. Corn (maize) is a good example of a monecius plant species. It has two types of flowers that develop of different parts of the plant. The male flower forms at the top of the plant and is called the tassle.

14. Flower is the reproductive part of the plant. It consists of female organ (whorl) made of carpels (Pistil/gynoecium), male organ (whorl) made of stamens (Androecium) and corolla made of petals, usually attractive part act as protective part also and outermost whorl-calyx, made of sepals, usually green but otherwise coloured in many cases. When flower has all these four whorls then flower is called as complete flower, missing any whorl make it incomplete.

15. Protandry is a state in hermaphroditic systems that is characterized by the development of male organs or maturation of their products before the appearance of the corresponding female product thus inhibiting self-fertilization and that is encountered commonly in mints, legumer and composites and among diverse groups of invertebrate animals.

17. Most plants sprout bisexual flower (which have both male and female parts), evolutionary biologists have recently discovered. Plants with male and bisexual flowers produce more seeds. Why this is true is new scientific mystery, but it probably has something to do with male flower hoarding less of a plant's energy (making more of it available to crack out seed)

18. In hypogynous flowers, the perianth and stamens are attached to the receptacle below the gynocism; the ovary is superior to these organs, and the remaining floral organs.

19. Insect pollinated flowers are brightly coloured and sweet smelling to attract insects to itself. This required the coevolution of insects and flowering plants in the development of pollination behaviour by the insects and pollination mechanisms by the flowers, benefiting both groups.

20. Cleistogamy (kleisto-closed, gamous marriage).

21. In Cleistogamy bisexual flowers never open therefore the pollengrains may only pollinate the stigma of the same flower e.g. commelina bengalenis (day flower)

22. Geitonogamy is the transfer for pollen grains from anthers of one flower to another flower of either the same plant or genetically similar plant or between two clones.

23. Self sterility, herkogamy and dichogamy are adaptation for cross pollination.

24. Dichogamy is the maturation of anther and stigmas of a flower at different times, e.g. sunflower.

25. Malacophily is cross pollination brought about by the agency of snails, slugs e.g. Arisaema (Cobra plant)

26. Vallisneria is sub merged, dioecius, fresh water plant. Hence pollinated in water.

27. In salvia (sage plant), a member of family labiatae pollination occurs by bees and there is a special mechanism called "Turn pipe mechanism" or Lever mechanism of pollination.

28. Wind pollination is common is grosses and gymnosperms.

29. Cleistogamy is the process of self pollination

30. Salvia has turn pipe or lever mechanism for pollination by honey bee.

31. Feathery stigma is characteristic of wind pollination.

32. Chiropterophily is pollination by bats e.g. Kigelia africana. Adansonia etc.

33. Anemophilous plants bear small and inconspicuous flowers. The pollen grains are small, light, smooth and dry.

34. Herkogamy are mechanical devices that prevent self pollination and favour cross pollination even in homogamous flowers.

35. Papaya is dioecious so that it prevents both Autogamy and Geitonogamy (method of self pollination).

36. Self pollination is favoured by cleistogamy.

37. Xenogamy is the cross pollination between two flowers of different plants.

38. Syngamy is fusion of one of the two male gametes with egg to produce diploid zygote (oospore)

39. Porogamy is the most common way in angiosperms e.g. Lily.

40. In mature female gametophyte, 3 antipodal cells, 2 Synergids, 1 egg and 1 diploid secondary nucleus are present.

41. Double fertilization was discovered by Nawaschin, (1898) in fritillaria and Lilium.

42. Because egg is the part of embryo sac.

43. In mesogamy pollen tube penetrates laterally through integuments (cucurbita) and funiculus (e.g. pistacia)

44. Because in gymnosperms, bryophytes and pteridophytes single fertilization is found.

45. Filiform apparatus of synergids secretes some chemical substance which is polysacchoride in nature which attract pollen tube.

46. Germination of pollen grains completes on stigma i.e., in vivo. It means in natural conditions or within the cell.

47. 5 i.e., 2 sperm nuclei, 2 pollen nuclei and one egg nucleus.

48. In angiosperms, male gametes reach the female gamete with the help of pollen tube. (Strasburger, 1884)

49. Generative cell divides into two male gametes, if it has not divided already.

50. Growth of pollen tube towards the embryo sac is chemotaxis because this movement is induced by chemicals like auxin hormone and carbohydrate.

51. Pea, bean and phaseolus seeds are non-endospermic because endosperm is fully consumed during their embryo development. It is an advance character of angiosperm.

52. All three type can be route of the pollen tube enters in the ovule as chalazogamy mesogamy and porogamy.

53. Double fertilization is found only in angiosperm. In which secondary nucleus form triploid cell and egg convert into diploid zygote. Triploid cell to form endosperm and diploid zygate to form embryo.

54. The formation of sporophyte from gametophytic cell without fertilization is called apogamy.

55. Endosperm is triploid (3n)

56. Synergids are short lived (one of them degenerated long before fertilization and second after entry of pollen tube into embryo sac)

57. After fertilization the outer integument forms testa, inner integument forms tegmen and ovary wall forms pericarp.

CHAPTER 3

Human Reproduction

Reproductive Systems

Male Reproductive System

The male reproductive system is classified into the following categories:

- Testes
  - Testes are the sex organ whose primary role is to produce testosterone and sperms.
  - Testes are found inside of scrotum in the upper thigh area.
  - The shape of testes is oval.
  - Testes are found outside of the body in a sack because it needs 2 to 3 degrees less temperature than body temperature for its optimal functioning.
  - There are two testes both having around 500 testicular lobules.
  - Every single lobule is stacked with connective tissue having around 2-3 semiferous tubules which are yellow in color.
  - These semiferous tubules are queued along with spermatogenic cells are also termed as sertoli cells.
  - These sertoli cells are responsible for optimal growth of spermatogenic cells and hence the term coined for it, is nurse cells. Sertoli cells provide nutrition to the developing sperm cells.
- Accessory Ducts
  - The four major constituent part of duct systems are:

    Rete testis

    epididymis

    vas deferens

    vasa efferentia
  - The tubules semiferous in nature open in vasa efferentia via rete testes.
  - Vasa efferentia is lead into opening of Epididymis.
  - Now the urethra originates at urinary bladder and ends in urethral meatus which is an opening end of penis.
- External Genetelia
  - Penis is the only major part of the external organ.
  - Penis is made up of special tissue.
  - This special tissue helps in erection of the penis which is needed for insemination.
  - The terminal end of penis comprises of foreskin.
- Accessory Glands
  - It comprises of several glands such as Cowper's gland, prostate gland, seminal vesicles etc.
  - Seminal plasma is the resulted secretion of these glands.
  - This seminal plasma is very rich calcium and fructose which ensure proper motility and nutrition of sperm.
  - Cowper's gland acts as lubricating agent for penis as their secretion is rich in mucus.

Female Reproductive System

The female reproductive system is classified into the following categories:

- Ovaries
  - Ovaries are the sex organ whose primary role is to produce estrogen and ova.
  - Ovaries are found in the lower abdomen.
  - The size of each ovary is around 3cm in length.
  - A ligament is used to link ovary to pelvic wall.
- Accessory Ducts

The three major constituent part of duct systems are:

Two oviducts: The oviducts are comprised of the following parts-

- Ampulla
- Isthmus
- Infundibulum
- Uterine Part

Uterus:

➢ Uterus is basically the womb. It is pyloric in shape.

➢ Uterus opens up in vagina by cervix.

➢ Uterus is responsible for the growth of the baby after fertilization.

Vagina: It is a tube shaped canal which connects the outer body with the uterus. It acts as a passage for movement of sperm. It also acts as a passage for childbirth.

- **External Genetelia:**

➢ Vagina is the major part of the external organ in females. It also constitutes of the following parts:

  - Clitoris
  - Hymen
  - Labia Minora
  - Mons pubis

➢ Mons pubis is the fatty tissue. It acts as a cusion and is overlapped by pubic hair and skin.

➢ The opening of vagina is Labia minora. It is basically two folds which are fleshy.

➢ Above the urethra opening there is a tiny finger like structure. This part is called as clitoris.

- **Mammary Glands**

➢ In the chest region there is a pair of mammary gland.

➢ This gland also contains a vital component known as Glandular tissue that helps to carry milk to the areolar region.

➢ Every single tissue has around 20 lobes which is actually a cell cluster also called as alveoli.

➢ In alveoli cavities milk is stored upto secrection.

➢ The alveoli opens up into mammary duct.

➢ These ducts combined together are connected to a lactiferous duct through which the milk is secreted out.

Gametogenesis

- The process in which the sex cells are produced is coined as gametogenesis.

- Gametogenesis is classified in following types:

  Spermatogenesis

  Oogenesis

Spermatogenesis

- The process which results in formation of sperms is called as spermatogenesis.

- It comprises of two stages:

  Spermatids formation: In this process the mother sperm cell results in formation of spermatids.

  Spermiogenesis: The spermatids formed in the above step results into formation of sperms.

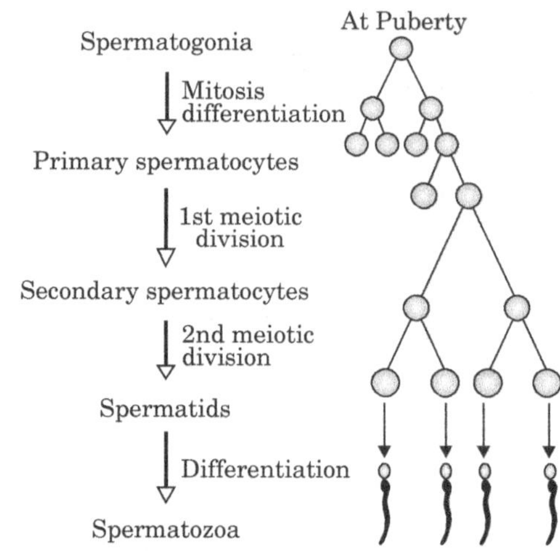

Fig.: Spermatogenesis mechanism

- Meosis-I is undergone by spermatocyte to produce secondary spermatocytes.

- Now Meosis-II is undergone by spermatocyte to produce haploid spermatids.

- Now using the process of spermiogenesis, the spermatids produced in the above step transforms into spermatozoa.

Structure of Sperm

- The length of a sperm is around 0.06 mm.

- The plasma encloses the sperm.

- The four basic parts of sperms are:

(*a*) **Head: The shape of the head is oval and the constituent part is acrosome and nucleus.**

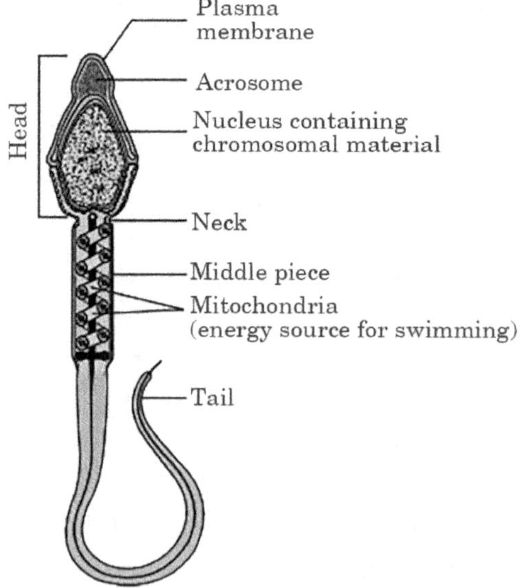

Fig.: Structure & various parts of Sperm

(*b*) **Neck: Distal and proximal centrioles is the basic part of neck. Neck is followed by the head.**

(*c*) Middle Part: The power house or mitochondria and cytoplasm comprises to make the middle part.

(*d*) Tail: It is a filament that is axial in nature. Tail is used for the movement by sperms. Accessory ducts are used to transport sperms.

- **Oogenesis**

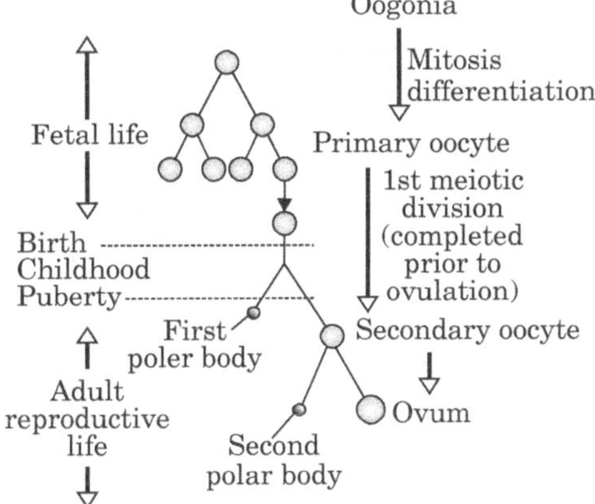

Fig.: Oogenesis mechanism

➢ The process which results in formation of ovum is termed as oogenesis.

➢ During the onset of embryo stage, oogenesis process initiates.

➢ During this process multiple of egg cells (oogonia) are produced in each ovary.

➢ Prophase I meiosis is undergone by these egg cells obtained in the above step and they result into several multiplied cells.

➢ The granulosa cells surround the egg cell to result into a primary follicle.

➢ As the ovary reaches the age of puberty, only around 70,000 primary follicles are left out which again are surrounded by granulosa cells to form secondary follicles.

➢ This process continues to form tertiary follicles.

➢ Unequal meiosis division is undergone by the egg cells inside the tertiary follicle and this results in to secondary oocyte and polar body.

➢ Now this polar body obtained in the above step either withers or survives by dividing itself.

➢ Now this secondary oocyte is released outside when it is being punctured by Graafian follicle.

➢ This releasing process is also termed as ovulation.

Structure of Ovum

- The shape is oval or it can be spherical.

- The radius of an ovum is around 0.1mm.
- It has got several membranes which are as follows:

Zona pellucida

Vitelline membrane

Corona Radiata

Plasma Membrane

Menstrual Cycle

- Human females undergo a reproductive cycle every month, this reproductive cycle is termed as menstrual cycle.
- This cycle usually starts the age of 13 to 15 years and this process is termed as menarche.
- This above cycle takes around 28 days.
- In each cycle a release of endometria lining takes place and is termed as menstrual flow. This flow occurs in between of a cycle and goes on for around three to five days.
- This cycle only takes place when the egg is not fertilized yet. If this cycle does not takes place, that means pregnancy might have occured.
- The menstrual flow begins when the lining of the uterus breaks itself as a result of the egg not getting fertilized as the level of progesterone drops.
- The next phase that is being followed by the menstrual phase is follicular. In this phase all the follicles become mature and results into formation of Graafian follicles.
- During this phase the secretion of estrogen also increases as a result of increased levels of gonadotropins.
- Now a third phase occurs after follicular is luteal phase. In this after the ovulation, the Graffian follicle degenerates into corpus luteum.
- There is no menstrual cycle taking place at the time of pregnancy.

Fertilization, Pregnancy and Embryonic development

Fertilization

- The process in which male and female gamete fuse together is termed as fertilization.
- The male gametes are sperms and the female gametes is ova. The sperms are being released in the vagina.

- As soon as the sperms enter the vagina, they swim towards the uterus. Then a fusion takes place at the oviduct on ampullary-isthmic junction.
- Now the sperms and ova fuse together to form zygote and that leads to pregnancy.
- For the formation of zygote the ova and sperms have to travel together.
- Now the sperms are ample, so when a sperm makes a contact with the zona pellucida, there are some changes made done to the membrane which results in no extra sperms entering in and ensures fertilization of ova with a single sperms.

Implantation

- The process in which the zygote just after fertilization moves and reaches the uterus and gets embedded in the uterine wall is called as implantation.
- Reaching the uterus, the zygote forms blastomeres i.e. daughter cells in group of powers of 2 (2,4,8,16,32).
- Morula is an embryo that has eight to sixteen blastomeres. This morula obtained keeps on getting divided to form blastocyst which is a group of so many cells together.
- Thropblast is the outer layer in which the blastomers are being arranged.
- The inner cells now gets differentiated in to the following germ layers:

      Inner endoderm   Middle mesoderm
      Outer ectoderm

- Conclusively in the process of implantation the blastocyst discussed above settles in uterus at endometrium.

Pregnancy and Embryo Development

- After the implantation of zygote in uterus, the female is said to be having pregnancy.

- The chorionic villi which is a finger like projection starts developing on the thropblast.
- This is also being surrounded by maternal blood and tissue. Placenta is also being developed in this stage.
- Placenta acts as a point of link in between the mother's body and the developing fetus which provides the required nutrition for the growth.

Parturition

- Parturition is defined as a process in which a female delivers a baby after 9 months of gestation period.
- Neuroendocrine system play an important role in parturition.
- When it is the time to deliver a child, the foetus and placenta sends a few signals in the form of uterine contractions.
- As a result oxytocin hormone is released, uterine wall starts to contract which results in the baby coming out of the vaginal passag.
- As the baby comes out, the placenta and the umbilical cord is being taken off the body of the baby.

Lactation

- After the baby is delivered, the mammary glands starts producing milk. This process as a whole is called as lactation.
- During the first few days after the onset of milk production, we find the milk to be yellow and is termed as colostrum.
- Several antibodies in order to develop the immune system is the essential part of the colostrum.
- This helps in providing the appropriate nutrition to the newly born child.

EXERCISE

1. The Primary sex organ is known as ______.
    (*a*) Regulate blood volume and composition
    (*b*) Synthesize glucose
    (*c*) Regulate blood Pressure
    (*d*) Gonads

2. The incomplete descent of the testes into the scrotum is called Cryptorchidism.
    (*a*) True   (*b*) False

3. Name the site of sperm maturation?
    (*a*) Epididymis   (*b*) Ductus deferens
    (*c*) Spermatic cord   (*d*) Urethra

4. Which of the following produces the male sex hormone?
    (*a*) rete testis
    (*b*) seminiferous tubule
    (*c*) leydig cell
    (*d*) scrotum

5. Which of the following is an energy source for the sperm?
    (*a*) Somatostatin   (*b*) Prostaglandin
    (*c*) Proteins   (*d*) Fructose

6. Mark the Incorrect statement about prostate gland?
    (*a*) Located interior to the Urinary bladder
    (*b*) Secretion is thin and milky colored
    (*c*) Secretion is acidic in nature
    (*d*) Function in increasing the mobility of the sperm.

7. The fluid from which of the following accessory gland neutralize the acidity in a vagina of the female?
    (*a*) Seminal vesicle   (*b*) Prostate gland
    (*c*) Cowper's gland   (*d*) Urethra.

8. Out of the following, which hormone does not secret from corpus luteum?
    (*a*) Estrogen   (*b*) Progesterone
    (*c*) Relaxin   (*d*) Testosterone

9. Name the process by which most of the oogonia degenerated before the birth.
    (*a*) Atresia   (*b*) Zone pellucida
    (*c*) Acrosome   (*d*) Granulosa cells

10. Name the hormone which is at peak during ovulation.
    (*a*) Progesterone   (*b*) Estrogen
    (*c*) FSH   (*d*) LH

11. Which of the following fertilization category is found is mammals?
    (*a*) Ovoviviparous   (*b*) Oviparous
    (*c*) Viviparous   (*d*) Segmentation

12. The process which begins after the fertilization is known as ________.
    (*a*) Cleavage   (*b*) Spermiogenesis
    (*c*) Organogenesis   (*d*) Embryogenesis

13. Which of the is Alecithal?
    (*a*) Reptiles   (*b*) Amphibians
    (*c*) Mammals   (*d*) Birds.

14. The nucleus of the sperm cell is highly condensed and transcriptionally inactive.
    (*a*) True   (*b*) False

15. The process of releasing the ripe female gamete from the ovary is called
    (*a*) Parturition   (*b*) Ovulation
    (*c*) Fertilization   (*d*) Implantation

16. Germ cells in Mammalia gonads are produced by
    (*a*) Only mitosis
    (*b*) Only meiosis
    (*c*) Mitosis and meiosis both
    (*d*) Without cell division

17. Polar bodies are formed during
    (*a*) Spermatogenesis   (*b*) Oogenesis
    (*c*) Gametogenesis   (*d*) Spermateleosis

18. In which phase of cell division is oogonia arrested
    (*a*) Anaphase II
    (*b*) Prophase I
    (*c*) Interphase
    (*d*) Both prophase I and II

19. Sperms formed from 4 primary spermatocytes are
    (*a*) 4   (*b*) 1
    (*c*) 16   (*d*) 32

20. Each primary oocyte on meiosis produces
    (*a*) One ovum   (*b*) Two ova
    (*c*) Four ova   (*d*) Three ova

21. 1st polar body is formed at which stage of oogenesis
    (*a*) 1st meiosis   (*b*) 2nd mitosis
    (*c*) Ist mitosis   (*d*) Differentiation

22. The breakage of the membrane surrounding the acrosome in a mammalian sperm is
    (a) Activation   (b) Cavitation
    (c) Agglutination   (d) Capacitation

23. Testis produce
    (a) Sperms   (b) Eggs
    (c) Seeds   (d) Spores

24. Acrosome of sperm is formed from.
    (a) Nucleus of spermatid
    (b) Mitochondria of spermatid
    (c) Golgi complex of spermatid
    (d) Centrosome of spermatid

25. What helps in the Penetration of egg by the sperm
    (a) Ferilizin
    (b) Antifertilizin
    (c) Sperm lysin
    (d) Fertilization membrane.

26. One of the minute cell which separates from the animal egg during maturation is known as
    (a) Primary spermatogonia
    (b) Secondary oogonia
    (c) Primary oogonia
    (d) Polar bodies

27. Fertilization occurs in human, rabbit and other placental mammals in
    (a) Ovary   (b) Uterus
    (c) Fallopian tubes   (d) Vagina

28. After a sperm has penetrated an ovum in the process fertilization, entry of further sperms is prevented by
    (a) Development of the vitelline membrane
    (b) Development of the pigment coat
    (c) Condensation of yolk
    (d) Formation of fertilization membrane

29. Development of an egg without fertilization is called
    (a) Gametogenesis   (b) Metagenesis
    (c) Oogenesis   (d) Parthenogenesis

30. The Phenomenon of fertilization was first perceived by
    (a) Weisman   (b) Leeuwenhoek
    (c) Robert Hooke   (d) Hertwig

31. The final event in the process of fertilization is
    (a) Fusion of gametes
    (b) Egg activation
    (c) Amphimixis
    (d) Organizational change in egg cytoplasm.

32. Fertilizin is a chemical substance produced from
    (a) Mature egg (ovum)
    (b) Acrosome
    (c) Polar bodies
    (d) Middle Piece of sperm

33. Movement of sperm is done by
    (a) Tail   (b) Head
    (c) Acrosome   (d) Middle piece

34. The sperm penetrates the ovum mainly
    (a) Mechanically   (b) Chemically
    (c) Electrostatically   (d) Thermally

35. Fertilization is depicted by condition
    (a) $n \rightarrow 2n$ (b) $2n \rightarrow 3n$
    (c) $2n \rightarrow 4n$ (d) $4n \rightarrow 8n$

36. Capacitation of sperms occurs in
    (a) Female genital tract
    (b) Vas deferens
    (c) Vas efferens
    (d) Vagina

Answer Keys

1. (d)	2. (a)	3. (a)	4. (c)	5. (d)	6. (c)	7. (c)	8. (d)	9. (a)	10. (d)
11. (c)	12. (d)	13. (c)	14. (a)	15. (b)	16. (c)	17. (b)	18. (b)	19. (c)	20. (d)
21. (a)	22. (d)	23. (a)	24. (c)	25. (c)	26. (d)	27. (c)	28. (d)	29. (d)	30. (d)
31. (c)	32. (a)	33. (a)	34. (b)	35. (a)	36. (a)				

Solutions

1. The reproductive system consists of primary sex organs, secondary sex organs, and accessory sex organ, Gonads are primary sex organs which produce gametes and harmones.

2. The testes descend to scrotum to lower the temperature upto 3°C which is viable for sperm production, but cryptorchidism is the condition when the testes do not descend into scrotum and remain in the abdominal cavity.

3. Epididymis lies along the posterior border of testes. It is a site of sperm maturation, the process by which sperm gets its mobility and ability to fertilize an ovum.

4. Male sex hormone, i.e., testosterone produces from the interstitial cells or leydig cells. These cells are located between the seminiferous tubule inside the lobule.

5. The fluid from the seminal vesicle contains fructose for an energy source, protein for coagulation reaction and prostaglandis for mobility and viability of the sperm.

6. Prostate gland lies inferior to urinary bladder and secrete alkaline fluid which is thin and milky color in appearance and it enhances the mobility of the sperm.

7. Cowper's gland or bulbourethal glands are small in size and located near the base of the penis. After getting sexual stimulation, these glands secrete alkaline fluid which neutralizes the acidity of the vagina.

8. Corpus luteum is the yellow body which left after the procedure of ovulation. It secretes four hormones, i.e., Progesterone, estrogen, relaxin, and inhibin. Testosterone is male hormone and it doesn't discharge from the corpus luteum.

9. In the female reproductive cycle, germ cell divides mitotically and produces millions of Oogonia. Most of the oogonia will undergo degeneration by the process known as atresia.

10. Leutilizing hormone secretes in a huge amount from the anterior pituitary on the 14th day of 28 day menstruation cycle. This hormone is responsible for the release of the ovum.

11. In Viniparous, fertilization is internal and nourishment is provided through placenta by the uterine wall of the mother.

12. Embryogenesis is the process of multiplication of cells by mitosis and formation of tissues and organs of a living baby. It starts once the egg has been fertilized.

13. Alecithal are those organism which have no yolk in their egg, e.g. mammals.

14. In the nucleus of the sperm cell normal histones are replaced by a special class of packaging proteins known as protamins which make the nucleus transcriptionally inactive.

15. Discharge of a mature ovum from graafian follicle is known as ovulation

16. Spermatogonia oogania 100 gamin are produced by mitotic cell division while spermatids and ova are produced after meiotic cell division.

17. Polar bodies are smaller cells produced during oogenesis that do not develop into egg cells.

18. The parent cells that produce oocytes are called oogonia. Oogania are diploid cells. All the Oogonia start the process of meiosis and form primary oocytes prior to birth. They are arrested in prophase I and remain this way until the female reaches puberty.

19. One primary spermatocyte produces four sperms so four spermatocytes will produce 16 sperms.

20. From one primary oocyte, one egg or ovum and 2 polar bodies are formed.

21. A polar body is a small haploid cell that is formed concomitantly as an egg cell during oogenesis, but which generally does not have the ability to be fertilized

22. Physiological changes that endow mammalian sperm with fertilizing capacity are known as sperm capacitation.

23. Testicles are male sex glands that produce sperm and sex hormones. Usually, both testicles are located in the scrotum. Undescended testicles means that either one or both testicles are missing from the scrotum and are situated in the groin or inside the lower abdomen.

24. The acrosome is an organelle that develops over the anterior half of the head in the spermatozoa (sperm cells) of many animal including human. It is a cap-like structure drived from the Golgi apparatus.

25. Sperm penetrates through egg wall in most of the organism by the help of sperm lysin formed from acrosome.

26. During maturation phase, the primary oocyte undergoes meiosis I producing two haploid cells (n) the larger one is secondary oocytes and the smaller one is first polar body, meiosis II of secondary oocyte result in the formation of functional egg or ovum and a second polar body.

27. In mammals (Rabbit and human beings), fertilization of the ovum occurs in fallopian tube, oviduct or uterine tube

28. Fertilization membrane prevents polyspermic fertilization by preventing further entry of spermetozoa.

29. Hyaluronidase, corona penetrating enzyme and acrosin are collectively called sperm lysin and are released from the acrosome during acrosomal reaction after the sperm entry.

30. Development of an egg (ovum) into a complete individual without fertilization by a sperm is known as parthenogenesis.

31. Entry of sperm stimulates the secondary oocyte to start the suspended meiosis-II resulting in the formation of one ootid and 2-3 polar body. ootid changes to become ovum, male and female pronuclei get mixed up. The process is called Amphimixis.

32. Fertilizin is a chemical secretion of uppermost layer of egg. It is mucopolysaccharide or glycoprotein that attracts sperms.

33. Tail is very long tapering vibratile part of sperm, so movement of sperm is done by tail.

34. In the first, meiotic division of the mammal oogenesis, the diploid primary oocyte divides into unequal haploid daughter cell a large secondary oocyte and small first polar body.

35. One primary specmatocyte produces four sperms so four spermatocyte will produce 16 sperms.

36. The first change in this cascade is capacitation. The sperm cells accomplish this during the ascension through the female genital tract. It has to do with a physiological maturation process of the sperm cell membranes, which is seen as the precondition for the next step to follow. namely the acrosome reaction.

CHAPTER 4

Reproductive Health

Reproductive Health- Problems and Strategies

Reproductive Health: The physical, emotional, behavioral and social well-being of reproduction is referred as reproductive health. To accomplish the social goal of total reproductive health, India has initiated 'family planning' programs in 1951.

- In present time, 'Reproductive and Child Health Care (RCH) programs are being operated as improved programs which cover wide reproduction-related areas.

- The primary steps to achieve the goal of reproductive health is counselling the people and making them aware them about adolescence, reproductive organs, changes associated with adolescence, safe and hygienic sexual practices, STDs (sexually transmitted disease) as AIDS etc.

- Some of the other facets of RCH programs are to provide care and medical facilities for the problems related to pregnancy, menstrual irregularities, delivery, STDs, birth control, post-natal child and maternal management, etc.

Population explosion and Birth control

- Reduction of maternal and infant mortality rates, assistance to infertile couples, early identification and cure of STDs, etc. indicate that reproductive health is improved in our country.

- A volatile population growth has been promoted by better living conditions and improved health facilities. That is why the intense propagation of contraceptive methods became necessary. Some natural as well as traditional, IUDs, pills, injectable, implants, surgical, barrier contraceptive options are available nowadays. These methods are useful to delay or avoid the pregnancy.

- In **natural methods** the chances of meeting the ovum and sperms are avoided by taking care of the period of menstrual cycle. In this method, the sexual intercourse from day 10 to 17 of the menstrual cycle is avoided as this is called the fertile period and this method is called Periodic abstinence. Withdrawal or coitus interruptus and lactational amenorrhea are the other natural methods.

- **Withdrawal or coitus interrupts:** Method in which the male partner removes the penis before ejaculating inside the women's vagina to avoid insemination.

- **Barrier** method helps to prevent the physical meeting of ovum and sperm. Condoms, diaphragms, cervical caps and vaults are the examples of barriers.

- **IUDs (Intra Uterine Devices)** are the devices which are inserted in the uterus of female through vagina which helps to prevent unwanted pregnancy.

- **Pills** are taken orally in order to prevent pregnancy. These are the small doses of progestogens or progestogen-estrogen combinations.

- **Sterilization** is a surgical method to prevent any more pregnancies. It is a terminal method which blocks gamete transport. In males, it is **Vasectomy** and in females it is **Tubectomy**.

Medical Termination of Pregnancy: Our country has legalized the medical termination of pregnancy (MTP). To get rid of unwanted pregnancy, MTP is performed. It is also performed in some cases where the need to discontinue the pregnancy is necessary as it could be harmful or fatal to either the mother, or the foetus or both. It can be done surgically or via medications.

Sexually Transmitted Diseases and Infertility

Sexually transmitted diseases or STDs are transferred through the sexual interactions. These are also called as **VD (Venereal Diseases)** or **RTI (Reproductive Tract Infections)**. Some complications of STDs are still birth, infertility, Pelvic Inflammatory diseases (PIDs). In order to cure these diseases in a better way, their early detection is necessary. Some precautions can be adopted to avoid STDs like use of condoms during sexual intercourse and avoiding it with multiple or unknown partners.

Some of the common STDs are syphilis, gonorrhoea, chlamydiasis, genital herpes, genital warts, hepatitis-B, trichomoniasis and HIV which leads to AIDS. Few principles to be free from such infections:

- Use of condoms during coitus.
- Avoiding sex with unknown partners/multiple partners.
- Visiting a qualified doctor for early detection of the disease and to get full treatment, if diagnosed with one.

Infertility: Infertility is the inability to conceive even when the sexual interaction is unprotected. Physical diseases, psychological reasons, drugs etc can be responsible for infertility. In present time, there are some methods and techniques available to help the couples who are dealing with infertility. These certain techniques are called assisted reproductive technologies (ART).

In vitro fertilization (IVF): In one of such methods, embryo is transferred into the female genital tract and is known as In vitro fertilization (IVF) and this program is called the 'Test Tube Baby' program.

ZIFT (Zygote intra fallopian transfer): Another method is ZIFT (Zygote intra fallopian transfer) in which a donor provides the ovum and it is then transferred into the fallopian tube of the female who cannot produce it but can give suitable environment for the fertilization and development process.

Intra cytoplasmic sperm injection (ICSI): is another technique to help the couples who are unable to produce a child because of infertility. In this technique an embryo is formed in the laboratory in which a sperm is directly injected into the ovum.

Artificial insemination (AI): Intra cytoplasmic sperm injection could be corrected by this technique, the semen is collected from either the husband or a healthy donor and is artificially introduced either into the vagina or into the uterus of the female also known as IUI (intra-uterine insemination).

There are many methods to help the couples dealing with infertility but they are not reachable to every class as not everyone can adopt these methods because of financial or some emotional and religious facts. So another method is adoption which is legal in our country now.

EXERCISE

1. Which of the following groups includes all STD?
   (a) Hepatitis-B, Hemophilia, AIDS
   (b) AIDS, syphilis, cholera
   (c) Gonorrhea, Hepatitis-B, Chlamydiasis
   (d) HIV, Malaria, Trichomoniasis

2. MTP is considered safe up to how many wreaks of pregnancy?
   (a) 8   (b) 12
   (c) 18   (d) 6

3. Which of the following is the widely accepted method of contraception in India?
   (a) IUDs   (b) Tubectomy
   (c) Cervical caps   (d) Diaphragms

4. The interferons are ______.
   (a) Antibiotics
   (b) Antibacterial Proteins
   (c) Immunosuppressive drugs
   (d) Antiviral Proteins

5. Which of the following test is used to detect AIDS?
   (a) Western blot and ELISA
   (b) Northern blot and ELISA
   (c) ELISA and Southern blot
   (d) ELISA and Immunoblot

6. Growth curve is normally ______.
   (a) J shaped   (b) S shaped
   (c) C shaped   (d) V shaped

7. Causative agent of syphilis is ______.
   (a) HIV
   (b) Neisseria
   (c) Treponema Pallidum
   (d) Trichomonas vaginalis

8. What is the function of copper-T?
   (a) Stops cleavage
   (b) Checks mutations
   (c) Stops gastrulation
   (d) Stops fertilization

9. Amniocentesis is a process of _______.
   (*a*) Know about brain disease
   (*b*) Grow cells on culture media
   (*c*) Determine disease of the embryo
   (*d*) Determine mutations

10. Saheli is _________.
    (*a*) An oral contraceptive for females
    (*b*) A diaphragm used by males
    (*c*) A surgical sterilization method
    (*d*) A diaphragm used by females

11. According to the World Health Organisation (WHO), reproductive health means a total well-being in all aspects of reproduction, that is
    (*a*) Physical
    (*b*) Social
    (*c*) Emotional and behavioural
    (*d*) All of the above

12. The 'family planning' programmes were periodically assessed over the past decades. Imporoved programmes covering wider reproductive-related areas are currently in operation under the popular name
    (*a*) RCH programmes
    (*b*) ART programmes
    (*c*) MTP programmes
    (*d*) Test tube baby programmes

13. RCH stands for
    (*a*) Routine Check-up of Health
    (*b*) Reproduction Cum Hygiene
    (*c*) Reversible Contraceptive Hyzards
    (*d*) Reprodutive and Child Health Care

14. Which has an explosive impact on the growth of population ?
    (*a*) Contraceptive devices
    (*b*) Increased health facilities
    (*c*) Better living conditions
    (*d*) Both (*b*) and (*c*)

15. Select the correct option which includes the steps implemented by government to control the ever increasing population.
    (*a*) Increasing the price of contraceptives so that they are available to all
    (*b*) Advertising the benefits of small family, slogans like, 'hum do hamare do', etc
    (*c*) Raising the marriageable age, females 18 years, males 21 years
    (*d*) Both (*b*) and (*c*)

16. Which of the following are the reasons for population explosion ?
    (*i*) Increased health facilities
    (ii) Rapid increase in MMR
    (iii) Rapid increase in IMR
    (iv) Rapid decrease in MMR
    (*v*) Decrease in number of people reaching reproducible age
    (*a*) (*i*) and (iv)   (*b*) (iii) and (*v*)
    (*c*) (ii) and (iv)   (*d*) (*i*) and (*v*)

17. MTP stands for
    (*a*) Medical Termination of Pregnancy
    (*b*) Mental Trauma Phase
    (*c*) Menstrual Pain
    (*d*) Menstrual Temporary Pain

18. MTP is of much risk in which phase of the pregnancy?
    (*a*) 2nd trimester   (*b*) 1st trimester
    (*c*) 1st week   (*d*) 2nd week

19. Nearly .....A...... to .....B..... million MTPs are performed in a year all over the world which accounts to .....C..... of the total number of conceived pregnancies.

	A	B	C
(*a*)	40	45	$1/5^{th}$
(*b*)	45	50	$1/4^{th}$
(*c*)	45	50	$1/5^{th}$
(*d*)	40	45	1/45

20. The other name for STDs are
    (*a*) Venereal diseases
    (*b*) Reproductive tract infections
    (*c*) Both (*a*) and (*b*)
    (*d*) None of the above

21. Which of the following STDs is/are curable ?
    (*a*) Chlamydia   (*b*) Syphilis
    (*c*) AIDS   (*d*) Both (*a*) and (*b*)

22. Which among the following STDs is most dangerous ?
    (*a*) Chlamydiasis   (*b*) Trichomoniasis
    (*c*) Hepatitis-B   (*d*) AIDS

23. Inability to conceive or produce children even after 2 years of unprotected sexual co-habitation is called
    (*a*) Sexuality   (*b*) ART
    (*c*) Fertility   (*d*) Infertility

25. In India, often the female is blamed for the couple being childless, but more often than not, the problem lies in the

(*a*) Male partner

(*b*) Female partner

(*c*) Both male and female partner

(*d*) Doctor

26. When the correction of infertility is not possible in infertility clinics then the couples could be assisted to have children through certain special techniques commonly called as

(*a*) RCH   (*b*) ART

(*c*) MTP   (*d*) RTI

Answer Keys

1. (*c*)   2. (*b*)   3. (*a*)   4. (*d*)   5. (*a*)   6. (*b*)   7. (*c*)   8. (*d*)   9. (*c*)   10. (*a*)

11. (*d*)   12. (*a*)   13. (*d*)   14. (*d*)   15. (*d*)   16. (*a*)   17. (*a*)   18. (*a*)   19. (*c*)   20. (*c*)

21. (*d*)   22. (*d*)   23. (*d*)   24. (*a*)   25. (*b*)

Solutions

1. STD is sexually transmitted diseases. It is a disease which is transmitted through sexual content and caused by bacteria, viruses or parasites. Gonorrhea, Hepatitis-B, Chlamydiasis are STDs.

2. MTP is medical termination of pregnancy. It is a medical way of getting rid of unwanted pregnancy. It is also called an induced abortion. MTP is considered safe up to 12 weeks of pregnancy.

3. IUDs are intrauterine device. It is a birth control device that is inserted into woman's uterus to recent pregnancy. IUDs is the widely accepted method of contraception in India.

4. The interferons are a group of signaling protein made and released by host cells in response to the presence of several pathogens like viruses, bacteria, parasites and also tumor cells.

5. ELISA is enzyme linked immunosorbent assay. It is a test that uses antibodies and color change to identify a substance. Western blot is used to detect specific proteins in a sample of tissue homogenate or extract.

6. Growth curve is an empirical model of the evolution of a quantity over time. It is S shaped curve. It has lag phase, log phase stationary phase and death phase.

7. Syphilis is a bacterial infection usually spread by sexual contact that starts as a painless sore. Causative agent of syphilis is Treponema pallidum.

8. Copper-T is a type of IUDs. It contains copper. It is used for birth control and emergency contraception. Copper-T stops fertilization and inhibits pregnancy.

9. Amniocentesis is a process in which amniotic fluid is sampled sing a hollow needle inserted into the uterus to screen for abnormalities in the developing fetus.

10. Saheli is worlds first and only oral non steroid contraceptive pill. It is also known as centchroman. It has zero side effects.

11. The term 'reproductive health' simply refers to healthy reproductive organs with normal functions. However, it has a broader perspective and includes the emotional and social aspect of reproduction also. According to the World Health Organisation (WHO), reproductive health means a total well-being in all aspects of reproduction, that is **physical, social, emotional** and **behavioural.**

12. The 'family planning' programmes were periodically assessed over the past decades. Improved programmes covering wider reproductive-related areas are currently in operation under the popular name 'Reproductive and Child Health Care (RCH) programmes.

13. Reproduction-related areas are currently in operation in India come under the popular name 'Reproductive and Child Health Care (RCH) programmes.

14. **Increased health facilities** and **better living conditions** have an explosive impact on the growth of population.

15. **(d)**

16. Increased health facilities and rapid decrease in Maternal Mortality Rate are among the various reasons of population explosion.

17. **(a)**

18. MTPs are considered relatively safe during the first trimester, i.e., upto 12 weeks of pregnancy. Second trimester abortions are much more riskier.

19. **(c)**

20. Diseases or infections, which are transmitted through sexual intercourse with infected persons are collectively called. Sexually Transmitted Diseases (STDs) or Venereal Diseases (VDs) or Reproductive Tract Infections (RTIs).

21. Bacterial infections are completely curable if detected early and treated properly.

22. **(d)**

23. Inability to conceive or produce children even after 2 years of unprotected sexual co-habitation is called **infertility.**

24. In India, often the female is blamed for the couple being childless, but more often than not, the problem lies in the male partner.

25. When the correction of infertility is not possible in infertility clinics then the couples could be assisted to have children through certain special techniques commonly called as **ART (assisted reproductive technologies).**

CHAPTER 5

Principles of Inheritance and Variation

Mendel's Laws of Inheritance

- **Genetics:** The inheritance and the variation of characters from parents to progeny are dealt in the branch of biology known as Genetics.
- **Inheritance:** The process of passing the characters from parents to offspring is called the inheritance which is the basis of heredity.
- **Variation:** The degree of difference of offspring from its parents is called the variation. Variation acts as raw material for evolution.

Mendel performed experiments on garden pea for 7 years in order to study the inheritance and gave the inheritance laws in living organisms. According to Mendel, the 'factors' (presently known as genes) are always found in pairs (called alleles) and they are responsible for regulating the characters. A definite pattern is followed in different generations by the expression of the characters in the progeny.

- **Principles or Laws of Inheritance:** It comprises two laws as follows:
- **Law of Dominance:**
- Discrete units called factors control the characters.
- Factors occur in pairs.
- One member of the pair dominates the other member in a dissimilar pair of factors.
- Dominative member is called dominant while the other is called recessive.
- **Law of Segregation:** The alleles or factors of a pair segregate from each other such that a gamete receives only one of the two factors.

A parent which produces all similar gametes is called a homozygous parent while the one producing two kinds of gametes each having one allele with equal proportion is called heterozygous.

All the characters do not show true dominance. Some of the characters show incomplete dominance while the others may show co-dominance. Dominance is dependent on the gene product, particular phenotype chosen to examine and the production of the particular phenotype.

Inheritance of one gene:

Mendel proposed that the units of inheritance are called factors (known as genes now) and they carry the required information in order to express a particular attribute. The genes which code for a pair of contrasting attributes are called alleles.

- **Monohybrid Cross:**
- Monohybrid cross is a cross involving two plants differing in one pair of contrasting characters.
- A tall and a dwarf pea plant were crossed to study the inheritance of one gene
- **Steps in making a cross in pea**
- Two pea plants were contrasting characters were selected.
- Emasculation: Anthers on one plant were removed in order to avoid self-pollination. This is called female parent.
- Pollination: It involves collecting pollen grains from male and transferring it to female parent.
- The pollen grains were collected and offspring was produced.
- Some factors were inherited from parent to offspring which were called as genes.
- The production of gametes by the parents, the formation of the zygotes, the $F1$ and $F2$ plants is understood from a diagram called Punnett Square.
- Following is the representation for monohybrid cross

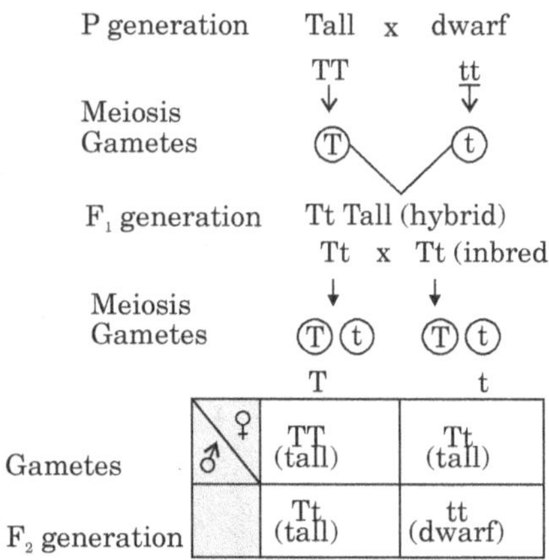

Fig.: Monohybrid cross

➢ Gametes T and t are produced in equal production when $F1$ is self-pollinated.

➢ Monohybrid Genotypic ratio is

Homozygous Tall : Heterozygous Tall : Homozygous Dwarf = 1 : 2 : 1

➢ Monohybrid Phenotypic ratio is Tall : Dwarf = 3 : 1

Non Mendelian Inheritance

- **Incomplete Dominance:**

➢ It refers to the inheritance in which heterozygous offspring shows intermediate character between to parental characteristics. Example: Flower color in snapdragon and Mirabilis Jalapa.

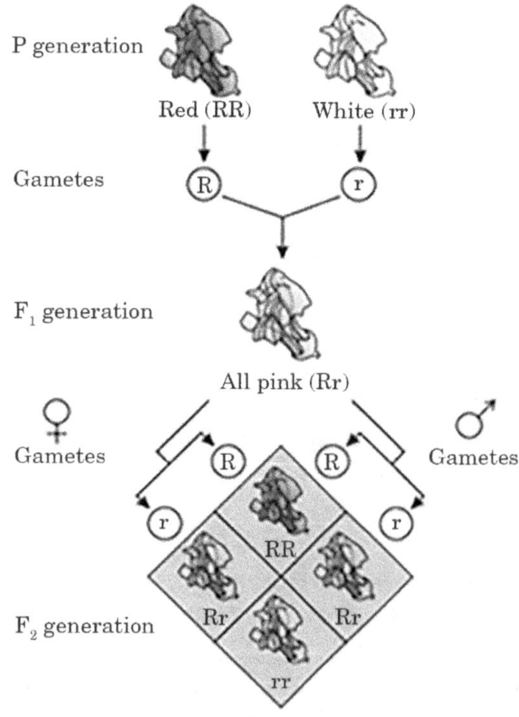

Fig.: Non Mendelian inheritance

➢ Genotypic Ratio = RR : Rr : rr = 1 : 2 : 1

➢ Phenotypic Ratio = Red : Pink : White = 1 : 2 : 1

- **Co Dominance:**

➢ It is the dominance in which both the alleles of a gene are expressed independently and equally in a hybrid that is both the alleles are dominant. Example: ABO blood group in humans.

➢ A gene I has three alleles I^A, I^B (the dominant alleles) and i (recessive allele)

➢ Antigen A and B are produced by I^A, I^B respectively and no antigen is produced by the recessive allele.

Allele from parent 1	Allele from parent 2	Genotype of offspring	Blood group of offspring
I^A	I^A	$I^A I^A$	A
I^A	I^B	$I^A I^B$	AB
I^A	i	$I^A i$	A
I^B	I^A	$I^A I^B$	AB
I^B	I^B	$I^B I^B$	B
I^B	i	$I^B i$	B
i	i	ii	O

Inheritance of two genes

- **Dihybrid Cross:**

➢ It refers to a cross between two parents who have two pairs of contrasting characters.

➢ Dihybrid cross between round pea plant with yellow seeds and wrinkled shaped pea plant with green seeds was studied by Mendel.

➢ The Punnett square is shown below:

Round Yellow   Wrinkled Green
P   RRYY   ×   rryy
Gametes RY   ry
F₁   RrYy (Dihybrid)
                     Round Yellow (selfed)
Gametes   RY   Ry   rY   ry
F₂

	RY	Ry	rY	ry
RY	RRYY Round Yellow	RRYy Round Yellow	RrYY Round Yellow	RrYy Round Yellow
Ry	RRYy Round Yellow	RRyy Round Green	RrYy Round Yellow	Rryy Round Green
rY	RyYY Round Yellow	RrYy Round Yellow	rrYY Wrinkled Yellow	rrYy Wrinkled Yellow
ry	RrYy Round Yellow	Rryy Round Green	rrYy Wrinkled Yellow	rryy Wrinkled Green

Fig.: Dihybrid cross (Punnett square)

➢ Dihybrid Phenotypic ratio is

Round yellow: Round green : Wrinkled yellow : Wrinkled green = 9: 3 : 3 :1

➢ Dihybrid genotypic ratio is

RRYY : RRYy :RrYY : RrYy : RRyy : Rryy : rrYY : rrYY : rrYy : rryy = 1:2:1:2:4:2:1:2:1

After this study, the Law of Independent Assortment was give which says that the factors are independently assorted and they combine in all permutations and combinations.

- **Chromosomes:** Chromosomes are the structures found in the nucleus. They double and divide just before each cell division. They also occur in pairs.

- **Chromosomal Theory of Inheritance:** Both gene and chromosome are found in pair. The two alleles of a gene pair are located on the same locus on homologous chromosomes. According to the argument of Sutton and Boveri that the pairing and segregation of a pair of chromosomes would lead to the separation of a pair of genes or factors they carried. The knowledge of chromosomal segregation was united with mendelian principles by Sutton and named as the chromosomal theory of inheritance.

Pleiotropy

- A single gene exhibiting multiple phenotypic expression is called as pleiotropic gene.

- Dominance depends on the production of a particular prototype and the gene product.

Example: Gene in pea plant which controls the wrinkled texture and roundness of the seeds influences the phenotype expression of the grain size of starch.

- **Linkage and Recombination:**

The physical association of genes on a chromosome is termed as linkage and the generation of non-parental gene combinations is termed as recombination. The genes are tightly linked when they are located on the same chromosome and show very low recombination.

Sex-Determination and Genetic Disorders

Sex Determination

The genes which were linked to sex chromosomes named as sex-linked genes. It was found out that both the sexes have a set of common chromosomes and a set of different chromosomes. The different chromosomes were called the sex chromosomes and the other set as autosomes. In many insects mammals (including man) XY type lof sex determination is observed in which both the sexes carry same number of chromosomes.

Sex Determination in Humans

- There are total 23 pairs of chromosomes in humans and 22 of them are exactly same and known as autosomes. In females, a pair of X chromosomes is present while XY in male. Two types of gametes or sperms are produced by male during spermatogenesis.

- 50% of them carry X chromosome while the other 50% carry Y chromosome. In female, only one kind of gamete or ovum carrying X chromosome only is produced.

- If the sperm which carry X chromosome fertilizes the egg, then the sex of the baby is female while if the one carrying Y chromosome fertilizes the egg, the sex of the baby is male.

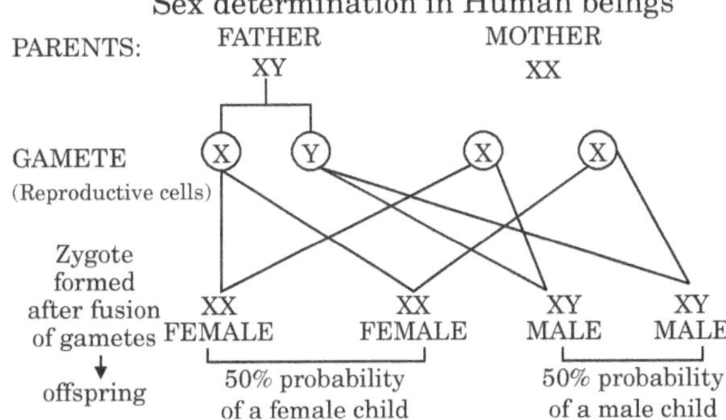

Fig.: Sex determination in human beings

Sex Determination in honey-bee (Haplodiploid sex-determination system)

- The males possess half the number of chromosomes than that of a female. The females are diploid having 32 chromosomes and males are haploid having 16 chromosomes.

- The sex determination in a honey bee is based on the number of sets an individual gets.

- A female is developed when there is a union of a sperm and an egg.

- A male is formed by parthenogenesis from an unfertilized egg.

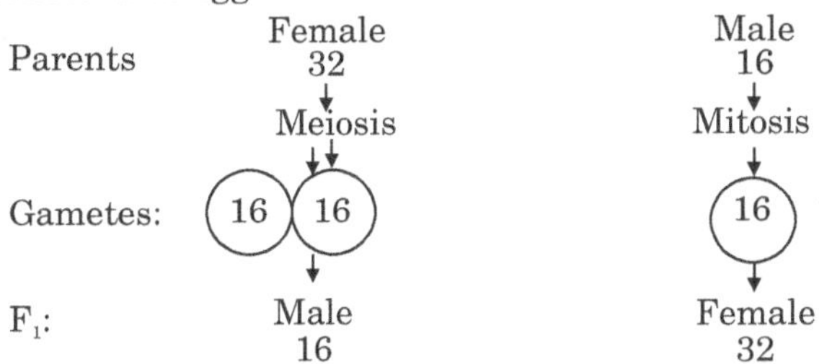

Fig.: Haplodiploid sex determination system

Mutation: A change in the genetic material is known as mutation. The result of this phenomenon is that it alters the DNA sequence and thus the change in the genotype and phenotype of an organism. If the mutation is due to the change in single base pair of DNA, then it is called the point mutation.

Genetic Disorders: Genetic disorders may be grouped into Mendelian disorders and Chromosomal disorders.

- **Pedigree Analysis:** The attribute analysis in a several of generations of a family is known as pedigree analysis. In this analysis, family tree over generations represents the inheritance of particular trait. It is useful in tracing the inheritance of a particular trait, disease and abnormality.

- **Mendelian Disorders:** Alteration in a single gene is responsible for Mendelian disorders. Through the Mendelian principles of inheritance, these are transmitted into generations. Their nature may be either dominant or recessive. Color blindness and phenylketonuria are the examples of Mendelian disorders. It also includes haemophilia (sex linked recessive disease), sickle cell anemia (an autosome linked recessive trait) and phenylketonuria (an inborn error of metabolism inherited as autosomal recessive trait).

  ➢ **Haemophilia:** In this, a single protein that is a part of the cascade of proteins involved in the clotting of blood is affected which results in nonstop bleeding in case of a simple cut.

  ➢ **Sickle-cell anaemia:** It is a recessive trait that can be transmitted from parents to the offspring when both the partners are carrier for the gene

  ➢ **Phenylketunuria:** In this, the affected individual lacks an enzyme responsible for converting amino acid phenylalanine into tyrosine.

  ➢ **Thalassemia:** It is an autosome linked recessive blood disease inherited by the offspring when both the parents are unaffected carrier for the gene. The defect is due to deletion or mutation. Abnormal haemoglobin is formed which results into anaemia.

  ➢ **Color blindness:** The defect is due to mutation in certain genes present in the X chromosome. It is a sex-linked recessive disorder which is due to defect in either red or green cone of eye resulting in failure to discriminate between red and green color.

- **Chromosomal Disorders:** The absence or excess of one or more than one chromosomes or their abnormal arrangement is the cause of this disorder. They are transmitted as the affected individual is sterile. Their nature is always dominant. The loss or gain of chromosome due to the failure of segregation of chromatids during cell division is known as aneuploidy. Two sets of chromosome called polyploidy are led due to the failure of cytokinesis.

Down's syndrome, Klinefleter's syndrome and Turner's syndrome are examples of chromosomal disorders.

➢ **Down syndrome:** The retardation in mental development is the result of Down's syndrome. The presence of additional copy of the chromosome number 21 is the cause of it.

➢ **Klinefleter's syndrome:** The reason of Klinefleter's syndrome is the presence of an additional copy of X-chromosome. Persons affected from it are sterile.

➢ **Turner's syndrome:** The person's having Turner's syndrome lack secondary sexual characters. The absence of one of the X chromosome is the cause of Turner's syndrome.

EXERCISE

1. Mendelism is related with
   (a) Heredity in living beings
   (b) Meiosis during sexual reproduction
   (c) Mutation in living organisms
   (d) None of the above.

2. The branch of botany dealing with heredity and variation is called
   (a) Geobotany   (b) Sericulture
   (c) Genetics   (d) Evolution

3. Term 'genetics' was given by
   (a) Mendel   (b) Morgen
   (c) Bateson   (d) Boveri

4. The first great "geneticist" was
   (a) Engler   (b) Mendel
   (c) Schwann   (d) Miller

5. Mendel was born in
   (a) 17th Century   (b) 18th Century
   (c) 19th Century   (d) 8th Century

6. Mendel was the native of
   (a) France   (b) Sweden
   (c) India   (d) Austria

7. Mendel proposed which of the following term for hereditary units
   (a) Factor (determiner)
   (b) Genome
   (c) Genetic particle
   (d) None of the above.

8. The resemblance of Individuals to their Progenitors is called
   (a) Heredity   (b) Genetics
   (c) Evolution   (d) None of these

9. In 1900 A.D. three biologists independently discovered mendel's principles. They are.
   (a) De vries, Correns and Tschermak
   (b) Sutton, Morgan and Bridges
   (c) Avery, Mc Leod and Mccarthy
   (d) Bateson, Punnet and Bridges

10. Law of Mendel which is not completely applicable is
    (a) Co-dominance
    (b) Law of segregation
    (c) Law of independent assortment
    (d) Law of dominance

11. Ratio of Progeny when a red coloured heterozygous is crossed with a white coloured plant in which red colour is dominant in white colour
    (a) 3 : 1   (b) 1 : 1
    (c) 1 : 2 : 1   (d) 9 : 3 : 3 : 1

12. How many type of genotypes are formed in F_2 Progeny obtained from self-pollination of a dihydrid f_1.
    (a) 6   (b) 3
    (c) 9   (d) 4

13. How many types of gametes may be produced by genotype D/d : E/e. F/f
    (a) 27   (b) 8
    (c) 3   (d) 6

14. Mendel chose pea plants because.
    (a) They were cheap
    (b) They were having seven pairs of contrasting characters
    (c) They were easily available
    (d) of great economic importance

15. How many pairs of contrasting characters in pea pod were chosen by Mendel.
    (a) 2   (b) 3
    (c) 4   (d) 7

16. The term "genotype" was coined by
    (a) H.J. Muller   (b) T.Boveri
    (c) W.S. Sultan   (d) W.L. Johansden

17. What type of *gametes* will form by genotype RrYy
    (a) RY, Ry, rY, ry   (b) RY, Ry, ry, ry
    (c) Ry, Ry, Yy, ry   (d) Rr, RR, Yy, YY

18. When two individuals are similar in external appearance but differ in their genetic makeup, they are called as
    (a) Phenotype   (b) Genotype
    (c) Homozygous   (d) Heterozygous

19. The term '*allelomorphic*' implied
    (a) Any two characters
    (b) A pair of contrasting characters
    (c) Sex linked characters
    (d) A pair of non-contrasting characters

20. Alleles which show independent effect are called
    (a) Supplementary alleles
    (b) Codominant alleles
    (c) Epistatic alleles
    (d) Complementary alleles.

21. An organism with two identical alleles for a given trait is
    (a) Homozygous   (b) Segregating
    (c) Dominant   (d) A hermaphrodite

22. Organisms phenotypically similar but genotypically different are said to be
    (a) Heterozygous   (b) Monozygous
    (c) Multizygous   (d) Homozygous.

23. The dwarfness in plants of F_2 generation is
    (a) Recessive   (b) Dominant
    (c) Both the above   (d) None of the above

24. Mendel formulated some laws which are known as
    (a) Laws of germplasm
    (b) Laws of origin of species
    (c) Laws of recapitulation
    (d) Laws of inheritance

25. The first law of mendel
    (a) Law of inheritance
    (b) Law of variation
    (c) Law of independent assortment
    (d) Law of dominance

26. The F_2 dihybrid ratio 9 : 3 : 4 is explained on the basic of
    (a) Epistatic gene
    (b) Supplementary gene
    (c) Allelic interaction
    (d) Complementary gene interaction

27. The phenomenon of incomplete dominance was observed by
    (a) De vries   (b) Correns
    (c) Tschermark   (d) None of the above.

28. What is the other name for "incomplete dominance"
    (a) Blending inheritance
    (b) Co-dominance
    (c) Pseudo-dominance
    (d) All the above

29. Complete dominance is absent in
    (a) Pisum sativum
    (b) Mirobilis jalapa
    (c) Lathyrus odoratus
    (d) Oenothera Lamarckiana

30. A plasmid
    (a) Lives together with chromosome
    (b) Shows dependent assortment
    (c) Can replicate independently
    (d) Cannot replicate

31. Kappa particles indicate
    (a) Nuclear inheritance
    (b) Cytoplasmic inheritance
    (c) Mutation
    (d) Nucleo-cytoplasmic inheritance

32. F_1 hybrid is intermediate between the two parents. The phenomenon is
    (a) Codominance
    (b) Dominance
    (c) Blending inheritance
    (d) Incomplete dominance.

33. It an albino man marries with a normal woman and 50 offsprings are albino and 50 are normal, the woman is
    (a) Heterozygous normal
    (b) Homozygous normal
    (c) Heterozygous carrier
    (d) None of these.

34. Which one in man is a wholly genetic trait
    (a) Diptheria   (b) Leucoderma
    (c) Albinism   (d) Tuberculosis

35. Mongolism Syndrome is caused by
    (a) One extra chromosome
    (b) One extra sex chromosome
    (c) One extra chromosome in 21st pair
    (d) One less sex chromosome

36. To be evolutionary successful, a mutation must be
    (a) Germplasm DNA   (b) Somatoplasm DNA
    (c) Cytoplasm   (d) RNA

37. Which of the following is a genetic disease
    (a) Phenylketonuria   (b) Blindness
    (c) Cataract   (d) Leprosy

38. Mutation is
    (a) Sudden charge in morphology
    (b) Charge in characters
    (c) Charge in heritable characters
    (d) None of these

39. The monosomic condition in human beings depicted as XO is referred to as

    (a) Criminal syndrome

    (b) Down's syndrome

    (c) Klinefelter's syndrome

    (d) Turner's syndrome.

40. The number of chromosomes in Turner's syndrome is

    (a) 45   (b) 43

    (c) 44   (d) 42

41. The point mutations A to G. C to T, C to G and T to A is DNA are

    (a) Transition, transition, transversion, and transversion respectively.

    (b) Transition, transversion, transition and transversion respectively.

    (c) Transversion, transversion, transition and transition respectively.

    (d) All four are transition.

42. The number of chromosomes in Down's syndrome is

    (a) 23rd pair with one less = 45

    (b) 21st pair with one more = 47

    (c) 17th pair with one more = 47

    (d) One extra sex chromosome = 47

43. A man having klinefelter's syndrome is

    (a) Intersex with secondary sexual characters on the side of female.

    (b) Male with secondary sexual characters of female

    (c) Female with secondary sexual characters of male

    (d) Normal fertile male.

44. Edward's syndrome, Patau's syndrome and Down's syndrome are due to

    (a) Mutation due to malnutrition

    (b) Change in sex chromosomes

    (c) Change in autosomes

    (d) Change in both sex chromosomes and autosomes

45. Trisomic condition of Down's syndrome arises due to

    (a) Triploidy

    (b) Translocation

    (c) Non disjunction

    (d) Dicentric bridge formation

46. An example of a disease of molecular mutation is

    (a) Erythroblastosis foetalis

    (b) Haemophilia

    (c) Anaemia

    (d) Sickle-cell anemia

47. Which of the following is not related to chromosomal aberration.

    (a) Euploidy   (b) AIDS

    (c) Aneuploidy   (d) Klinefelter's syndrome

48. When released from ovary human egg contain

    (a) One Y chromosome   (b) Two X chromosome

    (c) One X chromosome   (d) XY chromosome

49. Barr bodies (seen in saliva test in olympic games) are found in human are associated with

    (a) Male autosome

    (b) Female autosome

    (c) Female sex chromosome

    (d) Male sex chromosome

50. The chromosome responsible for the determination of sex are called

    (a) Autosomes   (b) Allosomes

    (c) Multiple alleles   (d) Heterosis

51. Sex chromosomes for the first time was discovered in which plant.

    (a) Sphaerocarpus   (b) Pisum sativum

    (c) Neurospora   (d) Lathyrus odoratus

52. The barr body is observed in

    (a) Basophils of males

    (b) Neutrophils of females

    (c) Eosinophils

    (d) Neutrophils of males

53. The sex determination pattern in honeybee is called

    (a) Female haploidy   (b) Haplodiploidy

    (c) Gametic diploidy   (d) Gametogony

54. The Genotype of a boy having sexual characteristics of a girl is

    (a) XXX   (b) XXY

    (c) XO   (d) XYY

55. The first plant in which chromosomal basic of sex determination was discovered is

    (a) Melandrium (Lychnis)

    (b) Rumex

    (c) Sphaerocarpus

    (d) Coccinia

56. Meta-females have
    (a) XX
    (b) XO
    (c) XXXX
    (d) XXXXXX

57. Barr bodies and drumstick are of what significance of genetists and biologists
    (a) They indicate the presence of abnormal sex cells
    (b) They indicate the presence of more than one X chromosome in the cells
    (c) They indicate male cells
    (d) They signify the presence of sex linked traits

58. Chromosomal abnormality of an unborn body (While in mother's womb) can be found out by a technique called.
    (a) Amniocentesis
    (b) CAT scanning
    (b) Ultrasound
    (d) Tissue culture

59. In human beings, sex is determined
    (a) Before fertilization of ovum
    (b) During 6th week of foetal life when androgens are produced
    (c) At the time of fertilization of ovum
    (d) During 7th and 8th weeks of foetal life when gonads differentiate into testis and ovary.

60. Male child will be born if
    (a) Mother provides both X chromosome
    (b) Sperm of male with Y chromosome fertilizes the egg
    (c) Sperm of male with X chromosome fertilizes the egg
    (d) None of the above

61. Barr body in mammals represents
    (a) All the heterochromatin in female cells
    (b) One of the two X chromosomes in somatic cells of female
    (c) All the heterochromatin in male and female cells
    (d) They Y chromosome is somatic cells of male.

62. A medical technician while observing a human blood smear under the microscope notes the presence of barrbody close to the nuclear membrane in the WBC. This indicates that person under investigation is
    (a) Colour blind
    (b) Haemophilic
    (c) Normal female
    (d) Normal male

Answer Keys

1. (a)	2. (c)	3. (c)	4. (b)	5. (c)	6. (d)	7. (a)	8. (a)	9. (a)	10. (c)
11. (b)	12. (c)	13. (b)	14. (b)	15. (d)	16. (d)	17. (a)	18. (a)	19. (b)	20. (b)
21. (a)	22. (a)	23. (a)	24. (d)	25. (d)	26. (b)	27. (b)	28. (a)	29. (b)	30. (c)
31. (b)	32. (d)	33. (c)	34. (c)	35. (c)	36. (a)	37. (a)	38. (c)	39. (d)	40. (a)
41. (a)	43. (b)	43. (b)	44. (c)	45. (a)	46. (d)	47. (b)	48. (c)	49. (c)	50. (b)
51. (a)	52. (b)	53. (b)	54. (b)	55. (a)	56. (c)	57. (b)	58. (a)	59. (c)	60. (b)
61. (b)	62. (c)								

Solutions

1. Gregor Johann Mendel was the first to formulate clear cut laws of heredity.

2. Genetics is the study of principles and mechanism of heredity and variations

3. Term genetics was first used by W.Bateson (1905)

4. Gregor Johann Mendel (1822 - 1884 Austria) is known as father of genetics, because of transmission of character from one generation to the other.

5. Mendel born in 1822 and died in 1884

6. He was an abbort (head) of Augustinian monastery of St. Thomas at Brunn, Austria in 1847.

7. Mendel factor now known as gene (Johannsen, 1905) is a unit of inheritance.

8. Heredity is the transmission of genetic characters from parents to be offspring.

9. Mendel died before his work could be appreciated by the rest of the scientific community. In 1900, three botanists, correns of Germany, De Vries of the Netherlands, and Tschermak of Austria rediscovered his work after reaching similar conclusions independently.

10. Linkage prevents independent assortment.

11. The cross of heterozygous dominant with its recessive parent is called test cross. The test cross gives 1 : 1 ratio in monohybrid condition whereas 1 : 1 : 1 : 1 in dihybrid condition.

12. Number of gene pair (n) = 2

    The number of F_2 genotype = $3^n = 3^2 = 9$

    Number of kinds of gamete = $2^n = 4$

13. Kinds of gametes may be calculated by following formula. Number of gemetes = $(2)^n$ n is number of alleles

    Example : D/d : E/e : F/f have trihybrid cross i.e., n = 3 than kind of gametes = $(2)^3 = 2 \times 2 \times 2 = 8$

14. Mendel selected these 7 characters-

    (1) Stem length   (2) Flower position

    (3) Pod shape   (4) Pod colour

    (5) Seed shape   (6) Seed colour

    (7) Seed coat colour.

15. Mendel in his experiment considered total 7 characters (3 characters of seed i.e. seed shape, seed colour, cotyledon colour, 2 characters of pod i.e., pod shape and pod colour and 2 characters of plant i.e., plant height and position of pods on the stem)

16. The genotype is the genetic constitutions of an organism

17. RrYy is a dihybrid, so four type of gametes are formed as RY, Ry, rY, ry.

18. Phenotype : Expresses the characters of individuals like form, sex colour and behaviour etc.

19. Individuals having a pair of contrasting characters are known as allelomorph.

20. In codominance, both the genes of an allelomorphic pair express themselves equally in F_1 hybrides, 1 : 2 : 1 ratio both genotypically as well as phenotytically in F_2 generation

21. The homozygote is pure for the character and breeds true, that is it gives rise to offspring having the some character on self breeding, e.g. TT or tt.

22. It is not pure and is called Hybrid. Heterozygote does not breed true on self fertilization. e.g. Tt.

23. The factor of an allelic pair which is unable to express its effect in the presence of its contrasting factor in a heterogygote is called recessive factor.

24. Law of segregation and law of independent assortment come under laws of inheritance.

25. Mendel gave only two laws of genetics. First law is segregation and second law is Independent assortment.

26. Two independent pairs of genes, which interact to produce a new trait together, but each dominant gene alone produces its own trait are called supplementary gene.

27. Correns (1903) while working with Mirabilis Jalapa found that when red flowered variety in crossed with white flowered variety the hybrid variety is pink and F_2 ratio is 1 red : 2 pink : 1 white. This shows that there is no complete dominance.

28. It is also called intermediate as mosaic inheritance

29. Mirabilis Jalapa shows incomplete dominance

30. Plasmid is an extra chromosomal circular DNA molecule which replicates independently in the host chromosome.

31. The transmission of traits from parents to offspring by means of plasmagenes is known as cytoplasmic inheritance.

32.

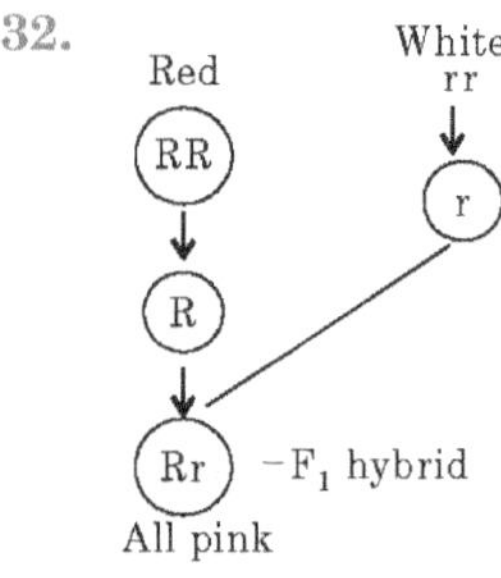

33. Albinism is an autosomal recessive trait. The genotype of such mother would by 'Aa' i.e. one recessive gene 'a' responsible for the absence of melanin and one dominant gene responsible for the presence of melanin would be present. So the mother would be heterozygotic carrier.

34. Albinism is most commonly due to recessive allele on long arm of chromosome 11 but can also be caused by another recessive allele of P-gene on long arm of chromosome 15.

35. Mongolism or Down's syndrome is caused by nondisjunction of 21st chromosome pair during anaphase I. As a result (n + 1) gametes are formed. Fertilization with normal gamete (n) result in trisomy (2n + 1)

36. Because germplasm DNA is inherited from one generation to another.

37. Phenylketonuria is homozygous autosomal recessive disorder.

38. Mutation are sudden stable inheritable/ transmissible discontinuous variations which appear in organism due to permanent change in their genotypes.

39. Individuals with Turner syndrome have on X chromosome (HH + Xo) due to non-disjunction of sex chromosome in their parents.

40. The chromosome number in Turner's syndrome is 2n = 45 due to fusion of (ZZ + 0) ovum with gynosperm (ZZ + X)

41. In transition, purine replaces purine and pyrimidine replaces pyrimidine and in transversion, a purine is replaced by pyrimidine or vice-versa.

42. The individuals with this syndrome are trisomic for chromosome 21. Chromosomal complement is 46 + additional chromosome 21 = 47

43. Phenotypically these individuals are males, but they can show some female secondary sexual characteristic and are usually sterile.

44. There is a large scale possibility of autosomal aneuploidy in human beings

45. Meiotic non-disjunction

46. In sickle-cell anaemia, due to mutation the beta chain amino acid sequence is changed causing change in molecular structure.

47. Because AIDS is caused b virus HIV. HIV also known as LAV = Lymphadenopathy associated virus.

48. The female contain two X chromosomes. The eggs are produced by the meiosis i.e., reduction division. So the egg contains one X chromosome when released from ovary. After fertilization the diploid phase is restored.

49. According to the British geneticist mary Lyon (1961), one of the two X-chromosomes of a normal female becomes heterochromatic and appears are Barr body.

50. Also called sex chromosome or heterosomes

51. Most flowering plants are monoecious and so do not have sex chromosomes. Sex chromosome has been reported in two plant species namely Melandrium (Lychnis) and sphaerocarpus.

52. The barr body is present in the neutrophil (Polymorphonuclear leucocytes) of 3 to 5% cells in females, but not is males.

53. Haplodiploidy is a type of sex determination in which the male is haploid while female is diploid. It occurs in some insects like honey bees, ants and wasps.

54. XXY genotype is found in klinefelters syndrome. It which individuals are male, but they can show some female secondary sexual characteristics and are usually sterile.

55. In melandrium, the sex is determined by the Y-Chromosome, when Y chromosome is present, the sex is male, when Y chromosome is absent, the sex is female.

56. Super or meta females have 47(44 + XXX), 48(44 + XXXX) or 49 (44 + XXXXX) chromosomes.

57. More than one X-chromosomes in females. is transformed into Barr bodies and drumsticks.

58. Amniocentesis is the most widely used method for prenatal detection of many genetic disorders

59. Sex is determined at fertilization by the nature of the sperm that fertilizes the egg.

60. Y-bearing sperms produce male embryo X-bearing sperms produce female.

61. Barr body is nothing but 'X' chromosome which has become heterochromatic, thus appear as deeply stained body. of the two 'X' chromosomes are remains normal while the other appears as a Barr body.

62. Barr body is characteristic feature of female.

CHAPTER 6

Molecular Basis of Inheritance

The DNA & RNA World

There are two types of nucleic acids found in living organisms, DNA (Deoxyribonucleic acid) and RNA (Ribonucleic acid). They are the building blocks of genetic material. Apart from some viruses, genetic material is RNA; mostly DNA is the genetic material in all the organisms. RNA functions as a messenger in most of the organisms.

DNA

Deoxyribonucleic acid also called as DNA is a long polymer of deoxyribonucleotides. The number of nucleotides define the length of DNA.

- **Structure of Polynucleotide Chain:**
  - Polymers of nucleotides are called as Polynucleotides. DNA and RNA are polynucleotides.
  - Nucleotide comprises of – a nitrogenous base, a pentose sugar (ribose in RNA, and deoxyribose in DNA) and a phosphate group.
  - Types of nitrogenous bases are- Purines and pyrimidines.
  - Purine comprises of Adenine (A) and Guanine (G). Cytosine (C), Thymine (T) and Uracil (U) comprise the pyrimidine.
  - N- glycosidic linkage links pentose sugar to a nitrogenous base to form a nucleoside.
  - Nucleosides in RNA-Adenosine, Guanosine, Cytidine and Uridine. Nucleosides in DNA-Deoxyadenosine, Deoxyguanosine, Deoxycytidine and Deoxythymidine.
  - Nucleoside along with phosphate group, which gets attached at 5'-OH, forms corresponding Nucleotide.
  - 3'-5' Phosphodiester bond links two nucleotides and forms dinucleotide. Similarly other nucleotides can be joined to form polynucleotide chain.

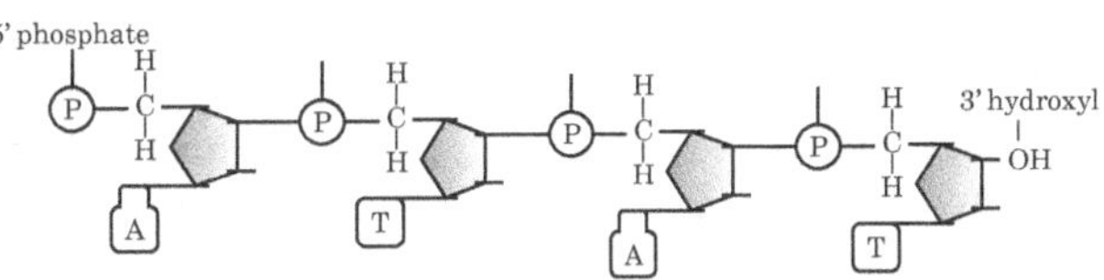

Fig.: 5' phosphate

- **Structure of DNA:**
  - DNA was identified in 1869 by Friedrich Meischer who called it "Nuclein".
  - On the basis of X-ray diffraction data given by Maurice Wilkins and Rosalind Franklin, the structure of DNA given by James Watson and Francis Crick. In the model two polynucleotide chains are coiled together in a right-handed fashion. The model is known as Double Helix model.
  - Links of sugar and phosphate together acts like a backbone (sugar-phosphate backbone).
  - Hydrogen bonds between Adenine (A) and Thymine (T) & Guanine (G) and Cytosine (C) keeps the two strands together.
  - A and T are linked by two hydrogen bonds ($A = T$) whereas G and C are linked by three hydrogen bonds ($G \equiv C$).
  - One chain has polarity of 5' → 3' and the other chain has polarity of 3' → 5' which means the two chains have anti-parallel polarity.

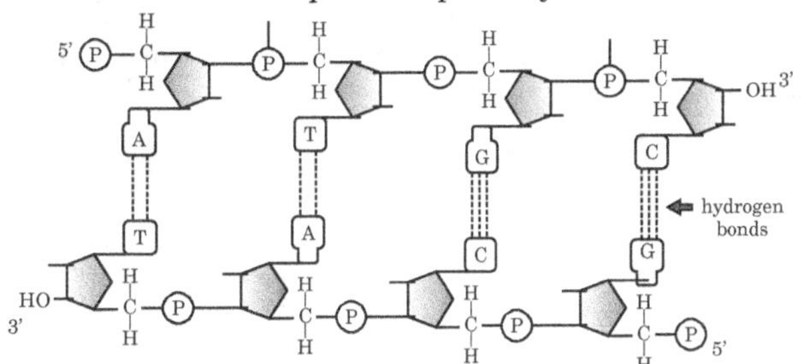

Fig.: Double stranded polynucleotide chain

- ➢ There are approximately 10 base pairs in each turn and the pitch of the helix is 3.4 nm. So, the distance between a base pair is approximately 0.34 nm.
- ➢ The ratio of Adenine-Thymine & Guanine-Cytosine is constant for a given species (Chargaff's rule).
- **Packaging of DNA Helix:**
- ➢ As DNA is negatively charged, so it is held in region called 'nucleoid' with some proteins which are positively charged, in prokaryotes, like E. coli.
- ➢ In eukaryotes, the positively charged protein is basic in nature and is called as Histones. It is rich in amino acid residues, lysines and arginines. They both carry positive charge in their side chains. Hence histone is positive and basic in nature.
- ➢ Histone octamer is a complex formed when histones organize to form a unit of eight molecules.
- ➢ The structure formed when a negatively charged DNA is wrapped around histone octamer is called nucleosome.

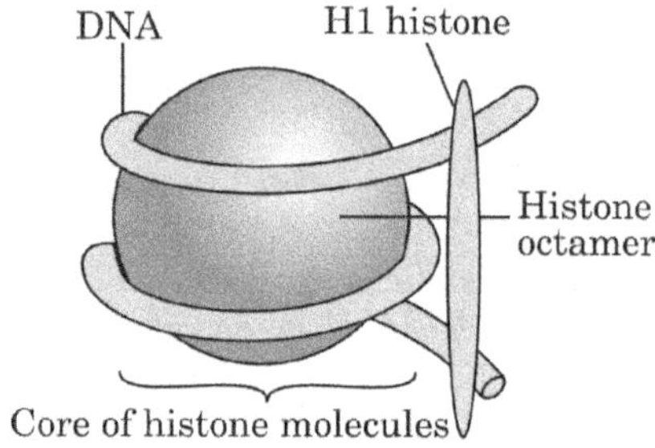

Fig.: Nucleosome

- **Nucleosome:**
- ➢ A nucleosome comprises of generally 200 bp.
- ➢ It constitutes the repeating unit to form a structure called Chromatin.
- ➢ Chromatins are packaged to form chromatin fibers which are further coiled and condensed to form chromosome at metaphase.
- ➢ Types of chromatins in nucleus- Euchromatin and Heterochromatin.

Euchromatins are transcriptionally active part of chromatin which are loosely packed. Whereas, heterochromatin is inactive part of chromatin and are densely packed.

The Search for Genetic Material

- **Transforming principle:**
- ➢ In 1928, Frederick Griffith used *Streptococcus pneumoniae* and mice for his experiment.
- ➢ *Streptococcus pneumoniae* bacteria were allowed to grow on a culture plate. Some of them produced rough colonies (R) while others produced smooth shiny colonies (S). This is because the S strain

bacteria has a polysaccharide mucous coating whereas R strain does not have the coating. The S strain is virulent whereas the R strain is non virulent.

- ➢ When S strain was injected into mice, it died. Whereas when R strain was injected in mice, it survived.
- ➢ When heat killed S-strain was injected into mice, it survived. However, when heat killed S-strain along with R- strain was injected into mice, it died.
- ➢ The conclusion made from this experiment was that, that some transforming principle' got transferred to R-strain from the heat-killed S strain. This might have enabled synthesize of smooth polysaccharide coat in the R strain and made them virulent. This must be due to the transfer of the genetic material.
- **Biochemical Characterization of transforming principle:**
- ➢ The biochemical nature of 'transforming principle' in Griffith's experiment was given by Colin MacLeod, Maclyn McCarty and Oswald Avery.
- ➢ They used suitable enzymes to purify the biochemicals, such as proteins, DNA, RNA etc. from the heat killed S cells.
- ➢ The discovery made from their experiment involved that:
  - Proteins and RNA were digested using proteases and RNases, but this did not affect transformation. They inferred that transforming substance was not a protein or RNA.
  - DNA was digested with help of DNases and this inhibited transformation. From this they concluded that DNA was the reason behind transformation of R-cells to S-cells.
- ➢ Hence, DNA was considered the 'transforming principle'.
- **The Hershey-Chase Experiment:**
- ➢ Experiment done by Alfred Hershey and Martha Chase in 1952 with bacteriophages, also proved that DNA is the genetic material.
- ➢ Some viruses were allowed to grow on a medium that contained radioactive phosphorus (P-32) and some others on medium that contained radioactive sulphur (S-35).
- ➢ E. coli bacteria were infected which radioactive phages, after which the cells were agitated gently and then the culture was centrifuged to separate virus particles from bacteria.
- ➢ It was found that:
  - Bacteria infected with viruses that had radioactive DNA were radioactive, showing that

DNA was the genetic material that passed from the virus to the bacteria.

- Bacteria infected with viruses that had radioactive proteins were not radioactive.

➢ They concluded that DNA is the genetic material.

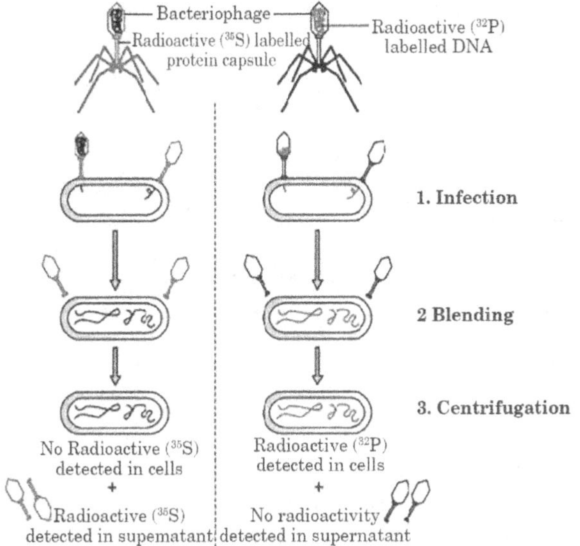

Fig.: The Hershey-Chase Experiment

• **Properties of Genetic Material:**

A molecule needs to possess following characteristics to be a genetic material-

➢ The molecule should be stable, structurally as well as chemically.

➢ There should be scope of slow changes which result in mutation which is essential for evolution.

➢ It should be able to replicate itself and create its replica by the process of Replication.

➢ It should possess the property to express itself as 'Mendelian Characters'.

• **DNA v/s RNA**

DNA	RNA
Chemically less reactive.	Chemically more reactive.
Structurally more stable.	Structurally less stable.
Less prone to mutation.	Prone to mutation.
Better for storage of genetic material.	Not good for storage due to instability.
Not suitable for transmission of genetic material.	Better for transmission of genetic material.
Depends on RNA for protein synthesis.	Can directly code for protein synthesis.
Double stranded.	Single stranded.

RNA

RNA or ribonucleic acid is a single stranded structure which is folded back upon itself forming helices. Nitrogenous bases of RNA are same as DNA except that it has uracil in place of thymine. It acts as genetic material for various viruses. RNA was the genetic material in early life forms after which it went into chemical modifications and evolved into DNA.

DNA Replication

It is the process of copying of DNA from the parent DNA. Watson and Crick proposed semi-conservative model of DNA replication. The model suggests the separation of two strands would and synthesis the new complementary strands by acting as a template. Once the replication is completed, each DNA molecule is left with one newly synthesized and one parental strand each. This scheme was termed as semi-conservative DNA replication.

• **The Experimental Proof:**

➢ In 1958, Matthew Meselson and Franklin Stahl performed an experiment to show that DNA replicates semi conservatively.

➢ *E. Coli* was grown in medium containing 15NH4Cl which resulted in 15N being incorporated into newly synthesized DNA and made it heavier. Then the cells were transferred into a medium with 14NH4Cl, which also got incorporated in both strands of DNA which made it lighter.

➢ The samples were studied at different time intervals. After 20 minutes when 15N had transferred to 14N, the sample was isolated and centrifuged. Its density came out to be intermediate between 14N DNA and 15N DNA.

➢ In the next generation, i.e. after 40 minutes, the DNA extract was composed of equal amount of hybrid DNA and of 'light' DNA.

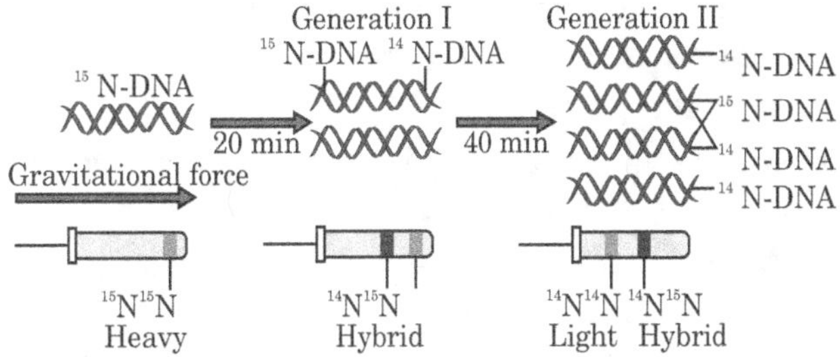

Fig.: Separation of DNA by Centrifugation

- **The Machinery and the Enzymes for replication:**
- ➤ DNA replication begins at a point called origin of replication. In this process both the strands unwind and *Helicase* enzyme break hydrogen bond between both the strands. The structure formed by breaking of bond and unwinding of strand is called as 'replication fork'.
- ➤ The process of DNA replication can be done only in 5' → 3' direction. In presence of enzyme *primase*, a small RNA primer is synthesized and then in presence of *DNA Polymerase* nucleotides join with one another to primer strand and result in polynucleotide chain.
- ➤ The replication is continuous on strand in which the template had polarity of 3' → 5' whereas it is discontinuous over 5' → 3'. *DNA ligase* helps in joining the discontinuous fragments called okazaki fragments.

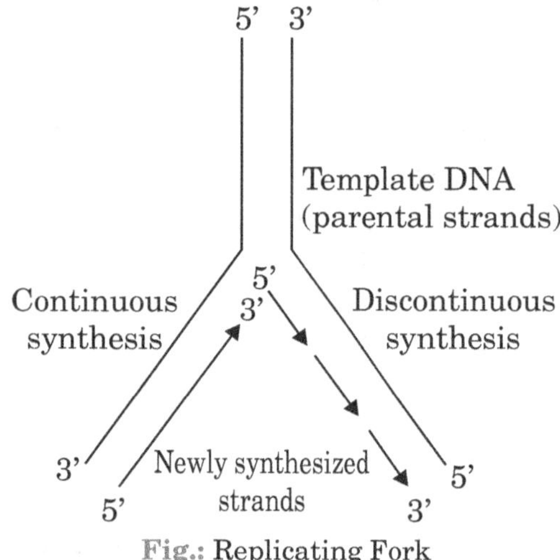

Fig.: Replicating Fork

Transcription

Transcription refers to the process of duplicating the genetic data from one strand of the DNA into RNA. Here also, the principle of complementarily governs the process of transcription, except the adenosine now forms base pair with uracil instead of thymine.

- **Transcription Unit:**

There are three main regions in a transcription unit in DNA, which are as follows:

- ➤ In a transcription unit, the promoter and terminator are found along with structural gene.
- ➤ The promoter is said to be located towards 5' –end (upstream) of the structural gene (the reference is made with respect to the polarity of coding strand).

- ➤ A DNA sequence helps in providing the binding site for RNA polymerase, and the template and coding strands are defined by the presence of a promoter.
- ➤ The explanation of coding and template strands can be switched by changing the position with terminator.
- ➤ The terminator defines the end of the process of transcription.

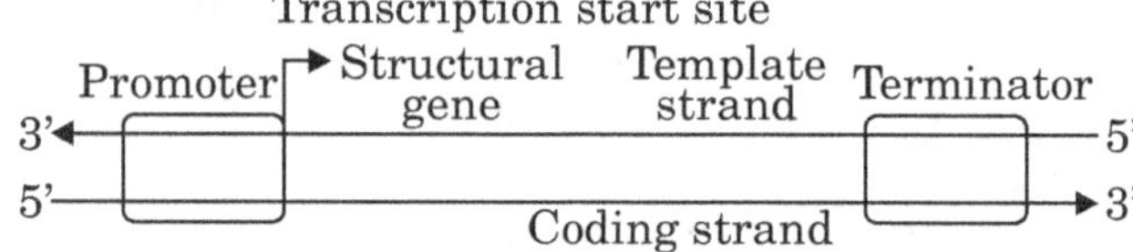

Fig.: Schematic structure of a transcription unit

- **Gene and the Transcription Unit:**
- ➤ A gene is considered as the functional unit of inheritance. Genes can also be called as DNA sequence coding for tRNA or rRNA molecules.
- ➤ Segment of DNA which codes for a polypeptide is called as cistron. There are two types of the structural gene in a transcription unit:
  - Monocistronic: It is found in eukaryotes, where the coding sequence or exons are split and are interrupted by introns, the intervening sequence
  - Polycistronic: It is found in bacteria or prokaryotes, where there's no split genes.
- **Types of RNA:**
- ➤ Bacteria have three types of RNAs: mRNA, tRNA and rRNA also known as messenger, transfer and ribosomal RNAs respectively.
- ➤ They are required for synthesizing a protein in a cell.
- ➤ The mRNA provides the template, tRNA brings amino acids and reads the genetic code, and rRNAs play structural and catalytic role during translation.
- **Process of transcription:**
- ➤ The first phase is initiation where RNA polymerase holds on to promoter and starts transcription.
- ➤ RNA polymerase follows the rule of complementarity where it uses nucleoside triphosphates as substrate and it is then polymerized into a template.
- ➤ It also helps helix to open up and keep on elongating.
- ➤ RNA polymerase enzyme is bound to a small part of RNA. Now the polymerase reaches the terminator region.
- ➤ The last phase is termination of transcription where the nascent RNA lowers down.

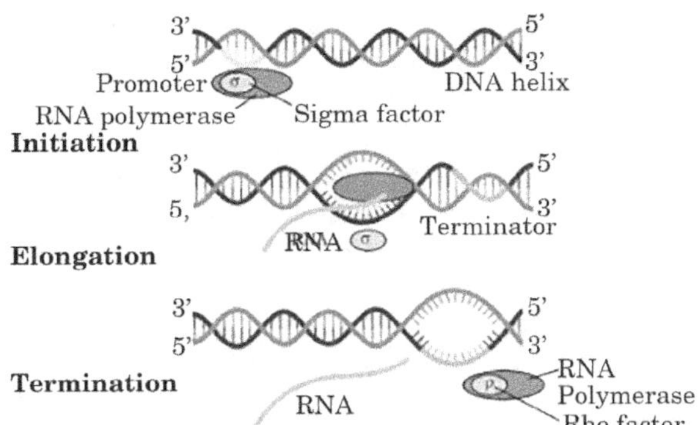

Fig.: Process of Transcription in Bacteria

- **Complexities in Eukaryotes:**
  - There exist non-functional exons and introns in the primary transcripts. Now, the exons are arranged in a set order and the introns are removed and this process is known as splicing. hnRNA goes through a process known as capping where an unusual nucleotide is added to 5' end of hnRNA. These are methylated guanine residues. It goes through another process called tailing in which adenylate residues (200-300) are added at 3'- end.
  - There exist three RNA polymerases in the nucleus. The RNA polymerase I, II and III transcribes rRNAs, precursor of mRNA and tRNA, 5S rRNA, and snRNAs, respectively.

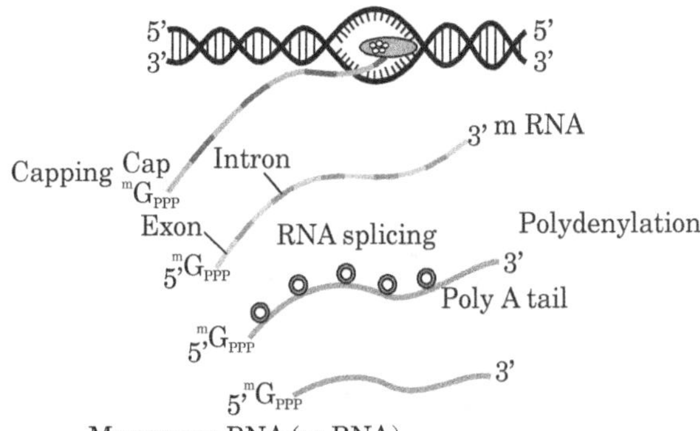

Fig.: Process of transcription in Eukaryotes

Genetic Code, Human Genome Project & DNA Fingerprinting

Genetic Code

Genetic code is the sequence of nucleotides in mRNA that contains information for protein synthesis.

- **Salient features of Genetic Code:**
  - The genetic code is a triplet code.

- One amino acid has only one codon code, hence, it is specific and undebatable.
- The code is almost universal and non-overlapping.
- Sometimes more than one codon is used to code amino acids and so the code is dissipated.
- No punctuation is used between adjacently placed codons.
- Exceptions to this rule have been found in mitochondrial codons, and in some protozoans

First position	Second position				Third position
	U	C	A	G	
U	UUU Phe	UCU Ser	UAU Tyr	UGU Cys	U
	UUC Phe	UCC Ser	UAC Tyr	UGC Cys	C
	UUA Leu	UCA Ser	UAA Stop	UGA Stop	A
	UUG Leu	UCG Ser	UAG Stop	UGG Trp	G
C	CUU Leu	CCU Pro	CAU His	CGU Arg	U
	CUC Leu	CCC Pro	CAC His	CGC Arg	C
	CUA Leu	CCA Pro	CAA Gin	CGA Arg	A
	CUG Leu	CCG Pro	CAG Gin	CGG Arg	G
A	AUU Ile	ACU Thr	AAU Asn	AGU Ser	U
	AUC Ile	ACC Thr	AAC Asn	AGC Ser	C
	AUA Ile	ACA Thr	AAA Lys	AGA Arg	A
	AUG Met	ACG Thr	AAG Lys	AGG Arg	G
G	GUU Val	GCU Ala	GAU Asp	GGU Gly	U
	GUC Val	GCC Ala	GAC Asp	GGC Gly	C
	GUA Val	GCA Ala	GAA Glu	GGA Gly	A
	GUG Val	GCG Ala	GAG Glu	GGG Gly	G

Fig.: The Codons for Various Amino Acids

- **Mutations and Genetic Code:**
  - Studying mutation explains the relationships between DNA and genes.
  - Deletion or rearrangement in DNA segment results in loss or gain of a gene and so its function.
  - Example of point mutation includes, change of single base pair in the gene for beta globin chain, results in the change of amino acid residue glutamate to valine which results into a diseased condition called as sickle cell anaemia.
  - If a base or two are inserted or deleted, it changes the reading frame from the point of insertion or deletion.

- **tRNA- The Adapter Molecule:**
  - Amino acids have no structural specialties to read the code uniquely. On one hand they read the code and on other hand would bind to specific amino acids.
  - An anticodon loop is present in tRNA which has basesthat are complementary to the code and amino acids are binded together by tRNA with the help of amino acid accepter end. There are specific tRNAs for each amino acid.
  - There is a specific initiator tRNA that helps in initiation. There are no tRNAs present for stop codons.

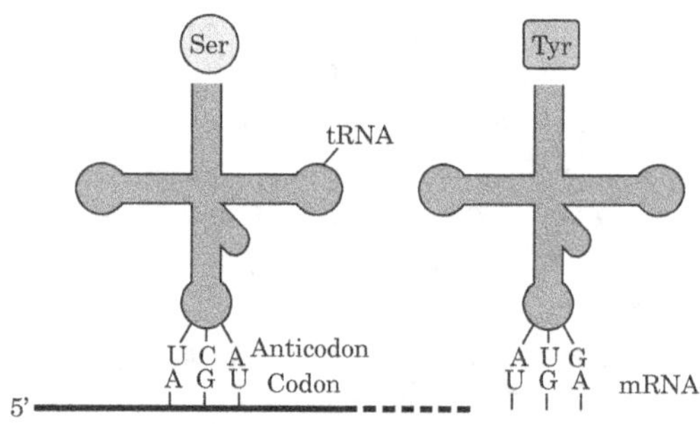

Fig.: tRNA – the adapter molecule

- **Translation:**
  - Polymerisation of amino acids to form a polypeptide is referred as translation.
  - In the first phase which is called as charging of tRNA, as energy is required from ATP for formation of peptide bond, so amino acids are activated in the presence of ATP and linked to their cognate tRNA in presence of *aminoacyl tRNA synthetase*. This step is also called as aminoacylation of tRNA or tRNA charging.

- In the next step called as initiation, the ribosome binds to the mRNA at the start codon (AUG) that is recognized by initiator tRNA.
- In the third phase of elongation, complexes which are formed by linkage of amino acids to tRNA, bind to appropriate codon in mRNAby forming complimentary base pairs with the tRNA anticodon.
- At the end, in last phase, the process of translation is terminated and complete polypeptide is released from the ribosome.

- **Regulation of Gene Expression:**
  - Polypeptide is formed as a result of gene expression. In eukaryotes, the regulation could be exerted at:
    - Transcriptional level (formation of primary transcript)
    - Processing level (regulation of splicing)
    - Transport of mRNA from nucleus to the cytoplasm
    - Translational level.

- **Lac Operon:**
- A polycistronic structural gene is controlled with the help of a common promoter and regulatory genes. In bacteria, this kind of an arrangement is quite common and is known as an operon. For example: val operon, trp operon, lac operon, etc.
- Lac operon which controls metabolism of lactose. Lactose is used as an inducer as it regulates switching on and off of the operon.

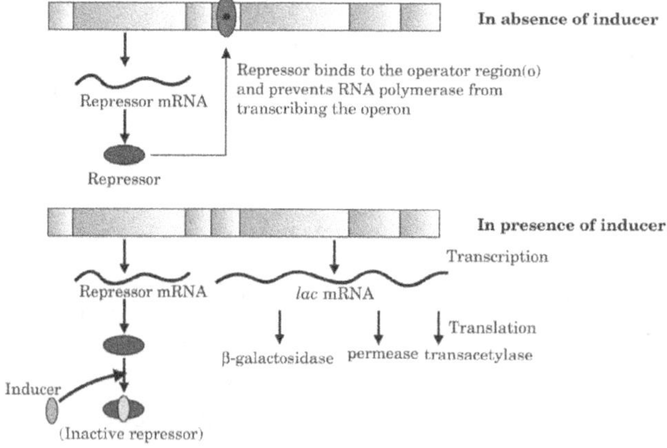

Fig.: The *lac* Operon

Human Genome Project

Genome is referred to as the complete DNA, found in the haploid set of chromosomes of an organism. Human Genome project (HGP) was the first effort in identifying the sequence of nucleotides and mapping of all genes in human genome.

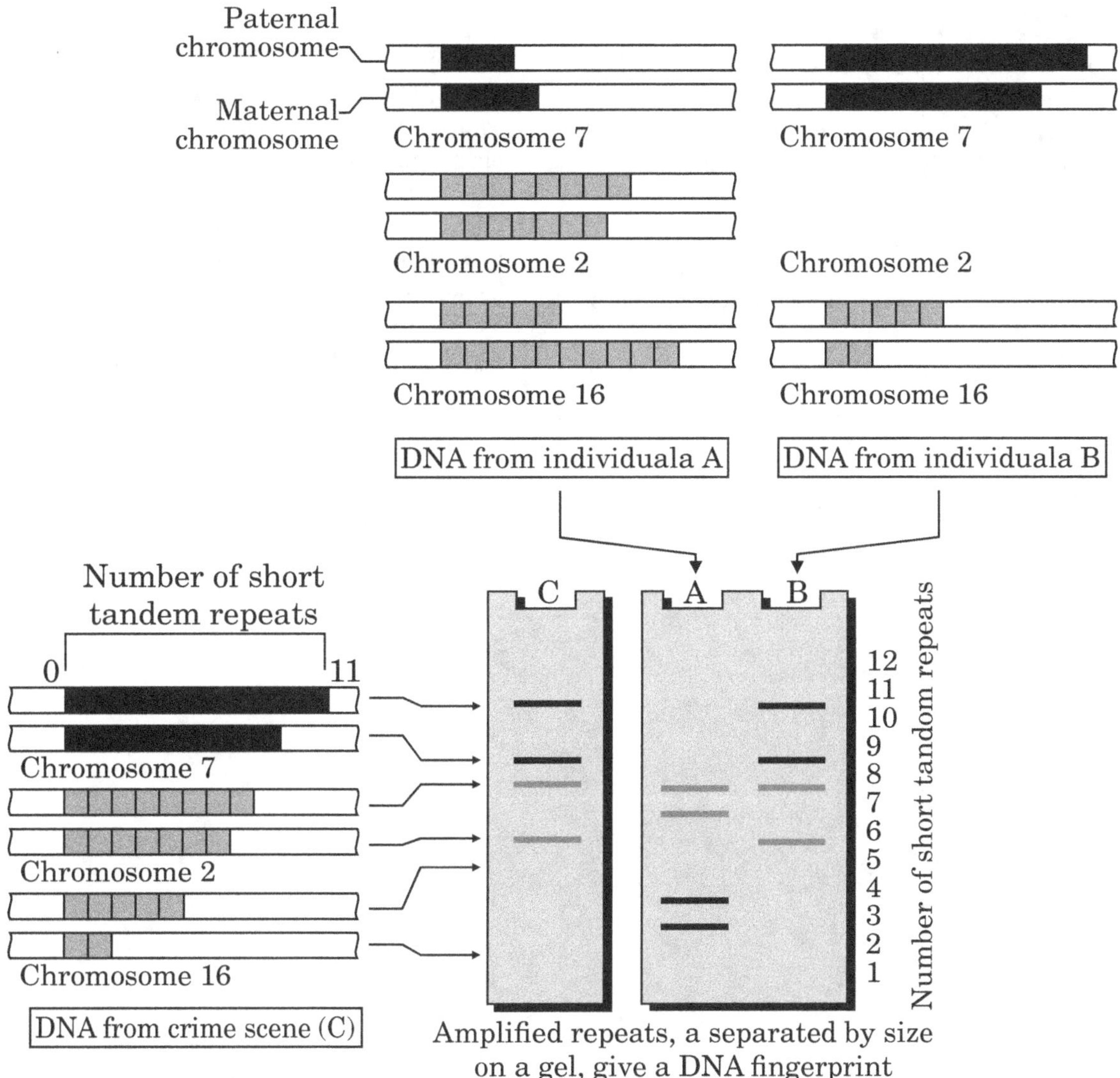

Fig.: Schematic representation of DNA Fingerprinting

- **Goals of HGP:**
- ➢ To determine the sequences of the 3 billion chemical base pairs that comprise of human DNA.
- ➢ To identify all the genes present in human DNA.
- ➢ To improve data analysis tools.
- ➢ To have a storage facility to safely keep this information in databases.
- ➢ To transfer related technologies to other sectors, such as industries.
- ➢ To deal with ethical, legal and social issues that may arise due to this project.
- **Methodologies:**
- ➢ One of the two methods focuses on recognizing all the genes that expressed as RNA.
- ➢ The second method takes the blind outlook of aligning the genome, containing all the coding and non-coding sequence, and are assigned different regions later in the sequence.

DNA Fingerprinting

DNA fingerprinting is a way to identify the similarities and differences in specific region of DNA sequence known as repetitive DNA, as in these sequences, a small stretch of DNA is repeated many times.

- **Basis of DNA fingerprinting:**
  - Polymorphism in DNA sequence is the basis of genetic mapping of human genome as well as of DNA fingerprinting. Polymorphism (variation at genetic level) arises due to mutations.

- **Steps of DNA fingerprinting:**
  - Firstly, isolate the DNA.
  - Then, DNA is digested by restriction endonuclease.
  - Then, DNA fragments are separated by electrophoresis.
  - After this, separated DNA fragments are transferred to synthetic membranes, such as nitrocellulose or nylon, also referred as blotting.
  - Then DNA fragments are hybridized using labelled VNTR probe.
  - Finally, hybridized NA fragments are detected by auto radiography.

EXERCISE

1. Who described the structure of DNA double helix?
   (a) Peter Mitchell
   (b) Andre Jagendorf
   (c) Ernest Uribe
   (d) Watson and Crick

2. Which form of DNA is described by watson Crick
   (a) B-DNA
   (b) Z DNA
   (c) A-DNA
   (d) Quadraplex DNA

3. How many base pairs are there in every helical turn of Watson-Crick double helix model?
   (a) 32.3
   (b) 11.6
   (c) 20
   (d) 10.4

4. Which one of the following statement is incorrect for Z-DNA?
   (a) Left-handed DNA
   (b) Mostly found in alternating Purine-Pyrimidine sequences
   (c) Only one deep, narrow groove
   (d) Anti glycosidic bond conformation

5. The third strand of triple helix is paired in which Scheme?
   (a) Hoogsteen base pair scheme
   (b) Intermolecular base pair scheme
   (c) Interamolecular base pair scheme
   (d) G-quartet scheme

6. Name the nitrogenous base which is found in abundance in G-quadruplex
   (a) Adenine
   (b) Guanine
   (c) Cytosine
   (d) Thymine

7. The stability and formation of G-quadruplex depends on ________.
   (a) Monovalent cation
   (b) Divalent cation
   (c) Bivalent cation
   (d) Pentavalent ion

8. Which of this factor is not responsible for thermal denaturation of DNA?
   (a) pH
   (b) Temperature
   (c) Ionic strength
   (d) Humidity

9. Double-stranded DNA with high GC content has higher thermal stability than that of lower GC content?
   (a) True
   (b) False

10. What is the term given to the supercoiling of circular DNA?
    (a) Twist number
    (b) Linking number
    (c) Writhe number
    (d) Cross-linking

11. Which of them is used to introduce negative supercoiling in DNA?
    (a) Type 1 topoisomerase
    (b) Ethidium bromide
    (c) Gyrase 1 type 2 topoisomerase
    (d) SYBR gold

12. Molecules which play the key role in the transfer of genetic information during protein synthesis are ________.
    (a) DNA
    (b) RNA
    (c) Nucleic acid
    (d) Lipids

13. Double helix formed by RNA is more stable than DNA.
    (a) True
    (b) False

15. Name the RNA molecular which is used to carry genetic information copied from DNA?
    (a) tRNA
    (b) mRNA
    (c) rRNA
    (d) snRNA

16. Which of the following RNA molecule convert information stored in the nucleic acid to protein?
    (a) mRNA
    (b) snRNA
    (c) rRNA
    (d) tRNA

17. Name the secondary structure of tRNA?
    (a) Cloverleaf
    (b) L-shaped
    (c) Duplex
    (d) Triple Helix

18. Name the RNA molecule which takes part in the formation of the ribosome?
    (a) mRNA
    (b) tRNA
    (c) rRNA
    (d) gRNA

19. Which of the following rRNA molecules have peptidyl transferase activity in prokaryotes?
    (a) 23 S rRNA
    (b) 28 S rRNA
    (c) 5 S rRNA
    (d) 18 S rRNA

20. Which of the following statement is incorrect about SnRNA?
    (a) It is small nuclear RNA
    (b) It helps in RNA splicing
    (c) It is also called snurps
    (d) It functions in RNA editing

21. What is the role of snRNA in eukaryotes?
    (*a*) Chemical modification
    (*b*) RNA splicing
    (*c*) Act as adaptor RNA
    (*d*) Forms component of the ribosome

22. Name the class of RNA which takes part in RNA editing?
    (*a*) snRNA   (*b*) tRNA
    (*c*) gRNA   (*d*) SiRNA

23. Which of the following is not a feature of the genetic code?
    (*a*) Triplet   (*b*) Degenerate
    (*c*) Non-Overlapping (*d*) Ambiguous

24. The codon is a ________.
    (*a*) Singlet   (*b*) Duplet
    (*c*) Triplet   (*d*) Quadruplet

25. Which of the following is not a termination codon?
    (*a*) UGA   (*b*) AGA
    (*c*) AGG   (*d*) UAC

26. In case of mitochondrial genetic code UGA is a ________ Codon
    (*a*) Tryptophan   (*b*) Arginine
    (*c*) Proline   (*d*) Stop

27. The wobble hypothesis was devised by ________.
    (*a*) Arthur Kornberg (*b*) Francis Crick
    (*c*) James Watson   (*d*) William Asbury

28. Which of the following genetic code shows ambiguity?
    (*a*) CGU   (*b*) AUG
    (*c*) GAC   (*d*) UGA

29. Which of the following is not true about the genome mapping?
    (*a*) It doesn't lead to the understanding a genome structure
    (*b*) It involves identifying relative locations of genes.
    (*c*) It involves identifying traits
    (*d*) It involves identifying mutations

30. Genetic markers are ________ Portions of a ________ Whose inheritance patterns can be followed.
    (*a*) Unidentifiable, genes
    (*b*) Unidentifiable, chromosome
    (*c*) Identifiable, chromosome
    (*d*) Identifiable, genes.

31. One centimorgan is defined as __________ Percentage of the total recombination events.
    (*a*) One
    (*b*) ten
    (*c*) 0.1
    (*d*) 0.01

32. Physical maps are maps of locations of identifiable landmarks on a genomic DNA __________ inheritance patterns.
    (*a*) remotely related to (*b*) related to
    (*c*) regardless of   (*d*) associated with

33. Which of the following is untrue about cytologic maps?
    (*a*) They cannot be directly observed under microscope
    (*b*) They refer to bonding patterns
    (*c*) They can be viewed on stained chromosomes
    (*d*) They can be directly observed under microscope

34. DNA finger printing was developed by
    (*a*) Francis Crick   (*b*) Khorana
    (*c*) Alec Jeffrey   (*d*) James Watson

35. DNA finger printing relies on
    (*a*) Difference in patterns of genes between individuals.
    (*b*) Difference in order of genes between individuals.
    (*c*) Difference in junk DNA patterns between individuals.
    (*d*) All of these

36. Minisatellites are
    (*a*) 10 – 40 bp sized short sequences within the genes.
    (*b*) Short coding repetitive regions on the eukaryotic genome
    (*c*) Short Non-coding repetitive sequences present
    (*d*) Are regions of chromosomes after secondary constriction.

37. The DNA fingerprint pattern of a child is
    (*a*) Exactly similar to that of both of the parents
    (*b*) 100% similar to the father's DNA print
    (*c*) 100% similar to the mother's DNA print
    (*d*) 50% bands similar to father and rest similar to mother.

Answer Keys

1. (*d*) 2. (*a*) 3. (*d*) 4. (*d*) 5. (*a*) 6. (*b*) 7. (*a*) 8. (*d*) 9. (*a*) 10. (*b*)

11. (*c*) 12. (*b*) 13. (*a*) 15. (*b*) 16. (*d*) 17. (*a*) 18. (*c*) 19. (*a*) 20. (*d*) 21. (*a*)

22. (*c*) 23. (*d*) 24. (*c*) 25. (*d*) 26. (*a*) 27. (*b*) 28. (*d*) 29. (*a*) 30. (*c*) 31. (*a*)

32. (*c*) 33. (*a*) 34. (*c*) 35. (*c*) 36. (*c*) 37. (*d*)

Solutions

1. DNA double helix was first described in 1953 by watson and crick using X-ray diffraction DNA fibers were obtained by franklin and wilkins. Watson crick ad wilkins were awarded a noble prize in 1962.

2. There are many forms of DNA which are biologically important, out of which watson crick double helix model describes the B form of DNA. The confirmation of DNA would depend on the hydration level, base modification etc.

3. Watson-crick double helix model consists of 10.4 base pairs per helical turn. Since one helical turn formed by 360° and there would be 34.3 twist angle per residue among adjacent base pair.

4. Anti glycosidic bond conformation is incorrect as in Z-DNA the sugar and glycosidic bond conformations alternate, anti for C and syn of G while in B form there is only anti glycosidic bond conformation.

5. Triple helix formed by three strands polypurine, polypyrimidine and the third strand which lay is the major groove of DNA and makes a hydrogen bond to duplex. The third strand is paired in hoogsteen base pairing scheme where the central strand is purine rich.

6. When nucleic acid sequences are rich in guanine and can form four stranded structure, it will term as G-quadruplex. It is a square arrangement of guanine, stabilized by hoogsteen hydrogen bonding.

7. A monovalent cation is responsible for the stability of G-quadruplex as it is present in the center of the tetrad. It can be formed in either DNA or RNA.

8. When DNA duplex is laid open to the specific conditions like temperature, pH, or ionic strength it will interrupt the hydrogen bond between strands and they are no longer held separates as individual coils and the double helix is denatured

9. There is three hydrogen bond in G : C while only two between A : T, this shows higher no. of hydrogen bonds and interaction in G : C than A : T. Higher G : C content has a higher melting temperature. So, it has more thermal stability as compared to A : T.

10. Linking number defines the no. of times one strand crosses other in closed circular DNA. It is the sum of twist number (total number of helical turn) and writhe number (supercoiling in the helix). LK = Tw + Wr.

11. Type 1 topoisomerase break only one strand of DNA while gyrase works on both the strands, it breaks and reseal both DNA strands and introduce negative supercoils. Ethidium bromide and SYBR gold are used to stain DNA molecules.

12. DNA has all the information which is confined to the nucleus, it is only transferred with the help of RNA during protein synthesis. RNA also has a diverse function in the body which is confined to the nucleus, it is only transferred with the help of RNA during protein synthesis. RNA also has a diverse function in the body which includes the enzymatic activity of ribozyme and storage of genetic information in RNA viruses.

13. The difference in their thermal stability is not clearly known but double stranded helical RNA needs higher temperature for denaturation than DNA.

15. Each type of RNA functions differently, among them mRNA which is also known as messenger RNA carries genetic information from DNA in the form of series of a three-base codon, which specifies the amino acid.

16. Transfer RNA (tRNA) plays a key role in protein biosynthesis and known as adopter tRNA. It acts as an interface between nucleic and language and protein language. Additionally, it also paritcipates in reverse transcription as a primer.

17. Based on their primary sequence tRNA folds into cloverleaf like secondary structure with well-defined loops and stems while tertiary structure further modified into the L-shaped structure.

18. rRNA is also known as ribosomal RNA which is a key component in the formation of a ribosome. rRNA molecules along with the ribosomal proteins in the nucleolus form pre-ribosomal subunit 40 S and 60 S respectively.

19. rRNA molecules have several roles in protein synthesis, one of them is peptidyl transferase activity. In prokaryotes, 50 subunit has 23 S rRNA which has a catalytic role and forms a part of peptidyl transferase activity. Similarly, eukaryotes have 28S rRNA in 60 subunits.

20. SnRNA is small nuclear RNA mainly found in the nucleus of eukaryotic cells. It takes part in RNA splicing and always remain associated with other proteins and referred to as snurps or snRNP. It functions in RNA editing is incorrect as RNA editing is done by guide RNA.

21. SnoRNA takes part in chemical modification like methylation of rRNA and other forms of RNA in eukaryotes. It forms a snoRNP complex with the proteins and guides it to the modification site of RNA.

22. gRNA is guide RNA which is an RNA gene that functions in RNA editing. It was reported in mitochondria of kinetoplastids, where mRNA edited by inserting or deleting stretches of uridylates.

23. The genetic code is non-ambiguous. This means that there is no ambiguity about a particular codon. A particular code will always code for the same amino acid wherever it is found.

24. The codon is a triplet. Singlet and doublet codes are not enough to code for 20 amino acids. Again in case of a quadruplet codon there will be 256 possible codon thus is the minimum requisite having 64 possible codons.

25. UGA, AGA and AGG are termination codons of which UGA is the universal termination codon and AGA and AGG are mitochondrial termination codons. But UAC is the universal codon for tyrosine.

26. In case of mitochondrial genetic code UGA is a tryptophan codon. But UGA is a stop codon in the universal genetic code.

27. In 1966, Francis crick devised the wobble hypothesis to explain the observation regarding base pairing. It states that the base at the 5 end of the anticodon is not as statically confined as the other two, allowing it to form hydrogen bonds with any of the several bases located at the 3 end of a codon.

28. UGA is one of the universal termination codon. But UGA codes for tryptophan in mitochondrial genetic code.

29. The first step to understanding a genome structure is through genome mapping, which is a process of identifying relative locations of genes, mutations or traits on a chromosome. A low-resolution approach to mapping genomes is to describe the order and relative distances of genetic markers on a chromosome.

30. For many eukaryotes, genetic markers represent morphologic phenotypes. In addition to genetic linkage maps, there are also other types of genome maps such as physical maps and cytologic maps, which describe genomes at different levels of resolution.

31. One centimorgan is one percentage of the total recombination events when separation of the two genetic markers is observed in a genetic crossing experiment. One centimorgan is approximately 1 Mb in humans and 0.5 Mb in Drosophila.

32. The distance between genetic markers is measured directly as kilobases (Kb) or Megabases (Mb). Because the distance is expressed in physical units, it is more accurate and reliable than centimorgans used in genetic maps.

33. Cytologic maps refer to bonding patterns seen on stained chromosomes, which can be directly observed under a microscope. The observed light and dark bonds are the visually distinct markers on a chromosome.

34. In September 1984, Dr. Alec Jeffreys, a geneticist from University of Leicester in great Britain developed the DNA fingerprinting.

35. DNA fingerprinting relies on the difference in Junk DNA patterns between individuals. The Junk DNA regions are made-up of length polymorphisms, which shows variations in the physical length of the DNA molecule.

36. Minisatellites are short Non-coding (10 - 60 base pairs long) of repetitive sequences throughout the chromosome. This number variation is exhibited in the number of repeated units, or stuthers' in the minisatellite sequence. The first minisatellite was discovered in 1980.

37. A child get half of his DNA from his father and half from his mother. STRs are therefore passed down from parents to their children.

CHAPTER 7

Evolution

Origin of Life on Earth and Various Related Exidences

Theories of origin of life: Many theories have been given by various scientists to explain the phenomenon of origin of life. Some of these proposed theories are as follows:

- Biogenesis
- Theory of sudden creation from inorganic material.
- Theory of special creation.
- Naturalistic theory
- Theory of spontaneous generation or Abiogenesis.
- Cosmozoic theory

Modern Theory by Oparin

- The main idea of the theory - "life could have originated from non-living organic molecules."
- In 1936, Oparin presented his ideas in his book "The origin of life".
- He proposed that, the origin of the Earth was about 4,500 million years ago. There was a reduced atmosphere which is also called as primitive atmosphere which had presence of nitrogen, hydrogen, ammonia, methane, carbon mono-oxide and water, when the earth was cooling down. Ultraviolet rays and electric discharges by lightening acted as the source of energy. Folded earth crust was formed during this process. For centuries, rains poured over the earth and got deposited in deep places of the earth crust.

Stanley Miller, an American biologist, performed an experiment known as Miller's experiment. He synthesized the basic compounds which are essential for life in the laboratory, on a small scale.

He made a specially designed flask which was containing hydrogen, ammonia and methane in the proportion of 2 : 1 : 2 respectively at 0°C. This proportion is the same as the proportion of gases that were present in the environment of primitive earth. A smaller flask, filled with water was connected to the flask that was containing the gases, with the help of glass tubes. Two tungsten electrodes were fitted and a current of 60,000 volts was passed through the gases to recreate the lightning storms that were there at the time of origin of life. This process was continued for seven days. On the last day when the vapours condensed, a red color substance was found in the tubes. On the analysis, it was found that the red substance was containing glycine, amino acids, and nitrogenous bases. These substances are found in the nucleus of a cell.

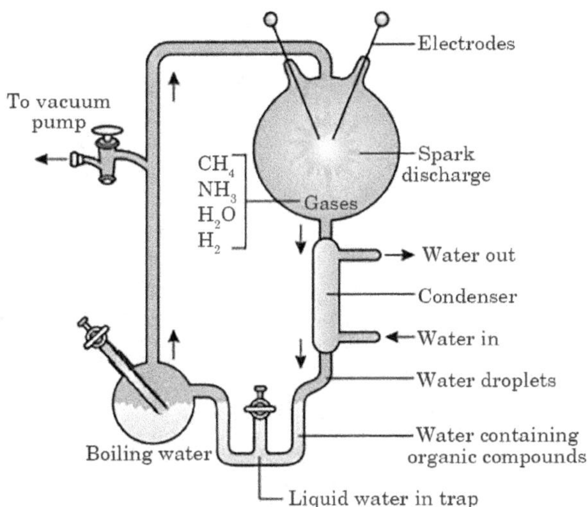

Fig.: Miller's experiment

Evolution of life forms

During a sea voyage, some observations were made. Charles Darwin concluded them all and proposed that current living forms have some similarities among themselves and also with life forms prevailing millions of years back. Quite a lot of them do not exist anymore. The geological history of earth matches up quite closely with the biological history of earth. Earlier it was a common conclusion that earth is very old, around thousands but in actual it is billions of years old.

Evidences for evolution

- **Divergent evolution:** Because of different needs, along different directions the same structures been developed.
- **Convergent evolution:** Different structures developed along same direction due to adaptation to perform similar functions.

Adaptive Radiation

In a given geographical area, evolution of different species from a point and diverging to different areas of geography. A number of marsupials, each different from the other evolved from an ancestral stock, but all within the Australian island continent

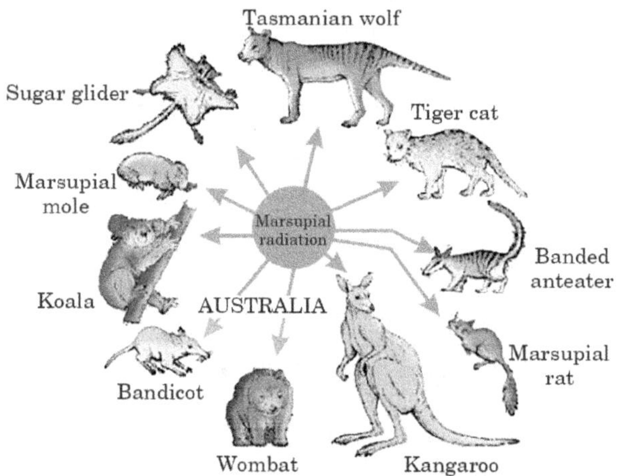

Fig.: Adaptive Radiation

Biological Evolution, Its Mechanism and Evolution of Man

Evolution by natural selection, in a true sense would have started when cellular forms of life with differences in metabolic capability originated on earth.

Lamarck, proposed that the evolution of various life forms happened but was driven by the use or disuse of the organs.

Darwinian Theory of natural selection, given by Charles Robert Darwin said that only the fittest species can survive the changing environmental and physical conditions. The two important concepts of Darwinian's Theory of Evolution: Branching descent and natural selection.

Mechanism of Evolution

Mutations are random and directionless while Darwinian variations are small and directional.

Evolution for Darwin was gradual while deVries believed mutation caused speciation and hence called it saltation (single step large mutation).

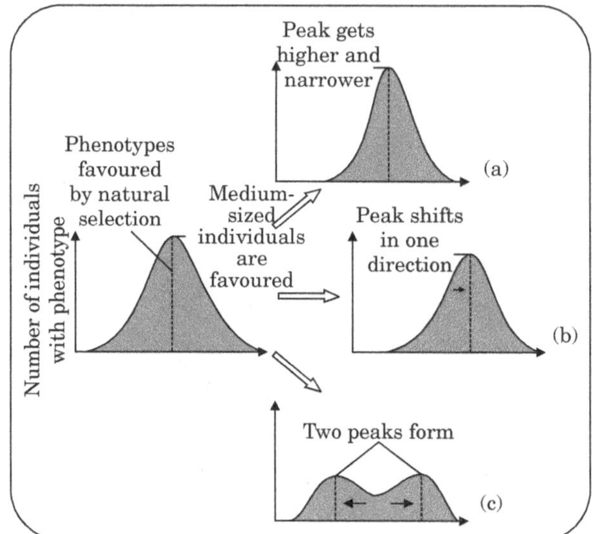

Fig.: Hardy weinberg principle

Hardy-Weinberg principle

The principle states that within a population, allele frequencies are stable and persistent from generation to generation.

In a population, total genes along with their alleles always remain a constant and this is referred to as genetic equilibrium. The total sum of every allelic frequency is 1.

Origin and Evolution of Man

- Primates called Dryopithecus (ape-like) and Ramapithecus (man-like) existed around 15 million years ago. They use to walk like chimpanzees and gorillas and were also hairy.
- According to few fossils found in Ethiopia and Tanzania, around three to four million years ago, man-like primates existed in eastern parts of Africa.
- Around two million years ago, the first human-like creatures were traced back and were called Homo habilis. They assumingly did not eat meat.
- Homo erectus, who is supposed to have a large brain, probably ate meat.
- Then came the age of Homo sapiens found first in Africa and they moved across continents and evolved into distinct races.
- Around 18,000 years ago, pre-historic cave art developed. Agriculture came into existence about 10,000 years back. After that the human settlement started.

EXERCISE

1. first life on earth was
   - (a) Cyanobacteria
   - (b) Autotrophs
   - (c) Photo autotrophs
   - (d) Chemoheterotrophs

2. One of the possible early sources of energy were/was.
   - (a) Green plants
   - (b) Carbon dioxide
   - (c) Chlorophyll
   - (d) UV rays and lightening

3. First experiment regarding evolution of life was performed by
   - (a) Watson and Crick
   - (b) Oparin and Haldane
   - (c) Urey and Miller
   - (d) Meselson and Stahl

4. Coacervates were formed by
   - (a) DNA
   - (b) radiations
   - (c) Polymerisation
   - (d) Polymerisation and aggregation

5. Miller and Urey performed an experiment to prove origin of life. They look for gases NH3 and H2 along with?
   - (a) N_2 and H2O
   - (b) H_2O and CH_4
   - (c) CO_2 and N_2
   - (d) CH_4 and N_2

6. According to oparin, which one of following was not present in the primitive atmosphere of the earth?
   - (a) methane
   - (b) hydrogen
   - (c) water vapour
   - (d) oxygen

7. Swan neck flask experiment was performed by
   - (a) Oparin and Haldane
   - (b) Darwin
   - (c) Aristotle
   - (d) Louis Pasteur

8. Coacervates were experiment produced by
   - (a) Urey and Miller
   - (b) Jacob and Monad
   - (c) Oparin
   - (d) Fischer and Huxley

9. Theory of spontaneous generation was put forward by
   - (a) Spallanzani
   - (b) F. Redi
   - (c) Van Helmont
   - (d) Pasteur.

10. Finding of Miller's experiment on origin of life has provided evidence for the
    - (a) theory of special creation
    - (b) theory of biogenesis
    - (c) theory of abiogenesis
    - (d) theory of organic evolution

11. A species inhabiting different geographical areas is known as
    - (a) Sympatric
    - (b) allopatric
    - (c) Sibling
    - (d) biospecies

12. According to De vries theory evolution is
    - (a) Jerky
    - (b) discontinuous
    - (c) Continuous and Smooth
    - (b) both a and b

13. Mutation may be described as
    - (a) Continuous genetic variation
    - (b) Phenotypic change
    - (c) Discontinuous genetic variation
    - (d) Change due to hybridisation

14. The theory of use and disuse was given by
    - (a) Stebbins
    - (b) Lamarck
    - (c) Aristotle
    - (d) Vavilox

15. The evolution of a species is based upon sum total of adaptive changes preserved by
    - (a) Natural selection
    - (b) Isolation
    - (c) Speciation
    - (d) Human conservation

16. Genetic drift is on account of
    - (a) Variations
    - (b) Mutations
    - (c) increase in population
    - (d) decrease in population

17. According to Neo-Darwinism, natural selection operates through
    - (a) Fighting between organisms
    - (b) Variations
    - (c) Killing weaker organism
    - (d) Differential reproduction

18. Sympatric speciation develops reproductive isolation without.

    (*a*) Geographic barrier

    (*b*) barrier to mating

    (*c*) barrier to gene flaw

    (*d*) genetic change

19. Quick change in phenotypes in a small band of colonisers is called

    (*a*) Founder effect

    (*b*) Genetic bottle neck

    (*c*) Genetic drift

    (*d*) Gene flow

20. Genetic drift is found in

    (*a*) Small population with or without mutated genes

    (*b*) large population with random mating

    (*c*) plant population

    (*d*) animal population

21. Which is related to reproduce isolations

    (*a*) genetic isolation

    (*b*) temporal isolation

    (*c*) behavioural isolation

    (*d*) all of these

Answer Keys

1. (*d*)	2. (*d*)	3. (*c*)	4. (*d*)	5. (*b*)	6. (*d*)	7. (*d*)	8. (*c*)	9. (*c*)	10. (*c*)
11. (*b*)	12. (*d*)	13. (*c*)	14. (*b*)	15. (*b*)	16. (*d*)	17. (*d*)	18. (*a*)	19. (*a*)	20. (*a*)
21. (*d*)									

Solutions

1. First living beings were formed in the environment of the sea having abundant organic molecules. They absorbed the Organic materials for the sake of nutrition and hence, were chemoheterotrophs.

2. UV rays and lightening were the only source of energy in the early time.

3. Miller-Urey experiment was a chemical experiment that simulated the conditions thought at the time to be present on the early earth, and tested the chemical origin of life under those condition.

4. Coacervates were formed through polymerisation and aggregation that leads to be formation of things into cluster.

5. The experiment showed that simple organic compounds of building blocks of proteins and other macromolecules can be formed from gases with the addition of energy.

6. In the primitive atmosphere of the earth nitrogen followed by carbon dioxide and hydrogen with almost no oxygen at all was considered.

7. Louis Pasteur used the Bottle en col de cygne (gooseneck bottle). He used a special flask whose neck was shaped like an S or the neck of swan, hence the name "Swan Neck flask".

8. Alexander Oparin was a Soviet biochemist who performed an experiment and produced coacervates.

9. The theory was put forwaded by van Helmont who held that living organism could arise from nonliving matter and that such process were commonplace and regular.

10. The theory of abiogenesis assumed that life was present in the form of resistant spores and applared on earth from other planet. Since the condition of earth was supporting the life, these spores grew and evolved into different organisms.

11. Allopatric refers to animal or plants, especially of related species or populations occuring in separate non-overlapping geographical areas.

12. The theory states that evolution is a jerky process where new varieties and species are formed by mutations (discontinuous variations) that function as raw material of evolution.

13. Mutation refers to the discontinuous genetic variation i.e a distinct form resulting from genetic mutation.

14. Lamarckism is the hypothesis that an organism can pass on characteristics that it has acquired through use or disuse during its lifetime to its offspring

15. Environmental change and sum total of adaptive changes preserved by Isolation play an Important role in evolution.

16. Genetic drift is common of after population bottlenecks, which are events that drastically decrease the size of population. In these cases, genetic drift can result in the loss of rare alleles and decrease the gene pool.

17. Natural selection of organisms adopted to a given environment will be most likely to survive to reproductive age and have offspring of their own. This process is popularly known as differential reproduction.

18. Sympatric speciation is the evolution of a new species from a surviving ancestral special while both continue to inhabit without any geographical barrier

19. The founder effect occurs when a small group migrants that is not genetically representative of the population from which they come to establish in a new area. ie.e Quick change in phenotype is a small bond of colonisers.

20. Variation in the relative frequency of different genotypes in a small population, owing to the chance disappearance of particular genes as individuals die or do not reproduce is called genetic drift.

21. Genetic isolation temporal isolation, behavioural isolation, all are related to reproductive isolation. The mechanisms of a reproductive isolation are a collection of evolutionary mechanisms, behaviours and physiological processes critical for specification.

CHAPTER 8

Human Health and Diseases

Health, Common Diseases in Human and Immunity

Health and Disease

- **Introduction:**
  - Health is a state of complete physical, mental, social and well-being. Human health can be affected by lifestyle, genetic disorders and infections. Good health is maintained by regular exercise, balanced diet and personal hygiene.
  - When functioning of one or more organs or systems of the body is affected, that state is called disease. Diseases are grouped as infectious and non-infectious.
  - The diseases caused by gene mutation, chromosomal aberrations or environmental factors are congenital as they are present in the body from birth.
  - The diseases which are developed after birth are acquired diseases which can further be of two types: Communicable and non-communicable diseases.
  - The diseases which are infectious and caused by bacteria, fungi, protozoa, etc. are communicable while the diseases which do not spread and remain confined to people like deficiency diseases, allergies, cancer and degenerative diseases are non-communicable diseases.

Common Diseases in Humans

Infectious diseases can be divided into five types: Bacterial, Viral, Protozoan, Fungal and Helminthic.

- **Bacterial Diseases:**
- **Typhoid:**

  It is caused by bacterium *Salmonella typhi* and the symptoms include stomach pain, high fever, weakness, headache etc.

- **Pneumonia:**

  It is caused by bacterium *Streptococcus pneumoniae* and *Haemophilus influenzae* and the symptoms include fever, cough, chills, headache, etc.

- **Dysentery:**

  It is caused by bacterium *Shigella bacillus* and the symptoms include abdominal cramps, diarrhea, stomach-ache, etc.

- **Viral Disease:**
- **Common cold:** It occurs due to rhino viruses. It is characterized by sore throat, cough, headache, nasal congestion, etc. It can be caused by transmission through contaminated objects.

- **Protozoan Diseases:**
- **Malaria:** Plasmodium is a protozoan which causes malaria. Plasmodium has four different species: *P. Vivax, P. ovale, P. malariae, P. falciparum*. The malignant, malaria caused by *P. falciparum* is the most serious one and can be fatal. Symptoms of malaria include, high fever, sweating, headache,, nausea, fatigue, etc.

- **Fungal Disease:**
- **Ringworm:** It is a type of fungal disease which is caused by fungi *Epidermophyton, Microsporum*, and *Trichophyton*. It occurs from use of comb, clothes, etc. of infected person or from soil. It grows in region like skin folds, in between toes by heat and moisture. Appearance of scaly, dry lesions on skin, scalp and nails, intense itching are some of its symptoms.

- **Helminthic Diseases:**
- **Ascariasis:** Intestinal endoparasite called *Ascaris* or common round worm is the main cause of Ascariasis. The eggs of parasite are excreted along with the faeces of infected person contaminate soil, water, plants, etc. which reaches to human beings and cause infection. Fever, internal bleeding, anemia are some of its symptoms.

- **Filariasis/Elephantiasis:** It is caused by filarial worms (*Wuchereria malayi, Wuchereria bancrofti*). The organs in which worm lives gets severely inflammated. Genital organs and limbs are deformed which are affected by it.

- **Prevention and Control of Diseases:**
- ➢ Maintaining personal hygiene by keeping the body clean, consuming clean drinking water, food, etc.
- ➢ Maintaining public hygiene by disposing of wastes and excreta properly, cleaning and disinfecting water reservoirs ad keeping a check on breeding places of vectors.

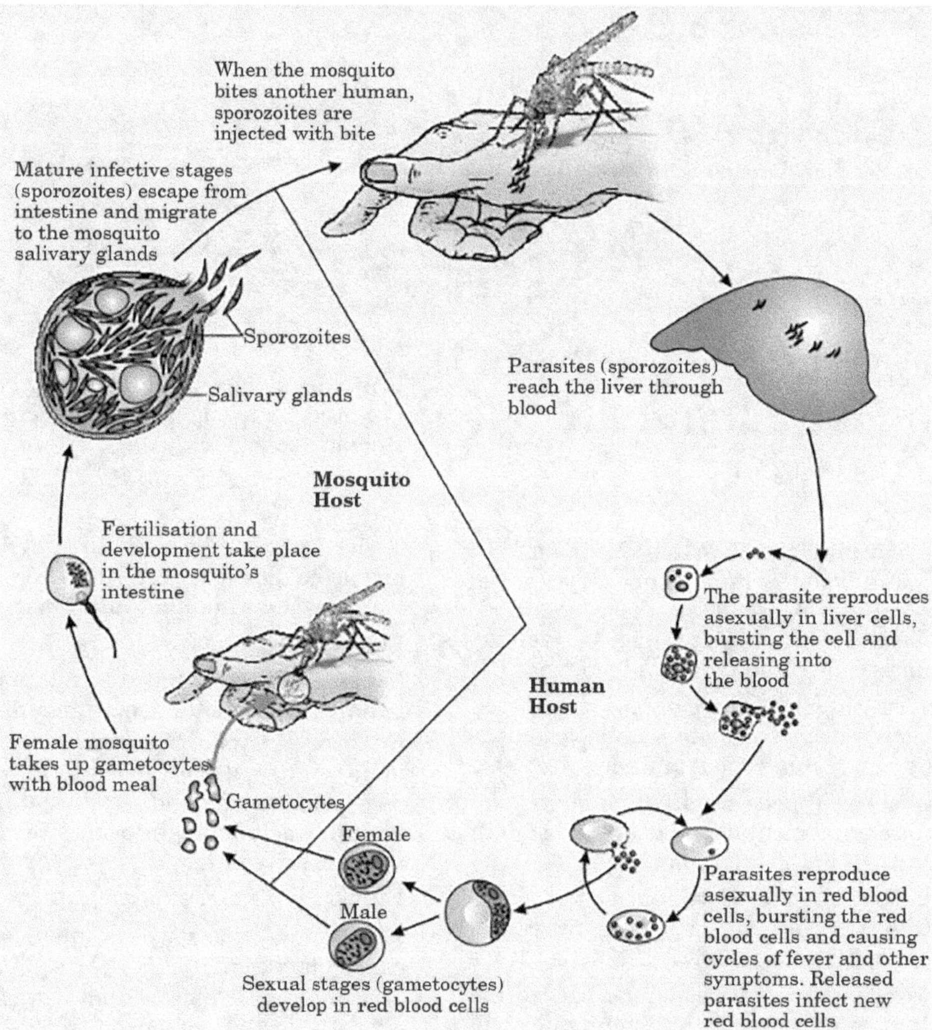

Fig.: Stages in Lifecycle of *Plasmodium*

Immunity

It is the immune system which can prevent us from these diseases. Entry of pathogens can be blocked by various defenses present in our body. There are some antimicrobial substances present in saliva, tears, mucous membranes, skin helps to protect us from the pathogens which might enter into our body. Antibodies and specified lymphocytes are produced to work against specific antigens. Immunity is basically of two types: **Innate** and **Acquired**

- **Innate immunity:**
- ➢ It is present in an individual since birth and remains throughout life and it is a non-specific defense system. The barriers could be of four types:

- Physiological barrier: Microbial growth in the body is prevented by physiological barrier like tears from eyes, acid in stomach, saliva in mouth, etc.
- Cytokine barrier: Virus infected cells which secrete protein called interferon protect non infected cells from further viral infection.
- Physical barrier: They prevent microorganisms to enter different parts of the body like gastrointestinal tracts, skin, etc.
- Cellular barrier: These destroy microbes. Example: Some natural killer cells in the blood, polymorpho-nuclear leukocytes, etc.

- **Acquired immunity:**
- ➢ It is acquired in the body of an individual after birth and can be short lived.

- ➤ If same pathogen is exposed several times then immune response would be quick as our immune system have a good memory.
- ➤ These responses are produced by B-lymphocytes (produce antibodies) and T-lymphocytes (help B-cells to produce antibodies).
- ➤ Structure of antibody: Antibody is represented as H2L2 as each antibody molecule has 4 peptide chains out of which two are small, called light chains and 2 are longer called heavy chains.
- ➤ There are two types of acquired immunity response – humoral immune response and cell- mediated immunity.

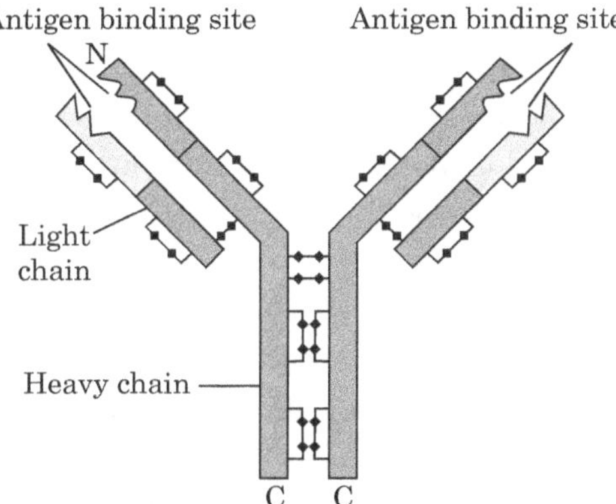

Fig.: Structure of an Antibody Molecule

- • **Active and Passive immunity:**
- ➤ Antibodies are produced in the host body as it is exposed to antigens present in the form of living or dead microbes. This type of immunity is called active immunity.
- ➤ In some cases, antibodies are prepared and just provided to the body to protect against foreign agents. This type of immunity is called passive immunity.
- • **Immunization:**
- ➤ Active Immunization: When a vaccine is introduced in body, the antibodies which are produced against the antigens neutralize the pathogenic agents during infection.
- ➤ Passive Immunization: It is pre-formed antibodies or antitoxin, introduced in body as injections for quick immune response.
- • **Allergy:**
- ➤ An amplified response to some antigens called allergens present in the environment is called allergy. Some of the allergens are mites in animal dander, dust, pollens, etc.
- ➤ Histamine and serotonin are some of the chemicals which are released from mast cells due to which causes allergy.

- ➤ Running nose, sneezing, difficulty in breathing are some of the symptoms of allergy.
- ➤ Anti-histamine, steroids and adrenaline are used to quickly reduce the symptoms of allergy.
- • **Auto Immunity:**
- ➤ Higher vertebrates can differentiate foreign organisms and foreign molecules.
- ➤ Body attacks self cells due to genetic and some other unknown reasons which is called auto-immune disease causing damage to the body.
- ➤ One of the example of auto-immune disease is Rheumatoid arthritis.
- • **Immune System in Human Body:**
- ➤ Immune system plays a vital role in identifying foreign antigens, remembering them and responding them. It is crucial in allergic reactions, organ transplantation and auto immune diseases. Immune system in human body comprises of lymphoid organ, tissues, cells and soluble molecules like antibodies.
- ➤ Lymphoid Organs: The organs where lymphocytes originate, mature and proliferate. They are of two types- primary lymphoid organs and secondary lymphoid organs.
- ➤ Bone marrow and thymus come under primary lymphoid organs, whereas spleen, tonsils, lymph nodes and MALT are examples of secondary lymphoid organs.
- • **AIDS:**

Fig.: Replication of Retrovirus

- A sexually transmitted disease called AIDS (Acquired Immune Deficiency Syndrome) kills number of people worldwide.

- A retrovirus which has RNA genome, Human Immunodeficiency Virus (HIV) is the causative agent for AIDS.

- Its infection can be spread by various ways like infected blood, sexual intercourse, contaminated needles, etc.

- There are various symptoms of AIDS like mononucleosis-like symptoms (high fever, chills, itchy rash, swollen lymph glands, etc.), weakness and weight loss.

- AIDS can be treated by antiretroviral drugs and it is only partially effective. It can prolong the life of the patient but cannot prevent death.

- AIDS is diagnosed by ELIZA test (Enzyme-linked immuno-sorbent assay)

- Prevention involves- controlling drug abuse, advocating safe sex, educating people about AIDS, etc.

- **Cancer:**

- It is the proliferation or uncontrolled growth of cells. These cells divide uncontrollably and are not affected by growth factors or property of growth inhibition.

- A large mass of cells is formed by repeated division called tumors. The cancer cells move from one part to other part of the body by body fluids. This is know as metastasis.

- There are two types of tumors- benign tumor which is confined to its place of origin and is less harmful and other is malignant tumor which keeps spreading to nearby tissues and is fatal.

- Agents which cause transformation of normal cells into cancerous cells are called carcinogens. They can be physical agents, chemical or biological.

- Cancer can be detected by various methods like:
  - Computed Tomography where a 3-D image is generated using X-rays.
  - It can be detected by histopathological studies and biopsy of the tissue.
  - Non-ionizing radiation and strong magnetic field is used for resonance imaging. It detects physiological and pathological changes in living tissue.
  - Different tests can be conducted like bone marrow and blood test for increased cell counts.
  - Cancer in internal organs can be detected using radiography by X-rays.

- Cancer can be treated by various methods:
  - Chemotherapy is done to kill cancer cells but the drugs used cause some side effects as well.
  - Surgery can be done for Tumors to avoid further spread of cells.
  - Immune system can be activated by some immunotherapy response modifiers.

Adolescence and Drug/ Alcohol Abuse

Drugs and Alcohol

Use of drugs and alcohol cause harmful effects on the body. Some commonly abused drugs are opioids, coca alkaloids and cannabinoids.

- **Opioids:**

- These drugs bind to the opioid receptors present in the central nervous system.

- Heroin which is chemically called diacetylmorphine is obtained from acetylation of morphine. It is a depressant which slows down body functions.

- **Cannabinoids:**

- These interact with receptors present in the brain called cannabinoid receptors.

- These are taken by oral ingestion or inhalation which affects cardiovascular system of the body.

- Natural cannabinoids are obtained from plant *Cannabis sativa*.

- **Cocaine:**

- It is obtained from the plant *Erythroxylum coca*. It has a stimulating action on the central nervous system.

- It interferes with transportation of neurotransmitter dopamine.

- **Alcohol:**

- Alcoholic drink is further divided into beverages and spirits. Wine, beer, etc. which have alcohol content between 5-15% come under beverages and whisky, brandy, etc. which have alcohol content more than 50% are types of spirits.

- Alcohol has various effects on human body. It hampers speech, thinking ability, movement, blurred vision, loss of body balance, vomiting, nausea etc. It causes cirrhosis and fatty liver.

Adolescence and Drug/Alcohol Abuse

- **Adolescence:**
- ➢ It is a phase is which child attains maturity for effective participation in society.
- ➢ This phase links childhood and adulthood, which makes it crucial and vulnerable stage of life.
- **Causes of Drug or Alcohol Use in Adolescence Period:**
- ➢ Curiosity, excitement, need for adventure are main causes of beginning drug or alcohol use by adolescents.

Addiction and Dependence

- **Addiction:**

  It is a psychological attachment to effects such as euphoria and temporary feeling of well being associated with drugs and alcohol.

- **Dependence:**

  The body's tendency to show a characteristic and unpleasant withdrawal syndrome because of regular dose of drugs or alcohol is dependence. It may lead to depression.

Effects of Drugs and Alcohol Abuse

- Showing reckless behavior, vandalism and violence are some adverse effects of drugs and alcohol abuse
- The chronic use of drugs and alcohol damages nervous system and liver this is termed as cirrhosis.
- Depression, fatigue, rebellious and aggressive behavior, withdrawal and isolation are some of the effects of alcohol and drugs.

Prevention and Control

- Measures like education and counseling, seeking help from parents and peers, avoid undue peer pressure, etc can be taken for prevention and control of drugs and alcohol abuse.

EXERCISE

1. What is called for the chemical emit with vinyl floors?
   - (*a*) Pathogens
   - (*b*) Vinyloxidize
   - (*c*) Phthalates
   - (*d*) Chorines

2. What is the other name of infectious diseases?
   - (*a*) Non-Communicable Diseases
   - (*b*) Communicable Diseases
   - (*c*) Non-transmissible diseases
   - (*d*) Heredity diseases

3. What is called the term which refers to an unhealthy intake of dietary nutrients?
   - (*a*) Healthy food
   - (*b*) Foul food
   - (*c*) Malnutrition
   - (*d*) Nutritious food

4. Which one of the following is a result of high exposure of radiation?
   - (*a*) Loss of white blood cells
   - (*b*) Hair Loss
   - (*c*) Tooth decay
   - (*d*) Ley fracture

5. The current rates of disease are increasing at alarming speeds and most are closely linked with known __________.
   - (*a*) Carcinogens
   - (*b*) Invigorating
   - (*c*) Organic farming
   - (*d*) Balanced diet

6. Which one of the following is an effect due to environmental pollution for human health?
   - (*a*) Increase in the male fertility
   - (*b*) Decrease in the carcinogen cells
   - (*c*) Decrease in the mental stress
   - (*d*) Decrease in the male fertility

7. Which one of the following can cause breast cancer in women?
   - (*a*) Breast feeding
   - (*b*) Being physically fit
   - (*c*) Using antiperspirant
   - (*d*) Eating healthy food

8. Degenerative diseases are those which develop due to
   - (*a*) Malfunction of hormones
   - (*b*) Degeneration of tissues
   - (*c*) Malfunction of certain body organs
   - (*d*) Degeneration of the infected organs.

9. 'Pathogens' are
   - (*a*) Substances produced against any disease causative
   - (*b*) Chemical substances produced by the host cells to kill the parasite animal
   - (*c*) Disease spreading factors
   - (*d*) Cells which kill the parasites

10. Sickle cell aneamia is more common in South Africa. This is due to
    (a) Change in beta-Chain of haemoglobin
    (b) More population of house flies
    (c) Change in alpha-chain of haemoglobin
    (d) Change in gamma-chain of haemoglobin

11. Black lung disease in common among
    (a) Coal miners
    (b) Refinery workers
    (c) Farmers
    (d) Petro chemical industry workers

12. X-rays are used in
    (a) ECG   (b) EEG
    (c) CT-Scan   (d) Endoscopy

13. Infantile amaurotic idiocy (Tay-sachs disease) is
    (a) They result of severe protein deficiency in diet and damages the muscle development in growing children.
    (b) An inherited disorder in which the spinal cord and brain are severely damaged within a few months of birth leading to paralysis and mental retardation, and finally the infant's death in 3 or 4 years.
    (c) A genetic abnormality which appear at the age of 25-30 years and damages the bones.
    (d) A chromosomal disorder in young children

14. Kwashiorkor disease develops due to
    (a) Malnutrition   (b) Over-eating
    (c) Catalysis   (d) Mutation

15. Epidemiology deals with the study of
    (a) Mode of transmission of diseases
    (b) Disease causing organism
    (c) Development of resistance against diseases
    (d) Skin ailments.

16. To have legal penalties removed.
    (a) Criminalyzed
    (b) Legalised
    (c) Codified
    (d) Decriminalized

17. _________ lead young people from less-harmful drugs to more-harmful drugs.
    (a) Gated drugs
    (b) Gateway drugs
    (c) Pathway drugs
    (d) Stepladder drugs

18. _________ is the most common mind-altering substance used during adolescence
    (a) Math   (b) Mushrooms
    (c) Alcohol   (d) Marijuana

19. _________ include (s) products that can be found in ordinary household chemicals.
    (a) Bleach   (b) Aspirin
    (c) Glucosamine   (d) Inhalants

20. Often, prescription drugs are used in conjunction with other substances, especially _________
    (a) alcohol   (b) inhalants
    (c) tobacco   (d) marijuana

21. Youth drug use is typically a_________ activity.
    (a) Solitary   (b) Private
    (c) Isolated   (d) Group

22. _________ brings a person's blood alcohol concentration to 0.08 gram percent or above.
    (a) Bungle drinking   (b) Binge drinking
    (c) Bounce drinking   (d) Bilge drinking

23. Neighborhoods with a high degree of _______ can protect their young people from crime, delinquency, and drag abuse.
    (a) Collective efficacy
    (b) Social disorganization
    (c) Strain
    (d) electronic monitoring

24. _______ is strongly linked to aggression.
    (a) Codeine   (b) Tobacco
    (c) Marijuana   (d) Alcohol

25. _________ suggests that the decision to use etc drugs or alcohol is based on the calculated casts and benefits of the actively.
    (a) Strain   (b) Rational choice
    (c) Life-Course   (d) Critical

Answer Keys

1. (c)   2. (b)   3. (c)   4. (a)   5. (a)   6. (d)   7. (c)   8. (c)   9. (c)   10. (a)

11. (a) 12. (c) 13. (b) 14. (a) 15. (a) 16. (d) 17. (b) 18. (c) 19. (d) 20. (a)

21. (d) 22. (b) 23. (a) 24. (d) 25. (a)

Solutions

1. Due to the addition of contaminates to the environment, it is contaminates to the environment, it is discovered that children who lives in homes with vinyl floors which can emit hazardous chemicals called phthalates. It develops signs of autism in kids.

2. Infectious diseases also known as transmissible diseases or communicable diseases comprise clinically illness resulting from the injection, presence and growth of pathogenic biological agents.

3. The term malnutrition refers to an unhealthful intake of dietary nutrients. Malnutrients may arise with inadequate or overabundant food intake, an imbalance of dietary nutrients or utilize the food we get.

4. High doses of radiation can be harmful or even it cause fatal to humans and it also damages environment. Doses above 100 rems usually cause the first sings of radiation. Loss of white blood cells happens due to more exposure of radiation.

5. The current rates of disease are increasing at alarming speeds and they are linked with carcinogens. Carcinogens have become abundant in our environment in the last several decades. It consists of particides, artificial hormone etc.

6. Male infertility has been linked to pesticides, air pollution, exposure to lead, household flame-retardant, surfactants and water pollution. Continuous exposure for such environmental pollution will lower the sperm amounts in males.

7. (c) Antiperspirants are applied near the breast and contain potentially harmful ingredients. Breast cancer can be caused by using antiperspirant a decrease in the occurrence and duration of breastfeeding and synthetic hormones found in food production.

8. Degenerative diseases are caused due to malfunctioning of our body organs these organs are pancreas, heart, kidney, eye lens and bone joints.

9. Any disease producing agent or micro-organism is termed pathogen.

10. Sickle cell aneamia is caused by a single gene mutation in the sixth place of β-chain of haemoglobin where glutamic acid is replaced by voline.

11. Due to deposition of carbon particles

12. CT scan is a radiographic technique where distinct images of internal structure are obtained by employing beams of X-rays

13. Tay-sachs disease is the most common GM_2 gangliosidosis occuring almost exclusively among north-east European Jews and specifically characterized by infantile onset (3-6 months) doll like facies, cherry red macular spot (90+ percent of the infants) early blindness, hyperacusis, macrocepholy, siezures and hypotonia; the children die between 2 and 5 years of age. It is caused by the deficiency of hexosaminidase A enzyme in tissue.

14. Kwashiorkar is a nutritional deficiency disease due to low protein diet.

15. Epidemiology is the study of the relationship of various factors determining the frequency and distribution of diseases in the human community.

16. Decriminalization is the lessening of criminal penalties in relation to certain act, perhaps radioactivity though perhaps regulated permits or fines night still apply.

17. Gateway drug used in early adolescence were significantly associated with marijuana use, illegal drugs and cocaine in older adolescence, but over the time these relationship were not consistent in adulthood.

18. Alcohol is the most commonly abused mind altering substance for the teenaged demographic. Alcohol is one of the few that's legal and at least for most teens, easily accessible.

19. Inhalant abuse includes the misuse of household Solvents, gases and anesthetics. Household inhalants can be anything from cleaning products to gasoline.

20. Alcohol is commonly used and abused with over-the-counter medications, prescription medications, and illicit drugs.

21. Drug addiction can start with experimental use of a recreational drug in social situation or group gathering.

22. Blood alcohol concentration is usually expressed as a percentage of ethanol in the blood in units of mass of alcohol per volume of blood or mass of alcohol per mass of blood, depending on the country.

23. Collective avoiding of drug and alcohol can protect our young ones from addiction of drug and alcohol.

24. Aggression and alcohol are strongly, related, most people who consume alcohol are found to be aggressive.

25. Strains shows the personal choice of the individuals on the consumption of alcohol and drug.

CHAPTER 9

Strategies for Enhancement in Food Production

Animal husbandry

It is the agricultural practice of breeding and raising livestock like buffaloes, cows, pigs, goats, etc.

Management of farms and farm animals

- **Dairy farm management:**
- It deals with the processes and systems that increase yield and improve quality of milk.
- For better yield from cattle:
- The cattle needs to be well fed, well housed get adequate water and remain disease free
- Special emphasis should be given to quality and quantity of fodder.
- Cleanliness and hygiene of cattle should be the main priority while milking and then while storing and transporting the milk.
- **Poultry farm management:**
- Poultry is the class of domesticated fowl used for food or for their eggs.
- Aspects of poultry farm management:
- The breed that is selected should be disease free and suitable for breeding and it also includes proper feed and water for domesticated birds, hygienic and health care of birds, proper and safe farm conditions.

Animal Breeding

It aims at increasing the yield of animals and improving the desirable qualities of the produce.

- **Inbreeding:**
- When mating is between animals of the same breed for 4 to 6 generations is called as inbreeding.
- Superior males and females of breed are mated in pairs to get superior progeny.
- Superior female is the cow or buffalo that produces more milk and superior male is the bull that helps in producing superior progenies.
- Inbreeding helps in increasing homozygosity to evolve a pure line animal. It also plays a role in accumulating superior genes and discarding less desirable genes.
- However, it also results in inbreeding depression, where the progeny may reduce productivity and fertility.
- **Outbreeding:**
- When breeding is between different breeds of animals or breeding of unrelated animals or different species altogether.
- Types of outbreeding:
- Out-crossing: Mating of animals within the same breed, but having no common ancestors on either side of their pedigree up to 4-6 generations. It helps in overcoming inbreeding depression.
- Cross-breeding: In this, superior males of one breed is crossed with superior females of another breed.
- Interspecific hybridization: In this method the male and female animals of two different species are crossed. The progeny attains desirable characters from both the parents.
- Controlled Breeding Experiments: It is carried out using artificial insemination. In this method the semen is collected from the male that is chosen as a parent and injected into the reproductive tract of the selected female by the breeder.

Bee keeping:

- It is also called apiculture. It deals with the maintenance of hives of honeybees for the production of honey and bee wax.
- Honey and bee wax both have industrial purpose. Honey is used in various medicines and for consumption as it is high in nutritional value. Bee wax is used in preparing cosmetics, polishes, etc.
- Bees also help in pollination of various flowering plants and crops.

Fisheries:

- This industry deals with the catching, processing or selling of fish, shellfish or other aquatic animals.
- In coastal area it is major source of employment and income, as it is the only source of livelihood for many.

Plant Breeding

It is the purposeful manipulation of plant species in order to create desired plant types that are better suited for cultivation, give better yields and are disease resistant.

- **Steps of Plant Breeding:**

  Breeding a new genetic variety of crop involves following steps:

- ➤ Collection of variability
- ➤ Evaluation and selection of parents
- ➤ Cross hybridization among the selected parents
- ➤ Selection and testing of superior recombinants
- ➤ Testing, release and commercialization of new cultivars
- **Wheat and Rice:**
- ➤ Due to development of semi-dwarf varieties of wheat and rice, their production increased enormously during 1960 to 2000.
- ➤ This variety of wheat was developed by Nobel Laureate Norman E. Borlaug
- **Sugarcane:**
- ➤ *Saccharum barberi* that grew in north India was crossed with *Saccharum officinarum* of south India as it had higher sugar content and thicker stem.
- ➤ Hybrid had desirable traits of both species; it had high sugar content with thick stems and had ability to grow in north India.
- **Millets:**
- ➤ Breeding hybrid varieties of maize, jowar and bajra has helped in developing high yielding varieties which are resistant to water stress.

Plant Breeding for Disease Resistance

Food production can be enhanced if the hybrid of plant is bred and developed in such a way that it is resistant to diseases. This will reduce the dependence on fungicides and bactericides.

- **Methods of breeding for disease resistance:**
- ➤ Breeding can be carried out by – conventional breeding techniques or by mutation breeding.
- ➤ A conventional breeding technique involves hybridization and selection. This method has restriction that limited number of disease resistance genes is available.
- ➤ Mutation breeding is the process of artificially inducing mutations through use of chemicals or radiations and selecting and using the plants that have the desirable character as a source in breeding.

Crop	Variety	Resistance to diseases
Wheat	*Himgiri*	Leaf and stripe rust, hill bunt
Brassica	*Pusa swarnim (Karan rai)*	White rust
Cauli-flower	*Pusa Shubhra, Pusa Snowball K-1*	Black rot and Curl blight black rot
Cowpea	*Pusa Komal*	Bacterial blight
Chilli	*Pusa Sadabahar*	Chilly mosaic virus, Tobacco mosaic virus and Leaf curl

- **Plant Breeding for Developing Resistance to Insect Pests:**
- ➤ Insect and pest infestation destroy crops on a very large scale. So various morphological, biochemical or physiological characteristics can help plant to become insect resistant.
- ➤ For example, hairy leaves in several plants, solid stems, etc. are some of the characteristics to keep the plant insect resistant.

Crop	Variety	Insect Pests
Brassica (rapeseed mustard)	*Pusa Gaurav*	Aphids
Flat bean	*Pusa Sem 2, Pusa Sem 3*	Jassids, aphids and fruit borer
Okra (Bhindi)	*Pusa Sawani, Pusa A-4*	Shoot and Fruit borer

- **Plant Breeding for Improved Food Quality**
  - As large number of people can't afford enough vegetables, fruits, meat, etc. So, breeding crops that are better in quality and high in nutritional value is necessary.
  - Biofortification: It is the practice of breeding crops with higher levels of vitamins and minerals, or higher protein and healthier fats to improve public health.
  - The main objectives of improving nutritional quality involves improving:
  - Protein content and its quality.
  - Micronutrients and mineral content.
  - Vitamin content
  - Oil content and its quality.

Single Cell Protein

- SCP or Single Cell Protein is one of the alternate sources of proteins for animal and human nutrition.
- *Spirulina* is easy to cultivate as it can grow on materials like straw, molasses, etc. It is rich in all nutrients. It also reduces environmental pollution.

Tissue Culture

- It is the technique of regenerating a plant from any part of plant in sterile condition under special nutrient media.
- Totipotency is the capacity to generate a whole plant from any cell/explant.
- The nutritional medium should provide a carbon source, inorganic salts, vitamins, amino acids and growth regulators.
- The process of producing thousands of plants through tissue culture is called micropropagation.
- Somaclones: The plants produced by the micro-propagation will be genetically identical to the original plant from which they are grown.
- When the plant is infected its meristem can be removed and can be grown in vitro to obtain a virus-free plant.
- The process of fusing the isolated protoplasts from two different varieties of plants each of which is having desirable characters to get a hybrid protoplasts, which can be further grown to form a new plant is called somatic hybridization and the hybrid is called somatic hybrid.

EXERCISE

1. Super-Ovulation and embryo transplantation are meant for improving
   - (a) Human race
   - (b) Livestock
   - (c) Poultry
   - (d) Plants

2. Selective breeding. progeny testing and improvement are taking place in
   - (a) Cattle
   - (b) Buffalo
   - (c) Sheep
   - (d) Annual food crops

3. One week old embryo can be preserved at
   - (a) 196°C
   - (b) 200°C
   - (c) 270°C
   - (d) None of these

4. Mule is
   - (a) Fertile
   - (b) Sterile
   - (c) Fertile after age
   - (d) Sterile after some age

5. Random and controlled breeding are included in the _______.
   - (a) Scientific method of breeding
   - (b) Natural method of breeding
   - (c) Both a and b
   - (d) Cultural method of breeding

6. First artificial insemination was done in India at
   - (a) National Dairy Institute, Karnal (Haryana)
   - (b) Indian Veterinary Research Institute, Izatnagar (U.P)
   - (c) Punjab Agriculture University Ludhiana (Punjab)
   - (d) Allahabad Agricultural Institute, Allahabad (U.P)

7. Superovulation and embryo transplantation techniques are being used for improving.
   - (a) Quality of milk breads of cows
   - (b) Breeds of sheep
   - (c) Breeds of goats
   - (d) All of these

8. Technique of cryopreservation is used for
   - (a) Preservation of various tissues
   - (b) Preservation of semen of good quality bulls
   - (c) Preservation of very young foetuses
   - (d) All of the above.

9. Exotic breeds are
   - (a) Used for cross breeding
   - (b) Allowed to multiply and replace local breeds
   - (c) Cheaper
   - (d) Resistant to local pests and pathogens

10. Drought breeds produce.
    (*a*) Good milk producing cows
    (*b*) Good working bullocks
    (*c*) None of these
    (*d*) Both a and b

11. Which of the following has been recently used for increasing productivity of super milch cow
    (*a*) Artificial insemination by a predigreed bull only
    (*b*) Superovulation of a high production cow only
    (*c*) Embryo transplantation only
    (*d*) A combination of superovulation, artificial insemination and embryo transplantation into a 'carrier cow' (surrogate mother)

12. The branch of biology dealing with the process of improvement of human race by selective breeding is called __________.
    (*a*) Euthenics   (*b*) Eugenics
    (*c*) Euphonics   (*d*) obstetrics

13. Plant breeding is a technique of improving __________.
    (*a*) Agricultural crops (*b*) Fodder crops
    (*b*) Fruit varieties   (*d*) All the above

14. Modern plant breeding started in
    (*a*) 1850   (*b*) 1880
    (*c*) 1900   (*d*) 1930

15. Plant breeding has close relationship with
    (*a*) Genetics   (*b*) Cytology
    (*c*) Biometry   (*d*) Both a and b

16. Sonora-64 and Lerma rojo are varieties of
    (*a*) Wheat   (*b*) Rice
    (*c*) Pea   (*d*) Maize

17. First successful pollen culture was done by
    (*a*) Guha   (*b*) Swaminathan
    (*c*) B.P. Pal   (*d*) H.Y. Mohav Ram

18. Pioneer worker in plants tissue culture is
    (*a*) Guha and Maheshwari
    (*b*) Steward
    (*c*) Haberlandt
    (*d*) Swaminathan

19. IR-36 was developed through breeding
    (*a*) Sin rice Varieties and Oryza nivara
    (*b*) 13 rice Varieties and Oryza nivara
    (*c*) Oryza indica and Oryza nivara
    (*d*) Oryza indica and Oryza sativa

20. The basis of green revolution is
    (*a*) Extensive cultivation
    (*b*) Plant breeding
    (*c*) Sowing at right time
    (*d*) Cultivation in black oil

21. Crop cultivation was first started in
    (*a*) Nile river valley
    (*b*) Chinese river valley
    (*c*) Northern plains of India
    (*d*) All of the above

22. Dwarf wheats were developed by
    (*a*) Vavilov   (*b*) Borlaug
    (*c*) Swaminathan   (*d*) None of these

23. Which of the following is not used for crop improvement
    (*a*) Inbreeding
    (*b*) Introduction
    (*c*) Hybridization
    (*d*) Mutations

24. The indica varieties of rice is crossed with iaponic varieties as these are.
    (*a*) High yielding
    (*b*) Resistant to diseases
    (*c*) Cheaper
    (*d*) Short life cycled annual

Answer Keys

1. (*b*) 2. (*a*) 3. (*a*) 4. (*b*) 5. (*b*) 6. (*d*) 7. (*d*) 8. (*d*) 9. (*a*) 10. (*b*)
11. (*d*) 12. (*b*) 13. (*d*) 14. (*c*) 15. (*a*) 16. (*a*) 17. (*a*) 18. (*c*) 19. (*b*) 20. (*b*)
21. (*d*) 22. (*b*) 23. (*a*) 24. (*b*)

Solutions

1. Super-Ovulation and embryo transplantation are the new techniques for cattle and other livestock improvement.

2. Mature cattle (over 3 years of age) should be used for selective breeding.

3. In superovulation and embryo transplantation foetuses can be preserved for several days at very low temperature ($196°C$)

4. Mule is the hybrid between male ass (Jack) and female horse (mare). It has the stamina of as and size of horse but is sterile.

5. Natural breeding may be random or controlled.

6. First buffalo calf produced by artificial insemination was born at the Allahabad. Agriculture institute on August 21, 1943.

7. Superovulation and embryo transplantation can also be carried out in sheep, goats, and other live stock.

8. Cryopreservation preservation at - $196°C$ (liquid nitrogen) can maintain tissue culture, embryos, animal cells/tissues, spermatoza indefinitely. The Cryoperserved material is revived through special technique when required.

9. Exotic breeds are foreign breeds of animals which are introduced in a country and required special environment.

10. Drought breeds, which give good working bullocks.

11. Superovulation (more ova and hence more embryo) embryo transplantation and surrogate mothers also help improve breeds.

12. Eugenics is the branch of science which deals with improvement of human race genetically. This aspect of human betterment aims to improve the human germplasm by encouraging the inheritance of best characteristics so that defective characters may be eliminated.

13. Plant breeding may be defined as "the branch which deals with improvement in heredity of crops and production of new crop varieties, which are superior to earlier over in all respects".

14. With the rediscovery of mendel's paper in 1900 which was originally published is 1866.

15. Plant breeding has close relationship with genetics because genetic engineering in part of plant breeding and it is the latest method of crop improvement in which instead of involving whole chromosomal set(genome), manipulation of a segment of DNA (gene) is done.

16. Dwarf wheat varieties like sonora-64, Lerma rojo-64 and Norin-10, which were introduced in India and Increased wheat production.

17. Haploid production through pollen culture was first made in Datura innoxia by Guha and Maheshwari (1964)

18. Tissue culture technique is based on totipotent nature of plant cell and concept of totipotency was given by Haberlandt (1902)

19. 13 rice varieties from six countries and oryza nivara (wild rice from central India) to produce early maturing, high yielding and resistant variety lR-36.

20. The basis of green revolution is plant breeding because it has been achieved through introduction of high yielding varieties increased irrigation facilities, fertilizer application, weed past and pathogen control and better agriculture management.

21. The earliest human civilizations around the river Nile is Eqypt, the chinese river valleys and the northern Indian plains are linked with crop cultivation.

22. Norman Borlaug (1963) of mexico produced triple dwarf wheats popularly called mexican wheats.

23. Introduction, hybridisation and mutations are methods of plant breeding.

24. Japonica is disease resistant because it is a wild variety.

CHAPTER 10

Microbes in Human Welfare

Microbes in Household Products, Industrial Products and in Sewage Treatment

- ➢ Microbes are diverse in nature; they include protozoa, bacteria, fungi, viruses, viroids and prions.
- ➢ Not all microbes are harmful, many microbes are useful to human in various ways.

- **Microbes in Household Products:**

- ➢ *Lactobacillus* and other LAB (lactic acid bacteria) help in formation of curd by producing acids during their growth that coagulates and partially digests milk proteins. LAB also keeps a check on disease causing microbes in our stomach.

- ➢ Various food items require microbes for their preparation. Dough of idli and dosa are prepared by bacteria. The fermentation of the dough used in making bread is done by using baker's yeast (*Saccharomyces cerevisiae*). Microbes are used in cheese to provide characteristic texture, flavor and taste.

- **Microbes in Industrial Products:**

- ➢ Alcoholic beverages are prepared by the process of fermentation using same yeast *Saccharomyces cerevisiae* which is used for bread making. Different drinks are obtained depending on the raw material used and whether or not distillation is required.

- ➢ Antibiotics are produced by microbes which kill or retard the growth of disease- causing microbes.

- ➢ Microbes are used in commercial production of acetic acids, citric acids, enzymes like lipase, pectinases and streptokinase.

- **Microbes in Sewage Treatment:**

- ➢ First the sewage undergoes primary treatment which involves filtration and sedimentation. During sequential filtration, floating debris is removed. Then grit is removed by sedimentation.

- ➢ The effluent from the primary settling tank then undergoes secondary treatment, where it is passed through large aeration tanks where air is pumped and constantly agitated. This activity results in strong growth of essential aerobic microbes into flocs, which are masses of bacteria along with fungal filaments that form mesh like structures. As this floc consumes major part of organic matter, so the biochemical oxygen demand, BOD reduces significantly.

- ➢ The effluent is then transferred to a settling tank where the bacterial flocs are allowed to sediment, this sediment is called an activated sludge. A part of it is pumped back in tank to act as inoculum and rest is pumped into anaerobic sludge digesters. Here, other bacteria digest the sludge and produce a mixture of gases which form biogas.

Microbes in Production of Biogas, as Bio-control Agents and Bio-fertilizers

- **The role of Microbes in Production of Biogas:**

- ➢ Biogas constitutes of methane primarily along with other mixture of gases. It is used as a fuel and is produced by the actions of microbes. Bacteria commonly found in anaerobic sludge and rumen of cattle are methanogens, which produce large amount of methane along with carbon dioxide and hydrogen.

➤ Biogas plant consists of a concrete tank, a floating cover and an outlet. Slurry and bio-waste is put in concrete tank. Floating cover rises when gas is produced in the tank due to microbial activity and the outlet helps to supply biogas to nearby houses through a pipe.

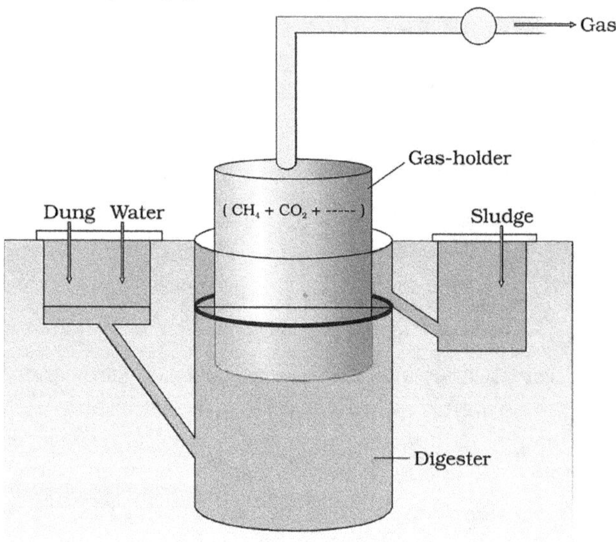

Fig.: A typical biogas plant

- **Microbes as Bio control Agents:**
➤ Plant diseases and pests can be controlled by the use of biological methods and this is referred as bio control. Organic farmers do not eradicate insects which are pests to their farms, instead they are kept at manageable level within a living and vibrant ecosystem.

➤ The use of bio-control measures will reduce our dependence on pesticides and other toxic chemicals. To control butterfly caterpillars the bacteria named Bt. or Bacillus thuringiensis is used.

- **The role of Microbes in Bio-fertilizers:**
➤ Bio fertilizers are nothing but the organisms that enhance the quality of nutrient in the soil. The microbes acting as bio-fertilizers are bacteria, fungi and cyanobacteria.

➤ *Rhizobium* found in nodules on the roots of leguminous plants fix atmospheric nitrogen into organic form for the plant to utilize as a nutrient.

➤ The symbiotic association between fungi and plants is known as Mycorrhiza. Phosphorus is absorbed from soil by fungal symbiont and passed on to plant as nutrient.

➤ Cyanobacteria are used in paddy fields as bio fertilizers.

EXERCISE

1. Which of the following microbe is used in the production of blue cheese
   - (a) Streptococcus thermophiles
   - (b) Lactobacillus bulgaricus
   - (c) Penicillium roqueforti
   - (d) Rhizopus stolonifer

2. Pickled cucumber is made from fermented self stock pickles.
   - (a) True
   - (b) False

3. Bacterial cell grown on hydrocarbon wastes from the petroleum industry are a sources of __________.
   - (a) Carbohydrates
   - (b) Proteins
   - (c) Vitamins
   - (d) Fats

4. How many tone of protein can be produced by algae grown in pond in a year?
   - (a) 1000
   - (b) 1
   - (c) 50
   - (d) 20

5. What is the range of protein content in yeast cells?
   - (a) 69%
   - (b) 12-15%
   - (c) 20-40%
   - (d) 40-50%

6. Which of the following micro organism have a high vitamin content?
   - (a) bacteria
   - (b) yeast
   - (c) algae
   - (d) protozoa

7. Which of the following micro organism produces dextran?
   - (a) Bacillus polymyxa
   - (b) Bacillus thuringiensis
   - (c) Leuconostoc mesenteroides
   - (d) Streptomyces olivaceus

8. Which of the following carbohydrates are mainly present in Whey?
   - (a) Glucose
   - (b) lactose
   - (c) fructose
   - (d) sucrose

9. Which of the following product is used for treatment of pernicious anemia?
   - (a) Insulin
   - (b) Streptokinase-streptodornase
   - (c) Cobalamin
   - (c) Sorbose

10. Insulin was isolated from which of the following organs of animals
    (*a*) Small intestine
    (*b*) tongue
    (*c*) pancreas
    (*d*) Stomach

11. Single cell protein (SCP) is the production of ?
    (*a*) Extracellular proteins
    (*b*) Fermentation of waste products
    (*c*) Intracellular proteins extraction
    (*d*) Metabolites

12. What do you mean by "Trophophase"?
    (*a*) Production of waste materials
    (*b*) Production of topical products
    (*c*) Production of primary metabolites
    (*d*) Production of secondary metabolites

13. What do you mean by "Idiophase"?
    (*a*) Production of waste materials
    (*b*) Production of topical products
    (*c*) Production of primary metabolites
    (*d*) Production of secondary metabolites

14. Which of the following does not have the property of production of secondary metabolites?
    (*a*) filamentous fungi
    (*b*) filamentous bacteria
    (*c*) Sporing bacteria
    (*d*) Enterobacteria

15. Which of the following is an upstream process?
    (*a*) Product recovery
    (*b*) Product purification
    (*c*) Media formulation
    (*d*) Cell lysis

16. Which of the following is a downstream process?
    (*a*) Product Recovery
    (*b*) Screening
    (*c*) Media formulation
    (*d*) Sterilization media

17. Which of the following is not a product of termination?
    (*a*) Oxygen
    (*b*) Carbon dioxide
    (*c*) Ethanol
    (*d*) Lactate

18. Alcoholic fermentation is carried by yeast known as __________.
    (*a*) Lactobacillus
    (*b*) Bacillus
    (*c*) Saccharomyces cerevisiae
    (*d*) Escherichia coli

19. Which of the following is not a prebiotic?
    (*a*) Fungi
    (*b*) Saccharomyces cerevisiae
    (*c*) Escherichia coli
    (*d*) Lactobacillus

20. Biofuels are products of fermentation.
    (*a*) True
    (*b*) False

Answer Keys

1. (*c*)	2. (*b*)	3. (*b*)	4. (*d*)	5. (*d*)	6. (*b*)	7. (*c*)	8. (*b*)	9. (*c*)	10. (*c*)
11. (*b*)	12. (*c*)	13. (*d*)	14. (*d*)	15. (*c*)	16. (*a*)	17. (*a*)	18. (*c*)	19. (*a*)	20. (*a*)

Solutions

1. For the production of blue cheese or Roquefort cheese, it is necessary to inoculate the curd with the micro Organism, penicillium, roqueforti which brings about the necessary changes.

2. Most commercial sweet, sour mixed. Pickles are made from fermented salt stock pickles. The other major type of pickled cucumber is the fermented dill pickle.

3. The micro organisms can be cultivated on industrial wastes or by- products as nutrients and yield a large cell crops that is rich in protein. Bacterial cell grown on hydrocarbon wastes from the petroleum industry are a sources of protein in france, Japan, Taiwan, and India.

4. Algae grown in ponds can produce 20 tons (dry weight) of protein per acre per year.

5. The protein content of microbial cells in very high. Yeast cells have a protein content in a 40 to 50 percent range.

6. Some micro organisms, particularly yeasts, have a high vitamin content. The growth medium for yeast cells consists of hydrocarbons supplemented with mineral salts.

7. Leuconostoc mesenteroides is the producer organism for dextran which acts as a stabilizes in food products and as a blood plasma substitute.

8. Whey represents a satisfactory medium for the growth of certain bacteria, since it contains lactose, nitrogenous substances including vitamins, and salts.

9. Cabalamin or vitamin B_{12} is used for treatment of pernicious anemia and also for food and feed supplements.

10. Commercial insulin for the therapy of diabetes was isolated from animal pancreatic tissue

11. Single-cell proteins develop when microbes ferment waste materials (including wood, straw, hydrocarbons, or human and animal excreta) Single-cell protein (SCP) refers to edible unicellular micro organisms. The biomass or protein extract from pure or mixed cultures of algae, yeasts, fungi or bacteria may be used as an ingredient or a substitute for protein - rich foods, and is suitable for human consumption or as animal feeds.

12. **Trophophase:** The phase in the active growth of a culture in which primary metabolites are formed.

13. **Idiophase:** The phase in the growth of a culture during which secondary metabolities are produced.

14. Not all micro organisms undergo secondary metabolism. It is common amongst the filamentous bacteria and fungi and the sporing bacteria but it is not found.

15. Upstream processing includes formulation of the fermentation medium, sterilisation of air fermentation medium and the fermenter, inoculum preparation and inoculation of the medium.

16. Downstream processing includes the recovery of the products in a pure state and the effluent treatment. Product recovery is carried out through a series of operations including cell separation by settling, centrifugation or filtration; product recovery by disruption of cells (if the product is produced intracellulary); extraction and purification of the product. finally, the effluents are treated by chemical, physical or biological method.

17. Fermentation is a metabolic process that consumes sugar in the absence of oxygen. The products are organic acids, gases or alcohol. It occurs in yeast and bacteria, and also in oxygen-starved muscle cells, as the case of lactic fermentation.

18. Saccharomyces Cerevisia is a species of yeast. It has instrumental to winemaking, baking, and brewing since ancient times. It is believed to have been originally isolated from the skin of grapes (one can seen the yeast as a component of the thin white film on the skins of some dark-colored fruits such as plums; it exists among the waxes of the cuticle).

19. Probiotics are live bacteria and yeasts that are good for your health, especially your digestive system (L. casei L. plantarum; L. lactis), Bifidobacterium species. (B. bifidum, B. brave, B. lactis), and others microbes like Bacillus cereus, Non pathogenic escherichia coli, saccharomyces cerevisial, enterococcus faecalis, and streptococcus thermophiles

20. Study and development of cell factories for production of biofuels (bioethanol, biobutanol, biodies-cl) and biochemicals (3-hydroxypropionic acid and ethylene). A common challenge for these cell factories is the requirement of high yield and productivity to make the potential production cost effective and competitive with petroleum based production. An efficient cell factory requires many rounds of metabolic ergineering as well as carefully designed and optimized fermentation process sachhoromyces cerevisiae, is commonly used.

CHAPTER 11

Biotechnology: Principles and Processes

Principles of biotechnology and tools of recombination DNA Technology

Introduction

Biotechnology deals with large scale production of products and processes that are useful to humans that makes use of live organisms, cells or enzymes. Karl Ereky coined the term 'biotechnology' in 1919.

Biotechnology helps in:

- Correcting a defecting gene
- Microbe-interceded process (making curd, bread, wine, etc.)
- Preparation of a DNA vaccine
- Synthesis and using of a gene
- *In vitro* fertilisation (test tube baby program)

Principles of Biotechnology

- **Genetic engineering:**

   This type of engineering uses different techniques that alter the chemistry of genetic material (DNA and RNA) which introduce these into host organisms and thus change the phenotype of the host organism.

The techniques of genetic engineering involve creating recombinant DNA, using gene cloning and gene transfer. This allows us to isolate and introduce only one or a set of desirable genes without introduction of undesirable genes into the target organism.

A recombinant piece of DNA cannot multiply itself in the progeny cells of an organism as the alien piece of DNA has the inability to replicate. So, it inherits and multiplies along with the host DNA as it gets integrated into the recipient genome. This process of making multiple copies of template DNA can also be termed as **cloning**.

Steps of genetically modifying an organism

- Recognise the DNA with desirable genes.
- Introduce those recognised DNA into the host medium.
- Maintain the recognised DNA in the host medium and then transfer DNA to its progeny.

Tools of recombinant DNA Technology

- **Restriction enzyme**

➤ They are also known as restriction endonuclease which cleaves DNA into fragments at recognition sites. The sequence at which the DNA is cut is known as recognition sequence.

➤ The first restriction endo nuclease was Hind II, isolated by Wileox, Kelley and Smith in 1968 from, *Haemophilis influenza* bacterium.

➤ It always cut DNA molecules at a particular point by recognizing a specific sequence of six base pairs which is called as Recognition sequence.

➤ There are two kinds of restriction enzymes: exonucleases (removes nucleotides from the ends of DNA) and endonucleases (makes cuts at specific positions within DNA).

Action of Restriction enzyme

Fig.: Steps in formation of recombinant DNA by action of restriction endonuclease enzyme - EcoRI

- ➢ Diagrammatic representation of recombinant DNA technology is shown below.
- ➢ Separation and isolation of DNA fragments:
- - The DNA fragments are formed by the cutting of DNA by restriction endonucleases and are separated by a technique called as gel electrophoresis.
- - DNA fragments are negatively charged molecules which are separated by forcing them to move towards the anode under an electric field through a medium/matrix.
- - Agarose is the most commonly used matrix which is a natural polymer extracted from sea weeds.

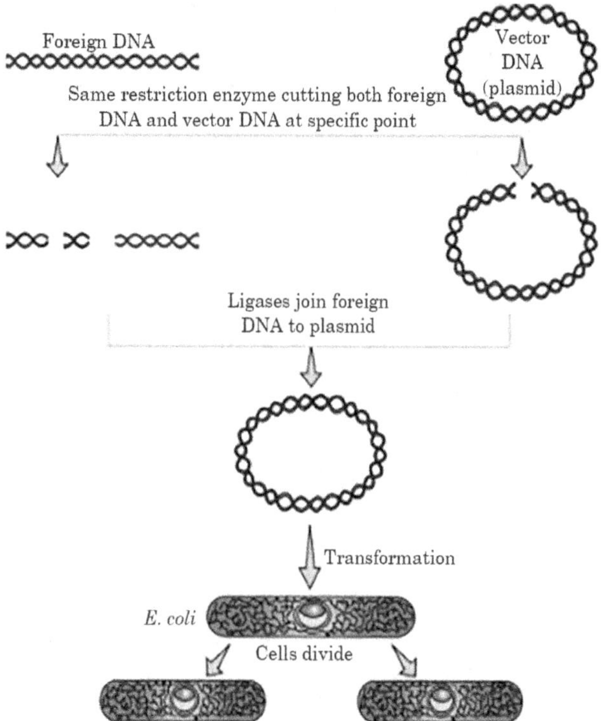

Fig.: Recombinant DNA Technology

- • **Cloning vectors:**
- ➢ DNA molecules which carry a foreign DNA segment and can replicate inside the host cells are called as cloning vectors. Example: Plasmids and bacteriophages.

The cloning of a DNA requires following features:

- ➢ Origin of replication (Ori): A DNA sequence from where replication begins is known as Origin of replication (Ori).
- ➢ Selectable marker: It helps in recognising and removing transformants and selectively allowing the growth of transformants. The procedure in which a DNA is introduced in a host is known as Transformation.
- ➢ Cloning sites: Vector needs to have recognition sites for linking alien DNA.

- ➢ Vectors for cloning genes in plants and animals: Genes of some pathogens can be changed into useful vectors for delivering genes to plants and animals. For plants, Agarobacterium can be used as vector and for animal Retrovirus Agarobacterium.
- • **Competent host:**
- ➢ To force bacteria to take up the plasmid, first the bacterial cell should be made component to take up DNA and for that they are treated with a specific concentration of a divalent cation, like calcium ions which improves the efficiency with which DNA enters the bacterium through pores in its cell wall.
- ➢ Alien DNA can be introduced into host cells in some other following ways:
- - Micro-injection: This is the process of directly injecting recombinant DNA into the nucleus of an animal cell.
- - Biolistics method: The process of bombardment of cells with high velocity micro-particles of gold or tungsten coated with DNA. It is a suitable method for the plants.
- - Disarmed pathogens vectors: Cells transfer the recombinant DNA into the host after getting infected by disarmed pathogens vectors.

Process of Recombinant DNA Technology

Introduction

Recombinant DNA technology involves many steps in a defined sequence which are –

Isolation of DNA, fragmentation of DNA by restriction endonucleases, isolation of a desired DNA fragment, ligation of the DNA fragment into a vector, transferring the recombinant DNA into the host, culturing the host cells in a medium at large scale and extraction of the desired product.

Isolation of the Genetic Material (DNA)

- • In order to get the DNA free from other macro-molecules, there is a need of treating bacterial cell/plant or animal tissue with enzyme.
- • Enzymes namely lysozyme is used to treat bacteria, cellulase to treat plant cells, chitinase to treat fungus.
- • The cell when broken, releases DNA along with other macro-molecules like proteins, lipids, RNA etc.
- • The RNA is removed on treatment with ribonuclease and proteins are removed by treatment with protease.
- • The purified DNA precipitates after chilled ethanol is added and can be collected as fine threads in the suspension. This is known as elution.

Cutting of DNA at specific locations

- At the optimal conditions, incubating purified DNA perform restriction enzyme digestions with the restriction enzyme.
- To check the progression of a restriction enzyme digestion, the technique adopted is agarose gel electrophoresis. As DNA is a negatively charged molecule, it moves towards the positive electrode.
- The source and the vector DNA are cut with specific restriction enzyme and then the cut out 'gene of interest' from the source DNA and the cut vector are mixed and ligase is added which forms recombinant DNA.

Amplification of Gene of interest using PCR

- Polymerase Chain Reaction (PCR) is a chemical reaction in which the multiple copies of the gene synthesizes in vitro with two set of primers and the enzyme DNA polymerase.
- The segment of DNA is amplified around 1 billion times if the process of replication is repeated several times.

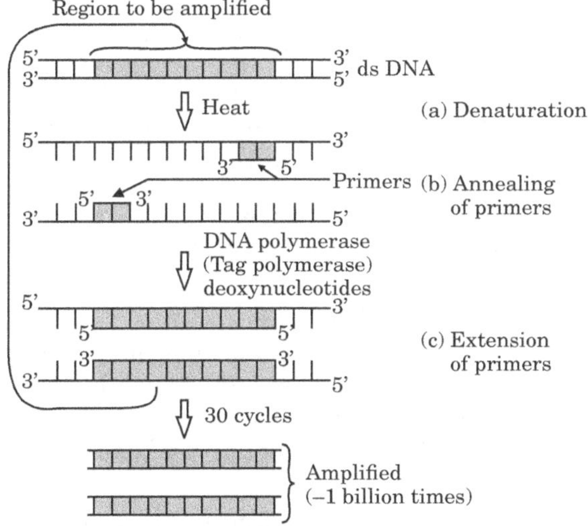

Insertion of Recombinant DNA into the host cell/organism

- There exist many methods to introduce the ligated DNA into recipient cells.
- The DNA present in the surrounding is taken by recipient cells.
- If a recombinant DNA bearing amplicillin resistant gene is transferred into E.coli cells, the host cell become amplicillin-resistant cells.
- But the untransformed recipient cell will die it the transformed cells are spread on agar plates containing ampicillin and only transformants will grow. The gene which is resistance to amplicillin in this case is called a selectable marker.

Obtaining the foreign gene product

- Recombinant protein is the protein encoded by Recombinant DNA which is expressed in a heterologous host.
- After the cloning of genes, the production of which can be done on a large scale, the fresh medium is obtained by separation technique and is added such that the cell maintain physiologically active phase and then produces a larger biomass leading to higher yields.
- Bioreactors:
- ➤ Bioreactor is a device used for biological conversion of raw materials into specific products like human cells, animal cells or microbial plants.
- ➤ Large volumes of cultures may be processed.
- ➤ The main components of a bioreactor are an oxygen delivery system, a foam control system and an agitator system.
- ➤ Desired conditions for the production of the product are provided like pH, vitamins, salts and temperature.
- ➤ Stirring type of bioreactors are mainly used which are usually cylindrical.
- ➤ A bioreactor is shown below:

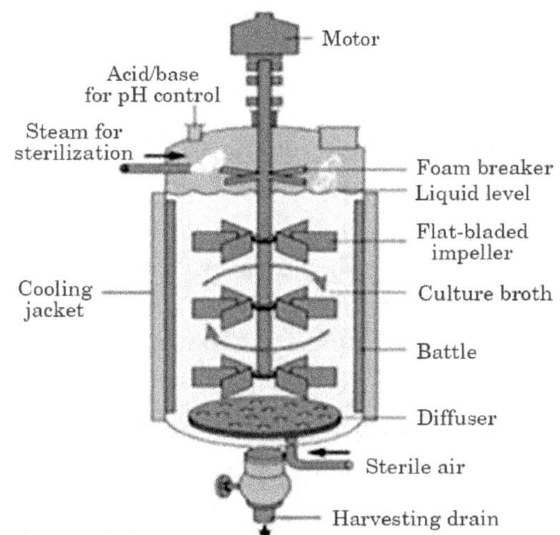

Fig.: Bioreactor

- In a recombinant protein, protein encoding gene is expressed in a heterologous host.

Downstream processing

Two main processes are referred as downstream processing which are separation and purification.

- Suitable preservations have to formulate the product.
- In case of drugs, formulation has to undergo thorough clinical trials and the process of quality control varies for every product.

EXERCISE

1. Which of the following involves remarkable capacity of short segment of DNA to move from one place to another?

   (*a*) DNA transposition   (*b*) DNA replication

   (*c*) Translation   (*d*) Transcription

2. Which of the following process occurs between DNA molecules of very similar sequences?

   (*a*) Homologous genetic recombination

   (*b*) Site specific recombination

   (*c*) Non-homologous recombination

   (*d*) Replicative recombination

3. Which of the following process occurs in regions where no large-scale sequence similarity is apparent?

   (*a*) Homologous genetic recombination

   (*b*) Site specific recombination

   (*c*) Non-homologous recombination

   (*d*) Replicative recombination

4. Which of the following process generates a new copy of the transposable element at a new location of DNA?

   (*a*) Homologous genetic recombination

   (*b*) Site specific recombination

   (*c*) Non-homologous recombination

   (*d*) Replicative recombination

5. What of the following occurs between particular short sequences present on otherwise dissimilar parental molecules?

   (*a*) Homologous genetic recombination

   (*b*) Site specific recombination

   (*c*) Non-homologues recombination

   (*d*) Replicative recombination

6. Which of the following promotes branch migration at higher rates than does Rec-A?

   (*a*) Rec-B   (*b*) Rec-C

   (*c*) Rec-D   (*d*) Ruv-A and RuV-B

7. Which of the following is called a resolvase?

   (*a*) Ruv-C   (*b*) Ruv-A

   (*c*) Ruv-B   (*d*) Rec-A

8. Which of the following does not code for an enzyme having both helicase and nuclease activity?

   (*a*) Rec-A   (*b*) Rec-B

   (*c*) Rec-C   (*d*) Rec-D

9. The sequences of the recombination sites recognized by site-specific recombinases are

   (*a*) Partially asymmetric

   (*b*) Partially symmetric

   (*c*) Symmetric

   (*d*) Palindromic

10. Which of the following contain only the sequences required for transposition and the genes for proteins that promote the process?

    (*a*) Insertion sequences

    (*b*) Complex transposons

    (*c*) Transposons

    (*d*) Chromosomes

11. The techniques of using live organisms or enzymes from organisms to produce products and processes useful to humans are called

    (*a*) Biopiracy   (*b*) Biotechnology

    (*c*) Bioprospecting   (*d*) Biomagnification

12. The EFB stands for

    (*a*) European Forum of biotechnology

    (*b*) Engineering Federation of biotechnology

    (*c*) European Function on biotechnology

    (*d*) European Federation of biotechnology

13. Which of the following statement is incorrect ?

    (*a*) Sexual reproduction preserves the genetic information, while asexual reproduction permits variation

    (*b*) Traditional hybridization procedures used in plant and animal breeding very often lead to inclusion and multiplication of undesirable genes along with the desired genes

    (*c*) In a chromosome there is a specific DNA sequence called the origin of replication, which is responsible for initiating replication

    (*d*) The ability to multiply copies of antibiotic resistance gene in *E. coli* was called cloning of antibiotic resistance gene in *E. coli.*

14. The technique of genetic engineering include

    (*a*) Creation of recombinant DNA

    (*b*) Gene cloning

    (*c*) Gene transfer

    (*d*) All of the above

15. Among the following, select the tools of recombinant DNA technology
    a. Restriction enzymes
    b. Polymerase enzymes
    c. Ligases
    d. Vectors
    e. Host organisms
    (*a*) a, b, c, d and e
    (*b*) a, c, d and e
    (*c*) a, b, c and d
    (*d*) a, b, c and e

16. In restriction enzymes (like *Eco*RI) the Roman numbers following the names indicate the:
    (*a*) Order in which the enzymes were discovered from that strain of bacteria.
    (*b*) Order in which the enzymes were isolated from that strain of bacteria.
    (*c*) Genus of the prokaryotic cell or bacteria.
    (*d*) Strain of the bacteria.

17. The enzyme which catalyses the removal of nucleotides from the ends of DNA is
    (*a*) Endonuclease
    (*b*) Exonuclease
    (*c*) DNA ligase
    (*d*) DNA polymerase/Hind II/EcoRI

18. Stickiness of the ends of the DNA facilitates the
    (*a*) Action of DNA ligase and these ends are joined together laterally
    (*b*) Action of DNA ligase and these ends are joined together end-to-end
    (*c*) Action of *Taq* polymerase
    (*d*) Action of restriction enzyme

19. In bacterial cells, the membrane is broken with the help of enzyme
    (*a*) cellulose
    (*b*) lysozyme
    (*c*) chitinase
    (*d*) lipase

20. Find the correct match for the breaking of the cell wall during isolation of genetic material in rDNA procedure.
    (*a*) Cellulase – Plant cell
    (*b*) Lysozyme – Fungus
    (*c*) Chitinase – Bacteria
    (*d*) All of these

21. The polymerase enzyme used in PCR is
    (*a*) DNA polymerase I
    (*b*) *Taq* polymerase
    (*c*) Reverse transcriptase
    (*d*) Restriction endonuclease

22. The first step in the PCR is
    (*a*) Denaturation
    (*b*) Primer extension
    (*c*) Annealing
    (*d*) Cooling

23. For large scale production of recombinant product the most commonly used bioreactors are of
    (*a*) Simple type
    (*b*) Stirring type
    (*c*) Both (*a*) and (*b*)
    (*d*) None of the above

24. Protein encoding gene which is expressed in heterologous host is
    (*a*) Foreign protein
    (*b*) Heterologous protein
    (*c*) Recombinant protein
    (*d*) Alien protein

25. A typical bioreactor has
    a. An agitator system
    b. An oxygen delivery system
    c. A foam control system
    d. A temperature control system
    e. A pH control system
    f. Sampling ports
    (*a*) a, b and c
    (*b*) a, b, c and d
    (*c*) a, b, b, d and e
    (*d*) a, b, c, d, e and f

26. After the biosynthetic phase, the product is separated and purified by the process called
    (*a*) Agarose gel electrophoresis
    (*b*) PCR
    (*c*) Downstream processing
    (*d*) Insertional inactivation

Answer Keys

1. (a)	2. (a)	3. (c)	4. (d)	5. (b)	6. (d)	7. (a)	8. (a)	9. (a)	10. (a)
11.(b)	12.(d)	13.(a)	14.(d)	15.(a)	16.(b)	17.(b)	18.(b)	19.(b)	20.(a)
21.(b)	22.(a)	23.(b)	24.(c)	25.(d)	26.(c)				

Solutions

1. A short segment of DNA with the remarkable capacity to move from one location in a chromosome to another.

2. Non-homologous recombination occurs in regions where no large-scale sequence similarity is apparent.

   Site specific recombination occurs between particular short sequences present on otherwise dissimilar parental molecules.

   Replicative recombination generates a new copy of the transposable element at a new location of DNA.

3. Site-specific recombination occurs between particular short sequences present on otherwise dissimilar parental molecules. Replicative recombination generates a new copy of the transposable element at a new location of DNA. Homologous genetic recombination occurs between DNA molecules of very similar sequences.

4. Homologous genetic recombination occurs between DNA molecules of very similar sequences Site-specific recombination occurs between particular short sequences present on otherwise dissimilar parental molecules. Non-homologous recombination occurs in regions where no large-scale sequence similarity is apparent.

5. Homologous genetic recombination occurs between DNA molecules of very similar sequences. Non homologous recombination occurs in region where no large- scale sequence similarity is apparent. Replicative recombination generates a new copy of the transposable element at a new location of DNA.

6. Ruv-A and Ruv-B protein form a complex that binds to Holliday intermediates, displays Rec-A protein and promotes branch migration at higher mates than does Rec-A.

7. Nucleases that specifically cleave Holliday intermediates are aften called resolvases, the Ruv-C protein is one of at least two such nucleases in E-coli.

8. In E coli, rec-B, rec-C and rec-D genes encode the Rec-BCD enzyme, which has both helicase and nuclease activities

9. The sequences of the recombination sites recognized by site-specific recombinases are partially asymmeteric (non-palindromic)

10. Complex transposons contain one or more genes in addition to those needed for transposition.

11. The techniques of using live organisms or enzymes from organisms to produce products and processes useful to humans are called **biotechnology**. The term 'biotechnology' was coined by a Hungarian engineer, **Karl Ereky** in 1917 to describe a process for large scale production of pigs.

12. The EFB stands for **European Federation of biotechnology**. The EFB has given a definition of biotechnology that encompasses (includes) both traditional view and modern molecular biotechnology. The definition given by EFB is as follows :

    "The integration of natural science and organisms, cells, parts thereof, and molecular analogues for products and services."

13. Asexual reproduction preserves the genetic information, while sexual reproduction permits variation.

14. The technique of genetic engineering include creation of recombinant DNA, use of gene cloning and gene transfer.

15. Recombinant DNA technology can be accomplished only if we have the key tools, i.e.

    a. Restriction enzymes

    b. Polymerase enzymes

    c. Ligases

    d. Vectors

    e. Host organisms

16. In restriction enzymes (like EcoRI) the Roman numbers following the names indicate the order in which the enzyme were isolated from that strain of bacteria.

17. Restriction enzymes belong to a larger class of enzymes called **nucleases**. These are of two kinds, **exonucleases** and **endonucleases**.

    Exonucleases remove nucleotides from the ends of the DNA whereas, endonucleases make cuts at specific positions within the DNA.

18. Stickness of the sticky ends of the DNA facilitates the action of DNA ligase and these ends joined together end-to-end.

19. **(b)**

20. In order to cut the DNA with restriction enzymes, it needs to be in pure form, free from other macromolecules.

    Since the DNA is enclosed within the membranes, we have to break the cell open to release DNA along with other macromolecules such as RNA, protein, polysaccharides and also lipids.

    This can be achieved by treating the bacterial cells / plant or animal tissue with enzymes such as:

    Lysozyme (bacteria),

    (ii) Cellulase (plant cells), and

    (iii) Chitinase (fungus).

21. *Taq* polymerase (isolated from bacterium *Thermus aquaticus*) which remains active during the high temperature, usually amplifies DMA-segments of upto 2 kb.

22. PCR is a technique used to amplify a small amount of DNA. It is followed in a sequence where denaturation, primer annealing and primer extension occurs.

23. For large scale production of recombinant product the most commonly used bioreactors are of stirring type. It can be used easily in research laboratories. Drawbacks in this bioreactor are that it is relatively expensive to run it.

24. If any protein encoding gene is expressed in a heterologous host, it is called a **recombinant protein**. Heterologous host is the host which expresses the protein in the cell lines where they are not supposed to be produced, e.g., *E. coli*, yeast, mammalian cells, etc. For example, a certain protein which is produced only in human cells can be expressed in the yeast and isolated.

25. A typical bioreactor has

    a. An agitator system

    b. An oxygen delivery system

    c. A foam control system

    d. A temperature control system

    e. A pH control system

    f. Sampling ports

26. After the biosynthetic phase, the product is separated and purified by the process called **downstream processing**.

CHAPTER 12

Biotechnology and Its Applications

Biotechnological Applications in Agriculture and Medicine

Biotechnology

Biotechnology is the science which is responsible for the manufacturing of different pharmaceuticals. These pharmaceutical products are produced from genetically modified fungi, animals, plants, microbes etc.

- **Applications of biotechnology:**
  - Therapeutics
  - Genetically modified crops for agriculture
  - Diagnostics
  - Bio remediation
  - Energy production
  - Waste treatment
- **Biotechnology Research Areas:**
  - Creating the optimal conditions which are required for a catalyst to work through engineering.
  - The purification of protein or organic compounds by downstream processing technologies.
  - Providing the top suitable catalyst as an improved organism such as microbes.

Biotechnological Applications in Agriculture

- Helped in increasing the production of food using the following:
  - Organic Agriculture
  - Genetically engineered crop based production
  - Agro-chemical based agriculture
- The Green Revolution increased the production of food by three folds.

- **Genetically Modified Organisms (GMO):**
  Genetically Modified Organisms are the flora and fauna whose genes are being modified to enhance them to be more productive according to the human needs.
  - Advantages of GMO in Plants:
    - The crop becomes more tolerant towards the physical climatic conditions i.e. weather, salinity pH etc.
    - The post-harvest losses are reduced enhancing more profit.
    - The nutrition value of the food also increases.
    - It increases the efficiency of the plant on the basic level which avoids early exhaustions.
- **Pest Resistant Plants:**
  - These plants cut the use of chemical pesticides by a huge amount and enable us to not use insecticides. Some of the examples of such plants are as follows:
- **Bt (Bacillus thuringiensis) Cotton:**
  - The Bacillus thuringiensis produces a few strains which kill insects such as worms, flies and mosquitoes (Lepidopterans).
  - The Bacillus thuringiensis produces an insecticidal protein while growing. This does not affect the bacillus as it is present in its inactive protoxin form.
  - When an insect eats the plant, the inactive toxin converts into an active toxin due to alkaline pH of gut of insect.
  - This whole process causes the cell to swell and as a result die.
  - The toxin binds to the midgut epithelial cells of the insect and creates pores.
  - The toxin is coded by a gene which is known as *cry gene.*

- **Nematode Resistance in Tobacco Plants**
  - *Meloidegyne incognitia* is a nematode which generally attacks the roots of the Tobacco plant causing a very less tobacco yield.
  - RNA interference is used to prevent this nematode attack.
  - The eukaryotic organisms use RNAi for their defence.
  - This prevents mRNA translation because of complementary dsRNA molecule.
  - The source of complementary RNA is from an infection by RNA virus.
  - Nematode specific genes are introduced into the host plant by Agrobacterium vectors.
  - Both sense and anti-sense bacteria are produced in the host cell.
  - These two complementary RNA initiates RNAi which silences the nematode. As a result the parasites are not able to survive this environment.

Biotechnological Applications in Medicine

The biotechnology is used for a mass production of pharmaceutical products and drugs using recombinant technology. Now a days there are thirty recombinant therapeutics officially throughout the globe among which twelve are being marketed in India.

- **Genetically Engineered Insulin**

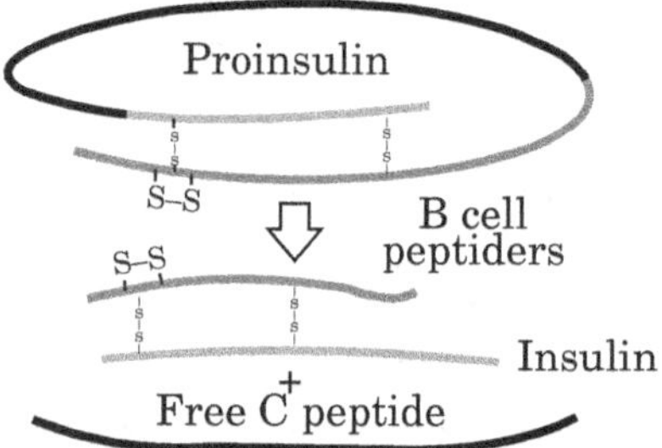

  - The diabetes in adults can be managed by taking insulin at regular intervals of time.
  - At the present moment we can produce insulin for humans synthetically.
  - The pancreas of different animals have insulins present in them but can cause allergy in humans.
  - Insulin consists of two polypeptide chains (Chain A and Chain B), which are connected by disulphide bridge.
  - In all the mammals the insulin is always produced in pro-hormone i.e. hormone which is in a stage of growth before it converts into a fully grown hormone.
  - These pro-hormones have C-peptide which is extracted at the time of maturation.

- **Gene Therapy**
  - It is a method using which a defect in a gene can be corrected.
  - In this method, the genes are inserted in to the cells externally in order to treat a hereditary disease.
  - It replaces the non functional gene causing the problem.
  - In the process patient blood's lymphocytes are cultured in culture.
  - The lymphocytes are introduced by a functional ADA cDNA.
  - This process is repeated unless all the cells are not immortal.
  - A permanent cure can be a result if ADA gene is introduced at early embryonic stage.

- **Molecular Diagnosis**
  - Using the conventional methods makes it is very difficult to make a diagnosis at an early stage.
  - Hence for early diagnosis tests like PCR, ELISA, recombinant DNA technology etc are done.
  - The presence of a pathogen is usually noted when the pathogen results in to the first symptom. At this time the density of pathogens is very high.
  - Using PCR the density of the pathogens is increased by amplification of nucleic acid.
  - PCR can be used to detect even minute concentration of pathogen.
  - PCR is vastly used to identify HIV or Cancer pathogens.
  - Antigen and antibody interactions is the principle on which ELISA works.
  - Infection produced by a pathogen can be detected by the presence of antigen or antibodies which are made to counter pathogens.

Transgenic Animals and Bioethical Issues

- **Transgenic Animals:** There are some animals in which an extra gene is expressed and possessed by DNA manipulation. Such animals are called transgenic animals. There are many animals of this type like rabbits, sheep, rats, cows, fish, etc. but most of them are mice.

These modifications lead to some benefits which are explained below:

- **Normal physiology and development:** These modifications in animals help us to understand about the regulation of genes and their effect of normal functioning of body.

➤ **Study of disease:** These modifications also help to understand their contribution for diseases. It helps us to investigate about the new treatments for various diseases like cancer, Alzheimer's, rheumatoid arthritis and cystic fibrosis.

➤ **Biological products:** Some products are used to treat certain diseases but are expensive therefore some transgenic animals are used to create those products. Some diseases which are treated by such products are phenylketonuria (PKU), emphysema, etc.

➤ **Vaccine safety:** Some of the vaccines are tested for safety on transgenic mice before being used by humans. If it is found reliable, mice are replaced by monkeys.

➤ **Chemical safety testing:** Transgenic animals are used to test toxicity of drugs. These animals are more sensitive to toxic substances. These animals are exposed to toxic substances and the effects are studied.

• **Ethical Issues:** There are some ethical standards to be followed so that the morality of human activities is evaluated. These are necessary because genetic modifications of organisms can have unpredictable results.

➤ GEAC (Genetic Engineering Approval Committee) is an organization set up by the Indian Government to determine the validity and safety of introducing genetic modification organisms for public services.

➤ Some companies are using products and technologies that have already been identified and used by some farmers and indigenous people.

➤ Rice is an example which is an important food grain and its varieties are produced in India. There are some varieties which were already derived by Indian farmers and the companies are using their patent rights.

➤ Biopiracy is used for the companies and organizations when they do not authorize from the concerned countries and people along with compensatory payment.

➤ Traditional knowledge of some developing and under developed countries is exploited for developing modern applications.

➤ Some laws are developed by some developed and developing countries to avoid unauthorized exploitation of traditional knowledge and bio-resources.

EXERCISE

1. Two bacteria most useful in genetic engineering are
   (*a*) Rhizobium and Azobacter
   (*b*) Nitrosomonas and Klebsilla
   (*c*) Escherichia and Agrobacterium
   (*d*) Rhizobium and Diplococcus

2. Transposon is known as
   (*a*) IS element　　　(*b*) Jumping gene
   (*c*) Conservation gene　(*d*) CO integrate gene

3. The uptake of plasmid DNA into the bacterial cell is facilitated by the presence of _____ in the medium
   (*a*) Calcium chloride
   (*b*) Potassium chloride
   (*c*) Magnesium chloride
   (*d*) None of these

4. The travel of gene expression and gene activation can be measured using which of the following?
   (*a*) Reporter gene　　(*b*) Marker gene
   (*c*) Gene sequences　(*d*) Promoter element

5. The enzyme required to obtained wall free/necked protoplasts are
   (*a*) Cellulase and proteinase
   (*b*) Cellulase and pectinase
   (*c*) Cellulase and amylase
   (*d*) amylase and pectinase

6. A synchronous culture is one in which the majority of cells proceed through
   (*a*) Lag phase
   (*b*) Log phase
   (*c*) exponential phase
   (*d*) each cell cycle phase (G_1, S, G_2 and M)

7. DNA molecules, identical except for different numbers of superhelical turns are called
   (*a*) Chain isomers
   (*b*) Topoisomers
   (*c*) Helical Isomers
   (*d*) Geometrical Isomers

8. Application of embryo culture is in
   (a) Clonal propagation
   (b) Production of alkaloids
   (c) Production of soma clonal variation
   (d) Overcoming hydridsation barriers

9. Haploid culture are obtained from
   (a) leaves   (b) root tips
   (c) pollen grain   (d) bud

10. Differentiation of shoot in plant tissue culture is controlled by
    (a) high auxin : cytokinin ratio
    (b) high cytokinin : auxin ratio
    (c) high gibberellin : cytokinin ratio
    (d) high gibberellin : auxin ratio

11. It the embryo is at one-cell stage then it is found in:
    (a) Ovary
    (b) Oviduct
    (c) Uterus
    (d) either ovary or uterus

12. Embryonic stem cells are also used for generation of transgenic organisms. They are obtained from ______ of a developing _________.
    (a) trophoectoderm, gastrula
    (b) trophoectoderm, blastula
    (c) inner cell mass, blastula
    (a) inner cell mass, gastrula

13. ES cells are used in order to ensure that insertion is done at required chromosomal location and it is called as:
    (a) gene targeting   (b) Knocking out
    (c) Knocking in   (d) gene disruption

14. It a gene is inactivated by gene targeting then it is called as:
    (a) Knock-in gene
    (b) Knock-out gene
    (c) gene disruption
    (d) insertional inactivation

15. Integration events may be insertional involving ________ crossover or replacement involving _______ crossovers.
    (a) single, single   (b) double, double
    (c) double, single   (d) single, double

16. For carrying out gene manipulation, use of cultured cells is _________ transgenic organisms.
    (a) less reliable
    (b) more reliable
    (c) may be less or more reliable
    (d) is same reliable as

17. The gene targeting approach produces individuals which are ________ for inactivation of gene.
    (a) homozygous
    (b) heterozygous
    (c) either only homozygous or only heterozygous
    (d) both heterozygous and homozygous.

18. If controlled inactivation of gene in carried out and same of the consequences when inactivation of a target is deleterious are avoided. It is referred as:
    (a) Specialized gene targeting
    (b) Controlled gene targeting
    (c) Conditional gene targeting
    (d) Specific gene targeting

19. Which principle best applies for euthanasia?
    (a) Beneficence   (b) Non-maleficence
    (c) Justice   (d) Autonomy

20. Terri schiavo
    (a) A patient diagnosed with brain death
    (b) A PUS patient
    (c) Has a diacephalus twin
    (d) A carniothoracophagus

Answer Keys

1. (c)	2. (b)	3. (a)	4. (b)	5. (b)	6. (d)	7. (b)	8. (d)	9. (c)	10. (b)
11. (b)	12. (c)	13. (a)	14. (b)	15. (d)	16. (a)	17. (b)	18. (c)	19. (d)	20. (b)

Solutions

1. Genetic engineering is the transfer of DNA from one organism to another using biotechnology The bacterial cells can be genetically modified so that they have the gene for producing human insulin some of these bacteria are escherichia and agrobacterium.

2. Transposable elements also known as Jumping genes are DNA sequences that move from on location on the genome to another.

3. Calcium Chloride (CaCl2) increases the ability of a prokaryotic cell to incorporate plasmid DNA allowing them to be genetically transformed.

4. Marker gene is a gene with a known location in a chromosome; used to track the insertion of DNA into organisms. It allows the travel of gene expression and gene activation.

5. The process of obtaining plant by the culture of isolated protoplast from the plant parts on an artificial media of known composition is known as protoplast culture. In order to culture the protoplast it is isolated from the explant. The protoplast, it is isolated from the explant. The protoplast is enclosed by the cell wall and plasma membrane in a plant cell so enzyme cellulose and pectinase are used to digest the cell wall which is composed of cellulose, hemicellulose and pectin.

6. synchronous culture consists of four phase: S, for synthesis, when the new DNA is made; M, for mitosis, when the cell splits into two; and two resting gap phases separating them, G1 before S phase and G2 between sand M.

7. topoisomers with different linking number may be reparated on an agarose get via gel electrophoresis.

8. Plant embryo culture has now been used to speed up breeding programme and to overcome the cross ability barrier in plant.

9. A method is presented by which hundreds of haploid plants of various species of Nicotiona can be raised from pollen grains. Stamens should be excised when pollen grains have been individualized, but are still uninucleate and free of starch.

10. High cytokinin to auxin ratio mean high conc. of cytokinin and low conc. of auxin which ultimately promote shoot production.

11. When embryo is at one cell stage it is found in oviduct. This is important for generation of whole organisms that are transgenic. Isolation of one cell embryo is done transgenic. Isolation of one cell embryo is done and then it is micro-injected into the pronucleaus.

12. Embryonic stem cells are also used for generation of transgenic organisms. They are obtained from inner cell mass of a developing blastula. A developing blastula composes of inner cell mass and it is surrounded by trophoectoderm.

13. Es cells are used in order to ensure that insertion is done at required chromosomal location and the process is termed as gene targeting. In some cases it is not necessary to ensure that integration is taking place at a normal chromosomal location.

14. If a gene is inactivated by gene targetting then it is called as knock-out gene. If a gene is replaced by some other gene then it is called as knocking in.

15. Integration can be done by either insertion or replacement. Insertion is carried out by using single crossover and replacement is carried out by double crossover.

16. For carrying out gene manipulation, use of cultured cells is less reliable than that of transgenic organisms. Thus, these transgenic organisms are used greatly.

17. The gene targeting approach produces individuals which are heterozygous for inactivation of gene. But it is necessary to generate homozygotes and they are produced by crossing heterozygous individuals and then screening is carried out.

18. Conditional gene targeting is the where controlled inactivation is carried out. If inactivation leads to deleterious effects then they are avoided.

19. Autonomy is the best principle applies for enthanasia as it is the right or condition of self government.

20. Terri schiavo was a PVS patient Her case was a right to die, legal case in the united states from 1990 to 2005.

CHAPTER 13

Organisms and Populations

Organisms and Their Environment

Ecology is a branch of biology, which gives us holistic perspective to biology. It is the study of relationships of living organisms with their environments abiotic and biotic components.

Organism and its environment

Physiological ecology is important as it explains how organisms adapt to their environment for survival and reproduction. Major abiotic or physical factors that affect the adaptation of the organisms are temperature, water, soil and light.

Major Abiotic Factors

- **Light:**
- ➢ Species of small plants like herbs and shrubs that grow in forests can photosynthesize optimally under very low light conditions.
- ➢ Some plants depend on sunlight to meet their photoperiodic requirement for flowering.
- ➢ Animals need light for timing their foraging, migratory and reproductive activities.
- ➢ Some plants present at the bottom of the ocean does not get sunlight so some of the color components are not available to them.
- **Temperature:**
- ➢ The average temperature decreases continuously as we move from plains to hilly areas and from the equator towards the poles.
- ➢ In some unique habitats like thermal springs, deep sea hydrothermal vents the average temperature exceed 100°C.

- ➢ Some factors like kinetics of enzymes, physiological functions, basal metabolism of the organism are affected by the temperature.
- ➢ The geographical distribution of different species is determined by the levels of thermal tolerance of the species. Some species are called eurythermal which can survive in wide range of temperatures while species called stenothermal can survive only in narrow range of temperatures.
- **Soil**
- ➢ The nature and properties of soil depend on the climate, weathering process, transportation of soil and the development of soil.
- ➢ Vegetation in an area is determined by the mineral composition, topography, pH of the soil.
- ➢ Water holding capacity of the soil is determined by the soil composition, grain size and aggregation.
- **Water**
- ➢ The amount of water available in a particular area determines the distribution and productivity of plants.
- ➢ Salt concentration in water varies for different areas like less than 5 in inland waters, 30 – 35 in the sea and more than 100 in hypersaline lagoons.
- ➢ Some aquatic organisms can grow in wide range of salt water, such aquatic organisms are called euryhaline and other can tolerate salinities in a narrow range, called stenohaline.

Responses to Abiotic Factors

- **Homeostasis:**

  A process of maintaining the constancy of its internal environment by the organism besides experiencing different external environmental conditions.

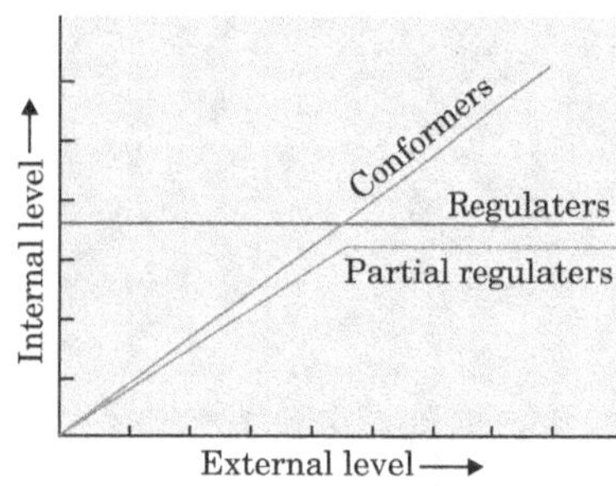

Fig.: Diagrammatic representation of organismic response

The various possibilities by which various organisms deal with the external environmental conditions are **regulate, conform, migrate** and **suspend**.

- **Regulate**
  - Constant body temperature, constant osmotic concentrations are the physiological means by which some organisms maintain homeostasis.
  - Success of mammals is largely due to their ability to maintain a constant body temperature and thrive whether they live in poles or in the arid deserts.
  - Humans maintain a constant body temperature of 37°C
  - In summers sweat cool due to evaporation and brings down the body temperature.
  - In winters we shiver which produces heat and raises body temperature.
- **Conform**
  - A constant internal environment cannot be maintained by plants and animals.
  - With change in water osmotic concentration, body temperature of aquatic animals also changes.
  - The animals and plants whose body temperature changes with ambient temperature are called conformers.
  - Thermoregulation is expensive energetically for many organisms that includes small birds like shrews and humming birds, because of which such organisms are conformers.
- **Migrate**
  - Some organisms move to favorable or more hospitable areas temporarily and return back once the stressful period is over in their own area this is called migration.
  - Many Siberian birds migrate from Siberia to Rajasthan in winters.
- **Suspend**
  - To help bacteria, fungi and lower plants to survive in unfavorable conditions various kinds of thick walled spores are formed that generate on availability of suitable environment.

- Some organisms escape time to avoid stress like bears goes into hibernation in winters and fishes and snails go into aestivation to avoid summer.
- Under unfavorable conditions many zooplankton species in lakes enter diapause, a stage of suspended development.

Adaptation

- It is any attribute of the organism (morphological, physiological, and behavioral) that enables the organism to survive and reproduce in its habitat. For example people living in higher altitudes have higher Red Blood Cell count because the oxygen level in higher altitudes is low because of which body produces more Red Blood Cells to allow increased level of transportation of gases.
- **Allen's rule:** According to Allen's rule, the limbs, ears and other appendages of the animals living in cold climates tend to be shorter than the animals of the same species living in warm climates to prevent loss of heat.
- Some dessert plants perform their photosynthetic function by stems are the leaves are reduced to spines. Some aquatic animals survive in hot springs while others may survive in Antarctic waters where the temperature is very less. These plants and animals adapt according to the conditions.

Population

- **Population**
  - When a group dwells in a well defined geographic area, share or compete for similar resources and interbreed, this represents a population.
  - A population has different attributes that an individual organism does not possess like birth rates, death rates and sex ratio.
  - The growth status of the population can be reflected by the shapes of the pyramids.

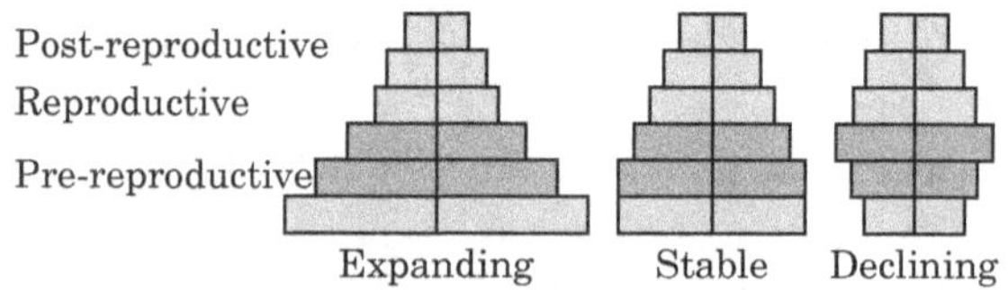

Fig.: Representation of age pyramids for human population

- **Population density:** Also known as population size, is the measurement of population per unit area or unit volume.
- **Population Growth:** The size of a population is not always constant, it varies with factors like food availability, adverse weather, predation pressure these factors provide insight into whether the population is declining or flourishing, these

variations in size of population is called population growth. The population fluctuations take place due to four basic processes.

➢ Natality- Number of births during a given period

➢ Mortality- Number of deaths in a given period

➢ Immigration- Number of individuals of the same species that have come into the habitat from some other place.

➢ Emigration- Number of individuals of the same species that left the habitat and shifted to a new place.

• **Growth models**

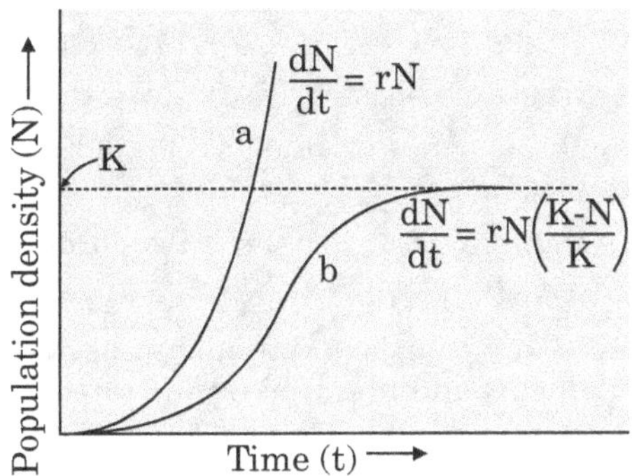

Fig.: Population growth curve

➢ Exponential growth: When the resources are unlimited population has exponential growth. If in a population of size N the birth rates are represented as b and death rates as d then the increase or decrease in N in a unit time period t will be

$$\frac{dN}{dT} = (b-d) \times N$$

Let $(b-d) = r$ then, $\frac{dN}{dT} = rN$

➢ Logistic Growth: When the resources are limited exponential growth is not possible, leading to competition between individuals for limited resources and only the fittest will survive and reproduce.

Verhulst-Pearl Logistic growth is given by

$$\frac{dN}{dt} = rN\left(\frac{K-N}{K}\right)$$

• **Life History Variation: Population Interactions**

➢ The various species of a habitat depend on each other for their survival. There is always a minimal requirement for any species to have one or more species on which it can feed. The populations interact with each other to survive in this ecology. Various population interactions can be understood by this table,

Species A	Species B	Name of Interaction
+	+	Mutualism
–	–	Competition
+	–	Predation
+	–	Parasitism
+	0	Commenalism
–	0	Amensalism

'+' for beneficial interaction

'–' for detrimental interaction

'0' for neutral interaction

• **Types of Interactions**

➢ **Mutualism:** This interaction benefits both the interacting species such as the plant-animal relationship. Plants offer pollen and nectar for pollinators and juicy and nutritious fruits for seed dispersers, for e.g. relationship between female wasp and fig species.

➢ **Competition:** It occurs when closely related species compete for same resource but sometimes totally unrelated species also compete for same resource. For example flamingoes and resident fishes compete for common food, i.e. zooplanktons in some shallow South American lakes. In this process, fitness of one species is lower in presence of the other. Gause's 'Competitive Exclusion Principle' states that two closely related species competing for the same resource cannot coexist indefinitely and the inferior one is eliminated.

➢ **Predation:** When one species is benefited harming the second species as it preys on it. For example for plants herbivores are predators. Predators maintain the species diversity in a community. If the predator makes the prey extinct then there are possibilities of predator becoming extinct as well.

➢ **Parasitism:** It is similar to predation where one species is benefited and the second species gets detrimented. The parasite obtains food and shelter from the host. For example lice on humans and ticks on dogs. Parasites have a complex life cycle as parasitisation of primary host is facilitated by one or two intermediate hosts. Ectoparasites are those parasites which feed on the external surface of host organism while endoparasites live inside the host body. An example of parasitism in birds is Brood parasitism where parasitic bird lay its eggs in the nest of the host.

➢ **Commensalism:** In this interaction one species is benefited while the other is neither harmed nor benefited. For example an orchid growing on a mango branch.

➢ **Amensalism:** In this interaction one species is detrimented/inhibited or destroyed while the other species is unaffected. For example bread mold penicillium and black walnut trees.

EXERCISE

1. The branch of Botany dealing with the distribution of plants on the earths surface is called
   - (*a*) Ecology
   - (*b*) Phytology
   - (*c*) Phytogeography
   - (*d*) Phytosociology

2. Biotic Potential refers to
   - (*a*) Increase of population under optimum conditions
   - (*b*) Increase of population under given conditions
   - (*c*) Increase of population under natural conditions
   - (*d*) Increase of population under climatic conditions.

3. Ecology takes into account only
   - (*a*) Environmental factors only
   - (*b*) Plant adaptations only
   - (*c*) Effect of environment on plants
   - (*d*) All of the above.

4. They plants and animals living in a given area form.
   - (*a*) Biological community
   - (*b*) Ecotone
   - (*c*) Biome
   - (*d*) Consociation

5. The term 'niche' of a species refers to
   - (*a*) Specific and habitual function
   - (*b*) Specific place where an organism lives
   - (*c*) Competitive power of an organism
   - (*d*) Specific function of organism

6. Which of the following statement is true regarding individuals of same species
   - (*a*) They are interbreeding
   - (*b*) They live in same niche
   - (*c*) They live in different niche
   - (*d*) They live in different habitate

7. Species are considered as.
   - (*a*) Real units of classification devised by taxonomists
   - (*b*) Real basic units of classification
   - (*c*) They lowest units of classification
   - (*d*) Artificial concept of human mind which cannot be defined in absolute terms.

8. Name the term used to describe a single dominant species that dictates community structure.
   - (*a*) Pioneer species
   - (*b*) Transitional species
   - (*c*) Key stone species
   - (*d*) Indigenous species

9. Habitat together with functions of species constitute its
   - (*a*) Trophic level
   - (*b*) Boundary
   - (*c*) Topography
   - (*d*) Niche

10. They organisms spending most of the time in transitional area between two communities are called.
    - (*a*) Exotic species
    - (*b*) Edge species
    - (*c*) Keystone species
    - (*d*) Critical link species

11. Population whose members reproduces asexually are termed as __________.
    - (*a*) Panimictic
    - (*b*) Amphimictic
    - (*c*) Apomictic
    - (*d*) Ecotype

12. The study of inter-relationship between living organisms and their environment is called
    - (*a*) Ecosystem
    - (*b*) Phytogeography
    - (*c*) Ecology
    - (*d*) Phytosociology

13. The carrying capacity of a population is determined by its __________.
    - (*a*) Birth rate
    - (*b*) Death rate
    - (*c*) Limiting resource
    - (*d*) Reproductive status

14. A Community is defined as
    - (*a*) A group of birds
    - (*b*) A collection of species
    - (*c*) Interacting populations
    - (*d*) An interactive ecosystem

15. Which of the following isolation is important for speciation
    - (*a*) Seasonal
    - (*b*) Tropical
    - (*c*) Behavioural
    - (*d*) Reproductive

16. Which one of the following is the most significant feature of the Indian population?
    - (*a*) Declining birth rate
    - (*b*) Improvement in the literacy level
    - (*c*) The size of its adolescent population
    - (*d*) Improvement in health condition

17. What was the population density of India according to 2001?
    - (*a*) 124 Person/km^2
    - (*b*) 244 Person/km^2
    - (*c*) 324 Person/km^2
    - (*d*) 424 Person/km^2

18. Which is the most populous country of the world?
    (*a*) India   (*b*) United states
    (*c*) China   (*d*) Russia

19. In how many years is the official enumeration of population carried out for census.
    (*a*) 1 year   (*b*) 5 years
    (*c*) 10 years   (*d*) 2 years

20. Name the union Territory having the highest density of population?
    (*a*) Chandigarh   (*b*) Delhi
    (*c*) Pondicherry   (*d*) Daman and Diu

21. The most populous state of India is
    (*a*) West Bengal   (*b*) Kerala
    (*c*) Uttar Pradesh   (*d*) Bihar

Answer Keys

1. (*c*)   2. (*a*)   3. (*d*)   4. (*a*)   5. (*b*)   6. (*a*)   7. (*b*)   8. (*c*)   9. (*d*)   10. (*b*)
11. (*c*)   12. (*c*)   13. (*c*)   14. (*c*)   15. (*d*)   16. (*c*)   17. (*c*)   18. (*c*)   19. (*c*)   20. (*b*)
21. (*c*)

Solutions

1. Apomixis is the formation of new individuals directly through asexual reproduction without involving the formation and fusion of gameter. So, those population whose members reproduce by the process of apomixi's are called apomictic

2. Biotic potential is the maximum capacity of a population to reproduces under ideal conditions (environmental).

3. Ecology is the branch of biology that deals with the inter relationships amongst organisms and interactions between organisms and their environment.

4. Biological community is the assemblage of interdependent and interacting populations of different species present in an area.

5. Ecological niche is specific habitat where an specific species lives.

6. Uniform interbreeding population or group of individuals which freely interbreed among themselves, constitute a species.

7. Species is the basic unit of classification only the species has a real existence, other units of classification are man made artificial groups.

8. According to paine (1969), keystone species are those whose role or activities determine community structure.

9. Niche is specific part of habitat occupied by individuals of a species which is circumscribed by its range of to tolerance, range of movement microclimate, type of food and its availability.

10. The species which are found primarily, most of their time in ecotone or community boundary are known as edge species.

11. Term phytogeography is made up of two words phyton = plant and geography i.e. geography of plant distribution.

12. The term ecology is derived from two greek words namely oikos and Logos. Oikos means home or habitation or a place to live in Logos means study or discourse? Hence literally speaking, ecology is the study of organisms at home.

13. The carrying capacity of a population is determined by its limiting resources. Carrying capacity is the upper limit of an ecosystem up to which it can provide the basic needs to the population under given circumstances.

14. A community is an assemblage of population of organisms that live in an area and interact with each other.

15. The interruption of gene flow (reproductive isolation) between populations is a pre-requisite for the formation of new species

16. The most significant feature of Indian population is that India has high population of young people and they are the future of India.

17. The measurement of population per unit area is 324 person/km^2

18. China is the most populous country with nearly 1.4 billion residents.

19. In India the census has been undertaken every 10 year's

20. Delhi is the most populous union Territory having estimated population of 18.6 million in 2016.

21. Uttar Pradesh is the most populous state of India with the total population density of 828 person/km^2

CHAPTER 14

Ecosystem

Ecosystem–Structure & Function, Productivity & decomposition

Introduction

The most basic part of nature where the living interact in between themselves and with the surrounding environment

Types of Ecosystems

- **Terrestrial:**
- ➢ Forest, grassland and desert are some examples of terrestrial ecosystems.
- **Aquatic:**
- ➢ Pond, lake, wetland, river and estuary are some examples of aquatic ecosystems.
- **Man-made ecosystems:**
- ➢ Crop fields and an aquarium may also be considered as man-made ecosystems.

Structure and Function

- An Ecosystem has two components:
- ➢ Biotic components: These are consumers, producers and decomposers
- ➢ Abiotic components: These are inorganic materials- air, water and soil
- Every ecosystem has characteristic physical structure derived from interaction of abiotic and biotic components.
- Stratification is vertical distribution of different species occupying different levels. These levels are called STRATA.
- The components of an ecosystem work as a unit by considering the following aspects:
- ➢ Productivity
- ➢ Decomposition
- ➢ Energy flow
- ➢ Nutrient cycling

Productivity

For ecosystems to sustain and function a basic input of solar energy is needed. The rate at which the biomass is produced is termed as productivity.

- **Primary productivity**
- ➢ During the process of photosynthesis, the amount of biomass produced per unit area by different plants is coined as primary productivity.
- ➢ The primary productivity can be illustrated in energy kcal m^{-2} or weight g^{-2}.
- ➢ Primary productivity can be divided into NPP (net primary productivity) and GPP (gross primary productivity).
- ➢ NPP of an ecosystems the remaining biomass after respiration (R) and GPP is the rate at which the biomass is produced under the process of photosynthesis.

GPP –R = NPP

The available biomass for heterotrophs to consume is NPP.

- **Secondary productivity:**
- ➢ The rate at which the new organic matter is formed is coined as secondary productivity.

Decomposition

The process in which complex organic compounds disintegrate to form inorganic simple compounds is termed as decomposition. The simple disintegrated compounds can be water, carbon gases etc. Detritus is formed from dead remains of animals and dead plants remains like bark, leaves, and flowers.

- **Steps are involved in decomposition**
- ➢ Fragmentation: Detritivores break down detritus into smaller particles which increases the surface area of detritus particles for microbial action. This process is called fragmentation.
- ➢ Leaching: The process in which inorganic nutrients goes into the ground and is stored in form of precipitation which cannot be accessed is called Leaching.

- ➢ Catabolism: The process in which detritus disintegrates into simple inorganic compounds with the help of fungal or bacterial enzymes is called Catabolism.
- ➢ Humification: This process results in accumulated humus. Humus is an amorphous substance which is black in colour. The decomposition of humus is also very slow.
- ➢ Mineralization: Mineralization is a process in which the humus produced decomposes to give inorganic simple compounds.
- **Factors affecting Rate of Decomposition:**
- ➢ Chemical composition of detritus: Decomposition rate is slower if detritus is rich in lignin and chitin, and it is quicker if detritus is rich in nitrogen and sugar.
- ➢ Climatic conditions: Warm and moist environment favours decomposition.

Energy Flow & Ecological Succession

Energy Flow

Energy flow is unidirectional. First, plants capture solar energy and then, food is transferred from the producers to consumers and then to decomposers. Organisms of different trophic levels in nature are connected to each other for food or energy relationship forming a food chain. To synthesize the molecules, ecosystem need a constant supply of energy.

- **Producers:**
- ➢ The green plants in the ecosystem which produces food are called producers.
- ➢ All living animals are dependent on the producers for their food; directly or indirectly.
- ➢ The solar energy trapped by the plants is either passed on to consumer or the organism dies.
- ➢ The detritus food chain starts when an organism dies.
- **Consumers:**
- ➢ The animals that depend on producers directly or indirectly for their food.
- ➢ They include:
- - *Primary Consumers*: These are herbivores that feed on producers. Example: birds, insects etc.
- - *Secondary Consumers*: They feed on herbivore. Example: fox, man etc.
- - Tertiary Consumers: They feed on primary carnivores.

- **Grazing Food Chain (GFC):**
- ➢ An example of grazing food chain (GFC) can be:

$$(\text{Producer}) \rightarrow (\text{Herbivore}) \rightarrow (\text{Carnivore})$$
$$\text{Grass} \longrightarrow \text{Deer} \longrightarrow \text{Lion}$$
$$(\text{Producer}) \rightarrow \left(\begin{array}{c}\text{Primary}\\\text{Consumer}\end{array}\right) \rightarrow \left(\begin{array}{c}\text{Secondary}\\\text{Consumer}\end{array}\right)$$

- **Detritus Food Chain (DFC):**
- ➢ This chain begins as soon as an organism die.
- ➢ This is made up of saprotrophs. For example: bacteria and fungi.
- ➢ These saprotrophs secrete enzymes that breakdown the dead and waste materials into simpler materials.
- ➢ Some animal are omnivores as well. For example: cockroaches, crow etc.
- ➢ These interconnections of food chains make a food web.
- ➢ The organisms have specific place in their ecosystem which is known as their trophic level.
- ➢ With every successive trophic level, the amount of energy decreases. Only 10% of energy is transferred to each trophic level from the previous one.

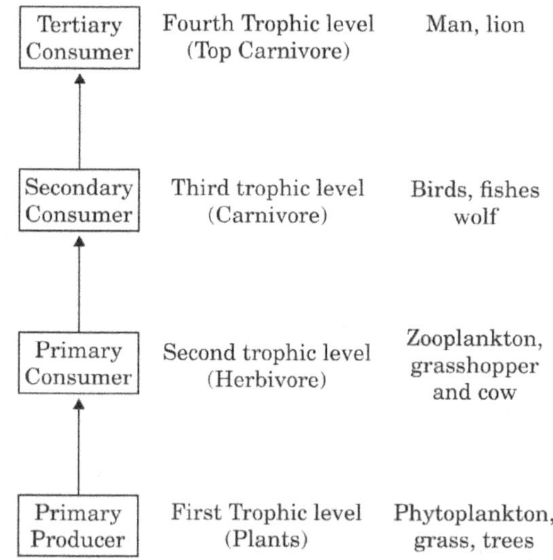

Fig.: Diagrammatic Representation of Trophic Levels in an Ecosystem

Ecological Pyramids

Expressing the relationship between organisms graphically in terms of biomass, energy or number results in ecological pyramids, where the base represents producers and the apex represents top level consumer.

- **Pyramid of Number:**
- ➢ It demonstrates the relationship between

organisms on the basis of their number.

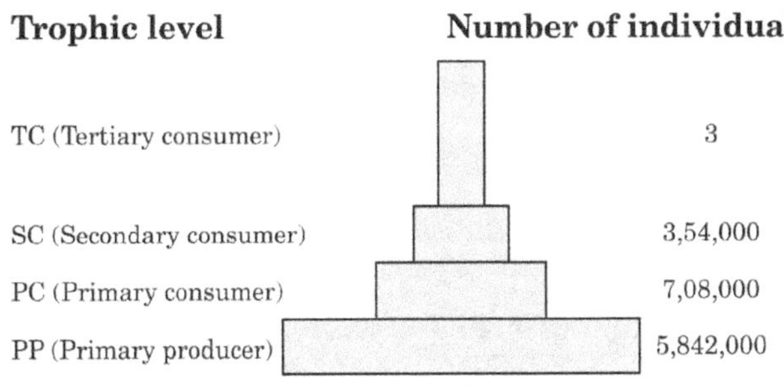

Fig.: Pyramid of Number

- **Pyramid of Biomass:**
- Sharp decrease in biomass at higher trophic levels can be seen in pyramid of biomass in grassland ecosystem.

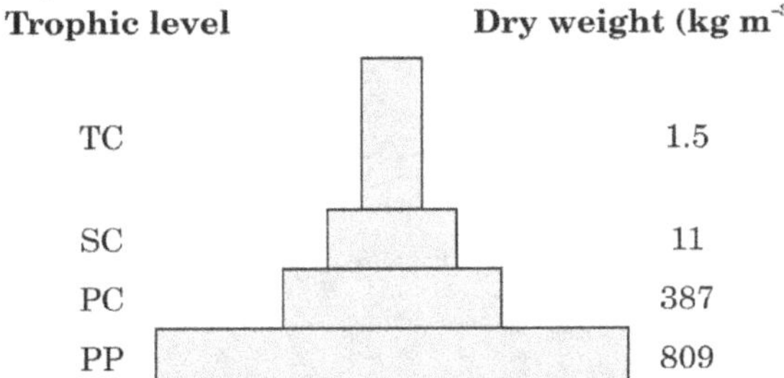

Fig.: Pyramid of Biomass (Grassland Ecosystem)

- Inverted pyramid of biomass is seen in aquatic ecosystem, where small standing crop of phytoplankton supports large crop of zooplankton.

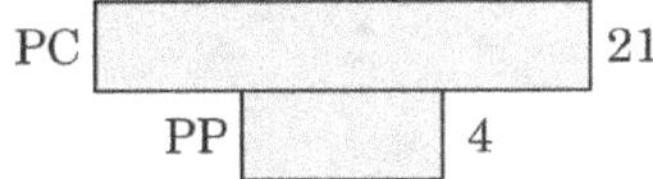

Fig.: Pyramid of Biomass (Aquatic Ecosystem)

- **Pyramid of Energy:**
- Only 1% of energy in sunlight is converted by primary producers.
- When energy flows from one trophic level to next, some amount of energy is always lost. So, pyramid of energy is always upright.

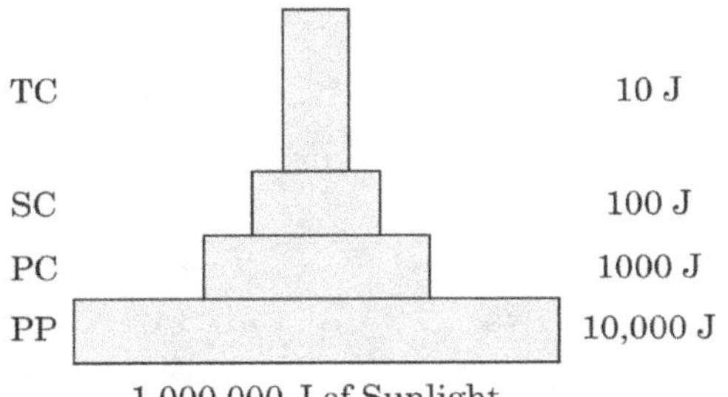

Fig.: Pyramid of Energy

- **Limitations of Ecological Pyramids:**
- It does not consider same species belonging to two or more trophic levels.
- It does not work for a food web.
- It does not accommodate saprophytes, though they play crucial role in ecosystem.

Ecological Succession

The biotic community is dynamic and undergoes changes with the passage of time. These changes are sequentially ordered and constitute ecological succession. Succession begins with invasion of a bare lifeless area by pioneers which later pave way for successors and ultimately a stable climax community is formed. The climax community remains stable as long as the environment remains unchanged.

- **Types of Succession:**
- Primary Succession: It occurs in areas where no living form ever existed, like bare rock or newly cooled lava, etc.
- Secondary Succession: It occurs where living form once existed but not any longer, like abandoned lands or burned forests, etc.
- **Succession of Plants:**
- Based on nature of habitat of plant, succession of plant is of two types: hydrarch succession and xerarch succession.
- Hydrarch succession: It occurs in wetter areas and the series progresses from too wet condition (hydric) to medium water (mesic) conditions.
- Xerarch succession: It occurs in dry places and series progresses from too dry (xeric) to medium water (mesic) conditions.
- Pioneer species are the first species that invade a bare area to begin an ecosystem.

Nutrient Cycling & Ecosystem Services

Nutrient Cycling

Nutrients are mandatory for living organisms in any ecosystem to survive and grow. The continuous movement of nutrients through the various components of an ecosystem is called nutrient cycling or bio-geochemical cycles.

- **Types of nutrient cycling:**
- Gaseous – the reservoir for the gaseous type of cycle is atmosphere or hydrosphere.
- Sedimentary- the reservoir for the sedimentary type of cycle is earth's crust.

- **Carbon Cycle:**
➢ 49% of dry weight of an organism is constituted by carbon. Reservoirs of carbon include- oceans, fossil fuels, etc. A large amount of carbon returns to atmosphere due to respiration, decomposition of waste material and dead organic matter also contribute carbon dioxide in atmosphere.

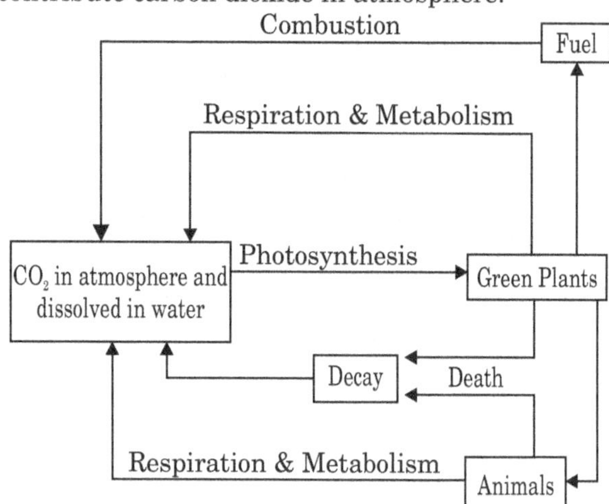

Fig.: Basic Carbon Cycle Flow Diagram

- **Phosphorus Cycle:**
➢ Rocks which contain phosphorus as phosphates are the natural reservoirs of phosphorus. Animals obtain this element from plants as plant roots absorb phosphates dissolved in soil solution.

Ecosystem Services

Benefits that organisms generally humans get from the environment and ecosystem come under ecosystem services.

For example:

- Purification of air and water by forests.
- Generating fertile soil.
- Maintaining biodiversity, etc.

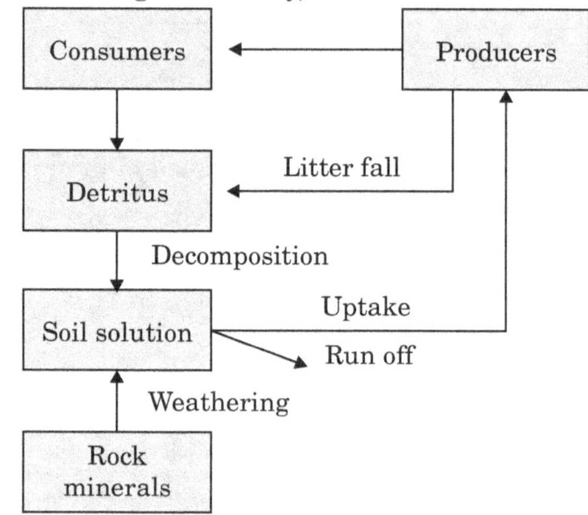

Fig.: Phosphorus Cycle

EXERCISE

1. Total organic matter Present in an ecosystem?
   (a) Biomass
   (b) Biome
   (c) Litter
   (d) Food

2. Puterfying organisms are
   (a) Producer organisms
   (b) Reducer organisms
   (c) Consumer organisms
   (d) Parasitic organisms

3. The most important organism for an ecosystem are
   (a) Herbivorous
   (b) Carnivorous
   (c) Green plants
   (d) Protozoa

4. A food chain consists of
   (a) Producers
   (b) Consumers
   (c) Decomposers
   (d) Producers and Consumers

5. Food chain always starts with
   (a) Photosynthesis
   (b) Respiration
   (c) Nitrogen fixation
   (d) Decay

6. Primary consumers are
   (a) Green plants
   (b) Herbivorous
   (c) Carnivorous
   (d) All the above

7. In parasitic food chain, the pyramid of number is
   (a) Linear
   (b) Upright
   (c) Inverted
   (d) Inverted upright

8. In Pyramid food, the producers occupy
   (a) The base
   (b) Position near the base
   (c) Apex
   (d) Position near Apex.

9. Energy flow in an ecosystem is
   - (a) Uni directional
   - (b) Bidirectional
   - (c) Multidirectional
   - (d) All the above

10. Secondary consumers are
   - (a) Green plants
   - (b) Herbivorous
   - (c) Carnivorous
   - (d) All the above

11. How many type of ecological succession are there?
   - (a) One
   - (b) Two
   - (c) Three
   - (d) Four

12. What is called for the term used to express a community in its final stage of succession?
   - (a) End community
   - (b) Final community
   - (c) Climax community
   - (d) Dark community

13. What is called for the term in which all the living organisms that occupy an area undergoing primary succession in the beginning stages?
   - (a) Climax community
   - (d) Settled community
   - (c) Dense community
   - (d) Pioneer community

14. What is called for the process when older communities of plants and animals are replaced by newer community?
   - (a) Evolution
   - (b) Deforestation
   - (c) Forestation
   - (d) Ecological succession

15. Which process occurs after a volcanic eruption?
   - (a) Primary succession
   - (b) Secondary succession
   - (c) Nitrogen fixation
   - (d) Oxidation

16. Soil changes due to erosion is an example of which of the following succession?
   - (a) Allogenic succession
   - (b) Autogenic succession
   - (c) Computational succession
   - (d) Emigrational succession

17. What is called for a pattern of vegetarian change in which a small number of species tend to replace each other over time in the absence of large scale disturbance?
   - (a) Primary succession
   - (b) Secondary succession
   - (c) Tertiary succession
   - (d) Cyclic succession

18. Which is the first process in ecological succession?
   - (a) Nudation
   - (b) Migration
   - (c) Escesis
   - (d) Aggregation

19. What is called for the succession occuring within a microhabitat?
   - (a) Primary succession
   - (b) Nudation
   - (c) Serule
   - (d) Climax succession

20. What is called for the climax which is governed by more than one climate?
   - (a) Climatic climax
   - (b) Catastrophic climax
   - (c) Sub climax
   - (d) Edaphic climax

21. The main nitrogen reservoir in the biosphere is
   - (a) rock
   - (b) Ocean
   - (c) Organism
   - (d) atmosphere

22. Which is the most common available form of S to plants
   - (a) S
   - (b) SO_2
   - (c) SO_4^{2+}
   - (d) H_2S

23. The Sedimentary cycle is
   - (a) oxygen
   - (b) nitrogen
   - (c) carbon
   - (d) Phosphorus

24. Phosphorus cycle in the form of
   - (a) HPO_3^-
   - (b) P_2
   - (c) PO_4^{2-}
   - (d) $AlPO_3$

25. Fixation occur with the help of
   - (a) Symbiotic bacteria
   - (b) With the help of nitrogenise enzyme
   - (c) leguminous modules
   - (d) all of these.

26. Nitrogen is critical elements of the ecosystem because it is.
   - (a) labile
   - (b) fixed by microbes
   - (c) abundant in atmosphere
   - (d) essential element

27. Which of the following atoms most often limits the primary productivity of an ecosystem?
   - (a) Carbon
   - (b) Nitrogen
   - (c) Sulphur
   - (d) Phosphorus

28. The natural place where the organism or communities live is known as
   - (a) Niche
   - (b) Habit
   - (c) Habitat
   - (d) Biome

29. Autoecology deals with
    (*a*) Ecology of species
    (*b*) Ecology of many species
    (*c*) Ecology of community
    (*d*) All the above

30. Energy flow ecosystem is
    (*a*) unidirection
    (*b*) Bidirectional
    (*c*) Multi directional
    (*d*) None of the above

Answer Keys

1. (*a*)	2. (*b*)	3. (*c*)	4. (*d*)	5. (*a*)	6. (*b*)	7. (*b*)	8. (*a*)	9. (*a*)	10. (*c*)
11. (*c*)	12. (*c*)	13. (*d*)	14. (*d*)	15. (*b*)	16. (*a*)	17. (*d*)	18. (*a*)	19. (*c*)	20. (*d*)
21. (*d*)	22. (*c*)	23. (*d*)	24. (*c*)	25. (*d*)	26. (*d*)	27. (*d*)	28. (*c*)	29. (*a*)	30. (*a*)

Solutions

1. Biomass is the total amount of organic matter present in anytrophic level.

2. Puterfying bacteria involved in puterfaction of living matter. Along with other decomposers, reduce organisms, they play a critical rule in recycling nitrogen from dead organisms.

3. The most important living things on our green plantet are single cell algae, they are the most important because they produce oxygen, more oxygen than anything else does.

4. A food chain consists of producers these include all green plants. These are also known as autotrophs since make their own food and consumer's include every organism that eat something. They include Herbivores, carnivores, scavengers and parasites.

5. A food chain always starts with producers, an organism that makes food. This is usually green plants, because plants can make their own food by photosynthesis.

6. Primary consumers are animals that eat primary producers; they are also called Herbivores (plant-eaters)

7. A parasitic food chain starts from herbivores but food energy passes from larger to smaller organism without upright killing as in case of predator food chain.

8. The bottom of on ecological pyramid is the broadest and is occupied by the producers which form the first trophic level. Producers are at the base level. Just as in food chain, the producers are consumed by the primary consumers.

9. The flow of energy in the ecosystem is Unidirectional The energy enters the plants through photosynthesis during the making of food. This energy then passed on from one organism to another in a food chain.

10. Secondary consumers eat primary consumers. They are carnivores (meat-eaters) and omnivores (animals that eat both animals and plants)

11. There are two types of ecological succession they are primary succession, secondary succession, and cyclic succession. Primary succession occurs when a new land is formed which provide habitant to colonized for first time. In secondary succession there is a recolonized in a previously occupied area.

12. The term climax community is used to express a community in its final stage of succession. The climax community may change if there are changed in climate or long term evolutionary changes in species.

13. When succession occurs in any particular area smaller species such as bacteria, fungi are usually first to come in. These first organisms that settle an area make up the pioneer community. These pioneer communities later lead to biological succession

14. Ecological succession can be defined as changing sequence of communities that live in an ecosystem during a given time period. The actual species involved in a succession in a particular area can control by geology, climate and other environmental factors.

15. Secondary succession refers to the concept of an ecosystem reviving itself after all has been destroyed. In an area where a volcano and tree life. If the land which was affected by volcanic rock, roots or plants parts in soil could renew.

16. Succession driven by the abiotic components of an ecosystem is known as allogenic succession. In contrast, an autogenic succession is driven by the biotic components of the ecosystem. Allogenic succession happens on a time scale that is proportionate with the disturbance.

17. Cyclic ecological succession happens within established communities and is merely a changing of the structure of the ecosystem on a cyclical basis. In cyclical replacement observation that made has provided evidence against end state climax community.

18. Nuclation is defined as the development of a bare site uninhabited by any organisms. This nudation is usually caused by disturbances in topographic, climatic or biotic factors. The areas formed can sustain only autotrophic organisms which can utilize in organic substrates

19. Micro-Organisms such as fungi and bacteria Occuring within a microhabitat known as serule. This type of succession occurs in newly available habitat. Changes of pH in a habitat could provide ideal conditions for a newly available habitat. Changes of pH in a habitat could provide ideal condition for a new species to inhabit the area.

20. Community in which climax is governed by more than one climax communities in a region, soil nutrients and animal activity is called as edaphic climax soil factors like salinity, alkalinity determined climax community.

21. Nitrogen is an incredibly versatile element existing in the atmosphere. The movement of nitrogen between the atmosphere, biosphere and geosphere in different form is called nitrogen cycle.

22. $SO^2 4+$ (sulfur dioxide) penetrates into leaves primarily in gaseous form through the stomata, although there is evidence for a limited pathway via the cuticle.

23. The phosphorus or sedimentary cycle is the biogeochemical cycle that describes the movement of phosphorus through the lithosphere, hydrosphere and biosphere.

24. The phosphorus cycle is show in the form of PO_4^{2-}

25. Fixation is the maintaining of the visual gaze on a single location with the help of symbiotic bacteria, nitrogenise enzyme, and leguminous nodules.

26. Nitrogen is a critical element of the ecosystem because it is labile. The form of nitrogen is labile in nature that is its is subjected to constant change because each organism needs nitrogen in a different form.

27. Because the quantities of phosphorus in soil are generally small, it is often the limiting factor for plant growth.

28. Habitat can be defined as the natural environment of an organism, the type of place in which it is natural for it to live and grow.

29. The ecological study of a particular species is known Autoecology.

30. The energy enters the plant through photosynthesis thus the flow of energy in the ecosystem is unidirectional.

CHAPTER 15

Biodiversity and Its Conservation

Biodiversity

Biologist Edward Wilson popularized the term Biodiversity to explain the combined diversity in every aspect of biological organization. It refers to the summation of diversity that exists in any respective level of biological organization. The most important among them are:

- **Genetic diversity:** One species would possibly show high diversity at the genetic level over its spatial arrangement vary. The medicinal plant Rauwolfia vomitoria shows a genetic variation. It grows in numerous mountain range ranges may well be in terms of the efficiency and concentration of the active chemical (reserpine) that the plant produces. There are over fifty thousand genetically different strains of rice, and 1,000 types of mango in India.

- **Species diversity:** It is the variation at the species level. For instance, the Western Ghats and Eastern Ghats differ in amphibian species diversity.

- **Ecological diversity:** This refers to the diversity at ecosystem level. India, as an example, with its deserts, rain forests, mangroves, coral reefs, wetlands, estuaries, and alpine meadows incorporates a bigger system diversity than a Scandinavian country like Serbia.

Number of species on Earth and in India

- Biodiversity and its conservation is currently the most important environmental problem with international concern as increasing number of folks round the world begin to grasp the vital importance of diversity for our survival and well-being on this planet.

- More than seventy per cent of all the species recorded are animals, whereas plants (including alga, fungi, bryophytes, gymnosperms and angiosperms) comprise no over twenty two per cent of the entire. Among animals, insects are the foremost species rich taxon, creating up over seventy per cent of the entire. That means, out of each ten animals on this planet, seven are insects.

- India constitutes 2.4 per cent of the world's total land area and also shares 8.1 per cent of the global species diversity. That makes India as one of the 12 mega diversity countries of the world. Nearly 45,000 species of plants and twice as many of animals have been recorded from India.

Patterns of Biodiversity

- **Latitudinal gradient:** The diversity of plants and animals isn't uniform throughout the planet however shows a rather uneven distribution. For several clusters of animals or plants, there are attention-grabbing patterns in diversity, the foremost well- famed being the angular distance gradient in diversity.

- **Species-Area relationships:** The increase in explored area will increase with the richness of the species within vicinity.

Importance of Species Diversity

An excessive amount of variation shouldn't be showed by a stable community in productivity from year to year; it should be either resistant or resilient to occasional disturbances (natural or man-made), and it should even be immune to invasions by alien species. Plots with additional species show less year-to-year variation in total biomass. Multiplied diversity contributes to higher productivity.

Loss of Biodiversity

- **Habitat loss and fragmentation:** The accelerated rates of species extinctions that the planet is facing currently are mostly because of human activities. Degradation of the many habitats by pollution threatens the survival of the many species. When massive habitats are shrunk into little fragments because of varied human activities, mammals and birds requiring massive territories and bound animals with migratory habits are badly affected, resulting in population declines.

- **Over-exploitation:** Many species extinctions within the last five hundred years (Steller's sea cow, passenger pigeon) were because of exploitation by humans. Presently several marine fish populations throughout the world are over harvested, endangering the continued existence of some commercially necessary species.

- **Alien species invasion:** When alien species are introduced accidentally or deliberately for any purpose, a number of them become invasive, and cause decline or extinction of native species.

- **Co- extinctions:** Whenever there is an extinction of any species, the animal and plant species linked to it become extinct. For example- mutualism in coevolved plant-pollinator, where the latter becomes extinct with the extinction of the first one or vice-versa.

Conservation of Biodiversity

- The barely utilitarian contentions for securing decent variety are self-evident; people infer multitudinous direct monetary benefits from nature sustenance (oats, beats, organic products), kindling, fiber, development material, mechanical item (tannins, greases, colors, gums, scents) and result of therapeutic significance.

- The broadly utilitarian argument says that diversity plays a significant role in several ecosystem services that nature gives. For the existence of humanity diversity is required because it provides oxygen and fruits and seeds created by pollination. There are alternative intangible benefits —we have a tendency to derive from nature–the aesthetic pleasures of walking through thick woods, looking at spring flowers fully bloom or rousing to a bulbul's song within the morning.

- The ethical argument for protecting diversity relates to what we have a tendency to owe to ample plant, animal and bug species with whom we share this planet. We've an ethical duty to worry for their well-being and gift our biological heritage in sensible order to future generations.

Reasons to conserve Biodiversity

- **In situ conservation:** Conservation and protection of whole ecosystem in order to protect the biodiversity at all levels. The species are protected in their natural environment so the complete ecosystem is protected. For example- To save the tiger, save the entire forest.

  There are more species that can become extinct in near future than the conservation resources available to conserve and protect them. Many conservationists have identified species rich zones known as 'biodiversity hotspots'. In India, Western Ghats and Eastern Himalayas come under this category out of total 34 in the world.

  Few traditional tribes of Jaintia and Khasi hills in Meghalaya have rituals in which they leave aside tracts of forests, given total protection and are known as 'sacred groves'.

- **Ex situ conservation:** In this type of conservation, the species that are endangered are shifted from their natural habitat to some artificial arrangements like botanical gardens, parks and wildlife sanctuaries. Strategies embody protecting maintenance of vulnerable species in zoological parks and biological science gardens, in vitro fertilisation, tissue culture propagation and cryopreservation of gametes.

EXERCISE

1. How many main goals are there in the convention on Biological Diversity?
   - (*a*) One
   - (*b*) Two
   - (*c*) Three
   - (*d*) Four

2. In which year the convention on Biological Diversity signed?
   - (*a*) 1990
   - (*b*) 1991
   - (*c*) 1992
   - (*d*) 1993

3. Where did the 10th conference of parties (COP) which happened to the convention on Biological Diversity take place?
   - (*a*) India
   - (*b*) China
   - (*c*) Russia
   - (*d*) Japan

4. What did the Cartagena protocol on Biosafety adopted?
   - (*a*) January 2000
   - (*b*) March 2000
   - (*c*) September 2000
   - (*d*) December 2000

5. The first ordinary meeting of the parties of conventional on Biological Diversity took place in the year 1994 (COP)
   - (*a*) True
   - (*b*) False

6. When did the Nagoya protocol on Access to Genetic Resource adopted?
   - (*a*) 19 June 2010
   - (*b*) 23 July 2010
   - (*c*) 29 October 2010
   - (*d*) 31 December 2010

7. Which event provided condition for high levels of biological diversity in India?
   - (*a*) Biological events in the atmosphere
   - (*b*) Geological events in the rivers
   - (*c*) Biological events in the rivers
   - (*d*) Geological events in the landmass

8. Into many terms Whittaker described for measuring biodiversity over spatial scales?
   - (*a*) One
   - (*b*) Two
   - (*c*) Three
   - (*d*) Four

9. Who introduced the term hotspot of diversity?
   - (*a*) Darwin
   - (*b*) Mclean
   - (*c*) Mike Housie
   - (*d*) Myers

10. How many mega diverse countries are there in the world?
   - (*a*) 11
   - (*b*) 17
   - (*c*) 25
   - (*d*) 34

11. One of endangered species of Indian medicinal plant is that of.
   - (*a*) Ocimum
   - (*b*) Nependenthes
   - (*c*) Garlic
   - (*d*) Podophyllum

12. Which endangered animal is the source of the world's finest, lightest, warmest and most expensive wool the shahtoosh?
   - (*a*) Nilgai
   - (*b*) Cheetul
   - (*c*) Chiru
   - (*d*) Kashmiri goat

13. What group of vertebrates comprises the highest number of endangered species?
   - (*a*) Mammals
   - (*b*) Fishes
   - (*c*) Reptiles
   - (*d*) Birds

14. Which one of the following is not included under is situ conservation?
   - (*a*) National park
   - (*b*) Botanic garden
   - (*c*) Statuary
   - (*d*) Biosphere reserve

15. According to IUCN Red list, what is the status of Red panda (Allures fulgens)
   - (*a*) Critically endangered species
   - (*b*) Extinct species
   - (*c*) Vulnerable species
   - (*d*) Endangered species

16. The world is highly prized wool yielding pashmina breed is
   - (*a*) Sheep
   - (*b*) Goat
   - (*c*) Goad-sheep cross
   - (*d*) Kashmir goat- Afgan sheep cross

17. The sheep is sheard from
   - (*a*) May to December
   - (*b*) August to September
   - (*c*) April to October
   - (*d*) Whole of the year

18. Term biodiversity was popularised by

    (*a*) Paul Ehrlich   (*b*) David Tilman

    (*c*) Edward Wilson   (*d*) Robert May

19. The most important component(s) of biodiversity is/are

    (*a*) Genetic diversity

    (*b*) Species diversity

    (*c*) Ecological diversity

    (*d*) All of the above

20. The pattern of biodiversity is affected by

    (*a*) Latitudinal gradients

    (*b*) Species-area relationships

    (*c*) Both (*a*) and (*b*)

    (*d*) None of the above

21. Latitudinal range of the Greenland and New York, respectively, would be

    (*a*) 41°S, 71°S   (*b*) 41°N, 71°N

    (*c*) 71°N, 41°N   (*d*) 71°S, 41°S

22. In the last 500 years, how many species of plants have become extinct from world?

    (*a*) 784   (*b*) 359

    (*c*) 338   (*d*) 87

23. Bali, Javan and Caspian are the three

    (*a*) Species of tiger   (*b*) Species of Cheetah

    (*c*) Species of lion   (*d*) Subspecies of tiger

24. The reason why should we conserve biodiversity, includes

    (*a*) Narrowly utilitarian

    (*b*) Broadly utilitarian

    (*c*) Ethical

    (*d*) All of the above.

25. Bioprospecting is related to

    (*a*) Narrowly utilitarian

    (*b*) Broadly utilitarian

    (*c*) Ethical

    (*d*) All of the above

Answer Keys

1. (*c*)	2. (*c*)	3. (*d*)	4. (*a*)	5. (*a*)	6. (*c*)	7. (*d*)	8. (*c*)	9. (*d*)	10. (*b*)
11. (*d*)	12. (*c*)	13. (*a*)	14. (*b*)	15. (*d*)	16. (*d*)	17. (*b*)	18. (*c*)	19. (*d*)	20. (*c*)
21. (*c*)	22. (*d*)	23. (*d*)	24. (*d*)	25. (*a*)					

Solutions

1. The convention on Biological Diversity (CBD) has three main goals including the conservation of biological diversity, the sustainable use of its components, and the equitable sharing of benefits arising from genetic resources.

2. The convention on Biological Diversity signed on 5 June 1992. It was signed in Rio-de-Janerio. As of now there are 196 parties and 168 signatories are there. Secretary General of the united nations is the depositary.

3. Though the convention on Biodiversity signed in 1992, it entered into force on 29 December 1993. In 2010, the 10th conference of parties to the convention on Biological Diversity in october in Nagoyo, Japan.

4. The cartagena protocol on Biosafety which is also known as the Biosafety protocol was adopted in January 2000. The Biosafety protocol clearly said that products from new technologies must be based on the precautionary principle.

5. The first ordinary meeting of the parties to the convention on Biological Diversity took place in the months of November and December 1994, in Nassau, Bahamas. It is known as 1994 conference of the parties (COP)

6. The Nagoyo protocol on access to genetic resources adopted on 29 October 2010 in Nagoyo, Japan, It entered into force on 12 October 2014. Its objective is the equitable sharing of benefits arising from the utilization of genetic resources.

7. Geological events in the landmass have provided conditions for high levels of biological diversity in India. A split in the single continent around 70 million and southern continents, with India as part of Gondwanaland along with other continents.

8. In 1972, Whittaker described three terms for measuring biodiversity over spatial scales. The three terms are alpha, beta and gamma diversity,

Alpha diversity refers to the diversity within a particular area.

9. In the year 1988, Myers introduced the term hotspot of biodiversity. Hotspots of biodiversity are areas which exhibit high species richness as well as high species endemism. To qualify as a hotspot a region must contain at least 1500 species of vascular plants and it should last at least 70 percent of its original habitat.

10. In 1998, conservation International identified 17 mega diverse countries. The term mega diverse country refers to any one of the group of nations that contains the majority of earth's species and high number of endemic species.

11. Podohyllum is an endangered and valuable medicinal plant which is found in few pocket of India cold desert.

12. Chiru is the source of shahtoosh

13. Mammals group of vertebrates comprises the highest number of endangered species.

14. Botanic gardens have collectively accumulated centuries of resources and expertise that now means they play a key role in plant conservation. Many of these activities contribute to ex situ conservation, but botanic gardens also play an important role in situ conservation.

15. Red Panda is listed on the IUCN Red list because the wild population is estimated at fewer than 10,000 mature individuals and continues to decline due to habitat loss and fragmentation poaching, and inbreeding depression.

16. The world's highly prized wool yielding pashmina breed is goat.

17. The recommended periods for shearing of wool are winter (February-March) and rainy (August-September) season when rich grazing ground is available.

18. Biodiversity is the term popularised by the sociobiologist **Edward Wilson** (1992) to describe the combined diversity at all the levels of biological organisation.

19. The most important components of biodiversity (Gk. *Bios* = life; *diversity* = form) are genetic diversity, species diversity and ecological diversity.

20. The pattern of biodiversity is affected by latitudinal gradients and species—area relationships.

21. Latitudinal range of the Greenland and New York, respectively, would be 71°N and 41°N.

22. IUCN Red list (2004) documents the extinction of 784 species in last 500 years (including: 359 invertebrates; 338 vertebrates and 87 plants).

23. Bali, Javan and Caspian are the three subspecies of tiger.

24. There are a number of reasons why should we conserve biodiversity, some are obvious and other not so obvious, but all equally important. These reasons can be grouped into three categories: narrowly utilitarian, broadly utilitarian, and ethical.

25. Bioprospecting is related to narrowly utilitarian. **Bioprospecting** is exploring molecular, genetic and species-level diversity for products of economic importance.

CHAPTER 16

Environmental Issues

Pollution, Solid and Radioactive wastes

Introduction

- Because of an explosion in the human population, the demand for food, water, home, electricity, roads, automobiles has been increased which leads to the pollution of air, water, and soil.
- Major issues relating to environmental pollution and depletion of valuable natural resources are different in local levels than that of regional or global levels.
- Any undesirable or harmful change in physical, chemical or biological characteristics of air, land, water or soil is known as pollution.
- The substances responsible for the pollution are called pollutants. The government of India has passed the Environmental (protection) Act, 1986 to protect and improve the quality of our environment (air, water, and soil).
- According to the Central Pollution Control Board (CPCB), the particulate which causes the greatest harm to human health is of size 2.5 micrometers or less in diameter (PM 2.5)

Air Pollution

- **Causes of Air Pollution:**
- Utilization of leaded petrol.
- Pollutants released from automobiles
- Particulate and gaseous air pollutants released by thermal power plants and other industries.
- **Harmful effects of air pollution:**
- It causes respiratory problems, irritation, inflammation and damage to lungs and premature deaths.
- Injuries to all living organisms are caused by air pollutants.
- The growth and yield of crops gets affected by air pollution and results in premature death of plants.

- **Controls of air pollution:**
- Catalyst converters should be used (having Platinum-Palladium and Rhodium as the catalysts)
- Pollutants must be separated out before releasing harmful gases into the atmosphere.
- Vehicles having a catalytic converter should use unleaded petrol.
- CNG is a better fuel than petrol or diesel because it burns more efficiently and very little of it is left unburnt.

Electrostatic Precipitator

- It is the most commonly used electrical device to remove particulate matter

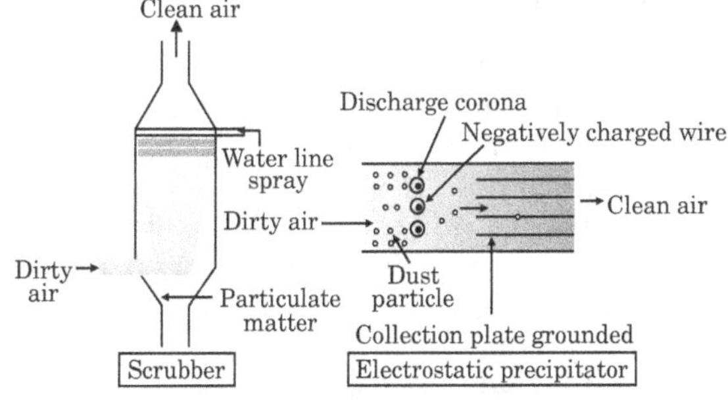

Fig.: Electro Static Precipitator (ESP)

- Electrode wires which are maintained at several thousand volts produce a corona which releases electrons.
- The dust particles get negatively charged as the electrons that are release get attached to them. These dust particles get attracted by grounded charged plates.
- The scrubber can remove gases like SO_2
- Over 99 percent particulate matter present in the exhaust from a thermal power point can be removed by this.

Noise Pollution:

- The undesired high level of sound is noise pollution. In 1987, the Air (Prevention and Control of Pollution) Act (1981) was amended to include noise as an air pollutant.

- **Causes:**
  - ➢ Loudspeaker, detonations, industries, led planes and rockets, music instruments, crackers, etc. are the causes of noise pollution.
- **Effects:**
  - ➢ Physiological and psychological disorders are caused by it.
  - ➢ Exposure to relatively higher or lower noise may damage hearing ability of humans.
- **Ways of control:**
  - ➢ Sound-absorbent material should be used in industries.
  - ➢ Delimit the timings and sound level of the crackers and loudspeakers.
  - ➢ There should be horn-free zone around hospitals and schools.
- **Laws in India to control vehicular pollution:**
  - ➢ Auto fuel policy
  - ➢ Euro II norms
  - ➢ The Bharat Stage II

Water pollution

- Human activities have polluted the lakes, ponds, stream, rivers, and oceans which is known as water pollution.
- Water (Prevention and Control of Pollution) Act, 1974 has been passed by the Government of India to safeguard the water resources.
- **Domestic Sewage and Industrial Effluents:**
  - ➢ Prevention of disposal of all kinds of waste in the water. Domestic sewage is the most common source of pollution of water bodies which reduces dissolved oxygen but increases biochemical oxygen demand of receiving water. It is rich in nutrients, especially, nitrogen and phosphorus, which cause eutrophication and algal blooms. The effect of sewage discharge on characteristics of a river are shown below.

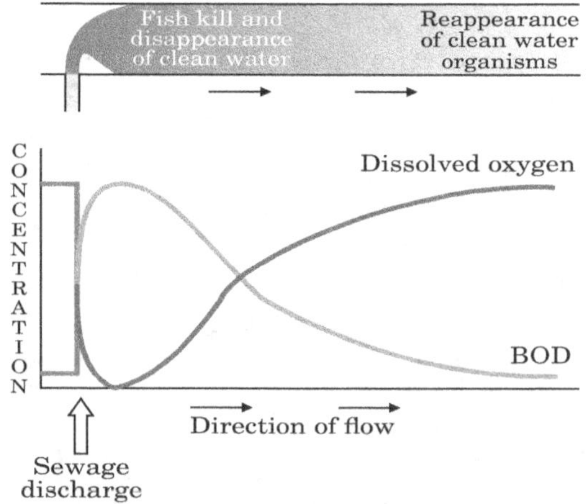

Fig.: Effect of sewage discharge on characteristics of a river

- ➢ Industrial waste waters are often rich in toxic chemicals, especially heavy metals and organic compounds. Industrial waste waters harm living organisms.

Using dry composting toilets, human excreta can be handled and this is called a sustainable system. This composite method allows human excreta to be recycled into a resource, which works as natural fertilizer.

- **Algal Bloom:**
  - ➢ Increase in amount of nutrients in water bodies result in excessive growth of algae, due to which quality of water degrades. Some of them are harmful to animals and humans.
- **Eutrophication:**
  - ➢ It refers to the natural aging of a lake by nutrient enrichment of the water.
  - ➢ Streams draining into the lake introduce nutrients like N_2, P_2 due to which the aquatic organisms grow.
  - ➢ The phenomenon where the pollutants (effluents from the industries) and homes accelerate the ageing process is called cultural or accelerated eutrophication.
- **Bio-magnification:**
  - ➢ It means the increase in concentration of the toxicant at successive trophic levels.

    $\text{Water}\,(\text{DDT}:0.03\,\text{ppm}) \longrightarrow \text{Zooplankton}\,(0.04\,\text{ppm})$
    $\longrightarrow \text{Small fish}\,(0.5\,\text{ppm}) \longrightarrow \text{Large fish}\,(2\,\text{ppm})$
    $\longrightarrow \text{Birds}\,(5\,\text{ppm})$

    This causes decline in bird population.

Solid Wastes

- Anything that goes in the trash is called solid waste.
- The wastes from homes, stores, offices, hospitals (like plastics, metals, glass etc.) are collected and disposed by the municipality are called Municipal solid wastes.
- In a sanitary landfill, the wastes are dumped in a trench after compaction.
- Bio-degradable, recyclable and non-biodegradable are the three types of solid waste.
- **Radioactive wastes:** Nuclear wastes emit radiation which causes mutation at a very high rate and creates various disorders such as cancer.
- **Plastic waste:** These are non-biodegradable wastes. Kabadi-wallas and rag-pickers help to separate material for recycling.

- **E-wastes:** The electronic good that cannot be repaired are called electronic waste (e-waste Recycling is the only solution to get rid of these wastes.

- **Agrochemicals:** The use of inorganic fertilizers and pesticides has increased manifold for enhancing crop production.

Pesticides, herbicides, fungicides, etc., are being increasingly used. These incidentally, are also toxic to non-target organisms which form the important components of the soil ecosystem.

- **Organic Farming:** In this, the waste products from one process are cycled in as nutrients for other processes.

Crop waste is used in creating compost, which can be used as a natural fertilizer or can be used to generate natural gas for satisfying the energy needs of the farm.

Greenhouse Effect, Ozone Depletion and Deforestation

Greenhouse effect and global warming:

- This is a natural phenomenon responsible for the heating of the Earth's surface and atmosphere. It allows the light to come in but restricts heat to go out. Earth's surface re-emit the heat as infrared radiation but a part of these radiations is absorbed by the atmospheric gases like CO_2, CH_4, etc. These gases cause the greenhouse effect.

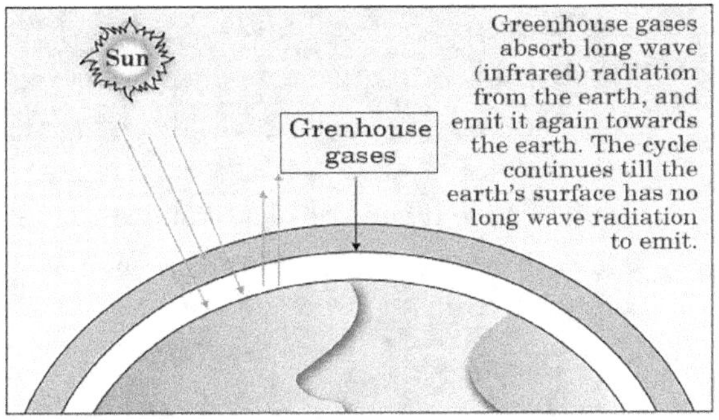

- Global warming is caused by the increasing level of the greenhouse effect. Earth's temperature has been increased by 0.6°C during the last three decades. Some of its effects are melting of polar ice caps, Himalayan snowcaps etc.

- Over many years, there will be a rise in sea level that will submerge many coastal areas.

- It can be controlled by reducing deforestation and planting more trees and reducing usage of fossil fuels.

Ozone depletion in the stratosphere

- "Good" Ozone acts as shield absorbing UV-rays from the sun, which cause mutation and is found in stratosphere.

- The "bad" ozone is formed in the troposphere.

- The balance in production and degradation of ozone in the stratosphere is disturbed due to Chlorofluorocarbons (CFCs) which move upward and reach the stratosphere. UV rays act on them releasing CI atoms. In the presence of CI (catalyst), ozone degrades molecular oxygen causing ozone depletion which has formed ozone hole over the Antarctic region.

- The thickness of the ozone in a column of air from the ground to the top of the atmosphere is measured in terms of Dobson units (DU).

- UV-B damages DNA and causes damage to skin cells, aging of skin and various types of skin cancers. Cornea of the eye absorbs UV-B radiation, and a high dose of UV-B causes inflammation of cornea, called snow-blindness cataract, etc.

- The Montreal Protocol was signed in 1987 to control the emission of ozone-depleting substances.

Degradation by improper resource utilization and maintenance

- **Soil erosion and desertification:**
  - Over-cultivation, deforestation, grazing and poor irrigation practices done by human are responsible for soil erosion. When large barren patches extend and meet over time, a desert is created

- **Waterlogging and Soil Salinity:**
  - Without proper drainage of water, the irrigation process leads to waterlogging which damages the agriculture. Water logging also draws salt to the surface of the soil.

Deforestation:
- Conversion of forest area to a non-forested area leads to deforestation and one of its hazardous effects is that concentration of CO_2 is enhanced because the tree is lost with deforestation who can hold a lot of carbon.

- Deforestation cause soil erosion and disturbance in hydrologic cycle.

➤ It can be controlled by reforestation which is restoring the forest that once existed in the past. It can speed up by planting more and more trees.

• **Participation by people for conserving the forests**

➤ Chipko Movement:

- It was started in 1974 by the local women in Garhwal, Himalayas.

- In order to protect the trees from the axe of the contractors, the women used to hug the trees.

➤ Bishnoi Movement:

- The king of Jodhpur in Rajasthan instructed his minister to arrange wood for constructing a new palace in 1731. The minister and workers went to a forest near a village where the Bishnois lived, to cut down trees.

- A Bishnoi woman Amrita Devi showed immense bravery by hugging a tree and daring king's men to cut her first before cutting the tree.

- Her three daughters and hundreds of other Bishnois followed her, and lost their lives saving trees.

- The Amrita Devi Bishnoi Wildlife Protection Award has been introduced by the Government of India for individuals or communities from rural areas that show dedication in protecting the wildlife.

EXERCISE

1. With reference to sources of water pollution, which of the following is true?

    (a) Natural sources

    (b) Domestic source

    (c) Agricultural sources

    (d) All of these

2. Which of the following chemical cause water pollution.

    (a) Arsenic　　　　(b) Zinc

    (c) Copper　　　　(d) All of these

3. Which gas is mainly produced due to incomplete burning wood?

    (a) CO　　　　(b) SO_2

    (c) NO_2　　　　(d) NO_3

4. Which of the following in a liquid form of aerosol?

    (a) Fume　　　　(b) Dust

    (c) Mist　　　　(d) Smoke

5. Which of the following is the physical monitoring of the lake?

    (a) pH　　　　(b) COD

    (c) BOD　　　　(d) Turbidity

6. For how many days is radioactive solid waste is kept under water at 6m deep for initial calling?

    (a) 15 days　　　　(b) 50 days

    (c) 30 days　　　　(d) 100 days

7. Absorption of radioactive element by human, affects their offsprings.

    (a) True　　　　(b) False

8. What are the ways in which most of radio activeness is removed?

    (a) Infusing them with other metal

    (b) Neutralizing them by diluting in chemical solutions

    (c) Storing them

    (d) Segregating them into small packs

9. The term 'Municipal solid waste' is used to describe which kind of solid waste?

    (a) Hazardous

    (b) Toxic

    (c) Non Hazardous

    (d) Non toxic

10. Why burning waste is not an acceptable practice of solid waste management?

    (a) Because it is very costly

    (b) Because it required modern technologies

    (c) Because it cause several environmental issues

    (d) Because it requires lot of space

11. How many main components are there in integrated waste management?

    (a) One　　　　(b) Two

    (c) Three　　　　(d) Four

12. Baval trees should be planted and used to prevent and control

    (a) Water pupation　　　　(b) Air pollution

    (c) Soil pollution　　　　(d) Noise pollution

13. Depletion of ozone layer causes, which of the following?
    (*a*) Cataract in eyes leading to blindness
    (*b*) Reduced productivity of forests
    (*c*) Lung Injection
    (*d*) Both a and b

14. The protocol which decided to completely phase out CFC is
    (*a*) Cartagena protocol
    (*b*) Skockolm convention
    (*c*) Montreal protocol
    (*d*) Kyoto protocol

15. Which of the following is not a green house gases?
    (*a*) Nitrous oxide   (*b*) ozone
    (*c*) Sulphur dioxide   (*d*) None of these

16. With reference to effect of green house gases, which of the following is true?
    (*a*) Change to plant growth and nutrition level
    (*b*) Ozone depletion
    (*c*) Smog pollution
    (*d*) All the above

17. Which of the following action takes place in the formation of ozone?
    (*a*) Action of daylight on oxygen
    (*b*) Action of daylight on nitrogen
    (*c*) Action of daylight on hydrogen
    (*d*) Action of daylight on phosphorous

18. How many oxygen particle are there in every atom of ozone?
    (*a*) One   (*b*) Two
    (*c*) Three   (*d*) Four

19. Which of the following is threat to the ozonosphere?
    (*a*) Nitrogen dioxide   (*b*) Oxygen
    (*c*) CFCs   (*d*) Carbon dioxide

20. In which layer of atmosphere ozone is very vital for all vegetation?
    (*a*) Upper atmosphere   (*b*) Below atmosphere
    (*c*) Ground level   (*d*) Below ground level

21. What is the full form of CFCs?
    (*a*) Chlorofluorocarbons
    (*b*) Chloride fluorocarbons
    (*c*) Chromate fluorocarbons
    (*d*) Chlorofluride carbons

22. Which treaty was signed in 1987 for the protection ozone layer?
    (*a*) The Montreal protocol
    (*b*) The kyoto protocol
    (*c*) Ozone summit
    (*d*) Wildlife consenvation Act.

23. Who among the following was associated with Bishnoi movement?
    (*a*) Amrita Devi
    (*b*) Gaura Devi
    (*c*) Govind Singh Rawat
    (*d*) Shamsher Singh Bisht

24. Who among the following was associated with chipko movement?
    (*a*) Sundarlal Bahuguna
    (*b*) Gaura Devi
    (*c*) Sudesha Devi
    (*d*) All of the above

Answer Keys

1. (*d*)	2. (*d*)	3. (*a*)	4. (*c*)	5. (*d*)	6. (*d*)	7. (*a*)	8. (*c*)	9. (*c*)	10. (*c*)
11. (*c*)	12. (*b*)	13. (*d*)	14. (*c*)	15. (*a*)	16. (*d*)	17. (*a*)	18. (*c*)	19. (*c*)	20. (*a*)
21. (*a*)	22. (*a*)	23. (*a*)	24. (*d*)						

Solutions

1. Water pollution is caused by a variety of human activities such as industrial, agricultural, and domestic, Natural sources of pollution of water are soil erosion, leaching of minerals from rocks etc.

2. Metals like lead, zinc etc in industrial waste waters adversely affect humans and other animals. Arsenic polluted water lead to accumulation of arsenic in the body parts like blood, nails etc and ultimately skin cancer.

3. CO is the colourless, odorless, toxic gas produced due to incomplete buring of wood.

4. Mist is a liquid form of aerosol whereas, fume, dust and smoke are a solid form of aerosol.

5. The turbidity of the water comes under the physical monitoring of the lake. Temperature, colour and solid also comes under the physical monitoring.

6. It is necessary to keep the radioactive solid waste first in the water of 6m depth nearly for 100 days. It was found that after 100 days cooling of radioactive waste of 28 MW plant in water still has a radioactivity equal to million grams of radium. About 50% radioactive elements disappear during cooling.

7. Absorption of neutron or radioactive elements by a tissue nuclear leads to radioactive nucleus which result change in chemical nature, malfunctioning of cell. Due to this, cell damages leading to genetic modification. Inhale of radioactive material through air, food, and water result radioactive hazard.

8. Most of the radio activeness of waste is removed just by storage. The storage problem is simplified by separating cersium and strontium which are extremely radioactive. These are generally stored in tanks which are buried in ground and them disposed into the sea after 13 years of storage.

9. The term 'municipal solid waste' is generally used to describe most of the non-hazardous solid waste from a city, town or village that requires routine collection and transport to a processing or disposal site.

10. Burning waste is not an acceptable practice, because if we look into environmental or health prospective buring waste creates lots of pollution and it is harmful to both environment and as well as organisms.

11. An integrated waste management strategy includes three main components they are source reduction, recycling and disposal. All these three types play an important role in the solid waste management.

12. Species of trees such as Baval (Acacia nilotica) which are least smoky should be planted and used to prevent and control air pollution.

13. Depletion of ozone layer permits passage of UV radiaction on earth's atmosphere which cause sunburn, cataract in eyes leading to blindness, skin cancer, reduced productivity of forests. Respiratory problem occur due to air pollution.

14. The Montreal protocol was amended in 1990 where it was decided to completely phase out CFC to prevent ozone layer depletion.

15. Atmospheric gases like carbondioxide, methane nitrous oxide, water vapour and chlorofluorocarbons are capable of trapping the out going infrared radiation from the earth.

16. Ocean acidification, smog pollution, ozone depletion as well as change to plant growth are nutrition levels.

17. Ozone is made by the action of daylight on oxygen. It forms a layer 20 to 50 km over the surface of the earth. This action of formation of ozone over the surface of the earth takes place naturally within the atmosphere.

18. Ozone is a type of oxygen that has three particles in every atom. The formation of ozone is extremely slow. Ozone gas is extremely toxic with a powerful order. This toxic gas is harmful to environment.

19. Ozone layer within the atmosphere protects life on earth from harmful ultraviolent radiation from the sun-chlorofluorocarbons (CFCs) that were used as refrigerants and aerosol spray propellants expose a threat to the ozonesphere.

20. Ozone in the upper atmosphere is vital to all forms of life as it protects the earth from harmful UV radiations. Ozone at ground level is considered a pollutant at ground level and causes harm to vegetation.

21. CFCs stands for chlorofluorocarbons. In the 1970s scientists discovered chlorofluorocarbons, which are used as refrigerants and aerosol spray propellants, pose a threat to the ozone layer.

22. The montreal protocol which was signed in 1987 is a treaty for the protection of the ozone layer, the use of CFCs was to be banned by the year 2000, after which the ozone layer is expected to slowly recover over a period of about 50 years.

23. Amrita Devi sacrificed her life along with her three daughters in the year 1730 during Bishnoi movement to save green trees being felled by the Maharaja of Jodhpur at a place known as Khejarli in Marwar, Rajasthan.

24. The Chipko movement or chipko Andolan was primarily a forest conservation movement in India that began in 1973. It was a movement that practised the Gandhian methods of satyagraha where both male and female activists played a Bachni Devi, Chandi Prasad Bhatt and Sunderlal Bahuguna.

www.ingramcontent.com/pod-product-compliance
Lightning Source LLC
La Vergne TN
LVHW081305210726
843509LV00019B/378